IRISH MANAGEMENT 2.0

IRISH MANAGEMENT 2.0

New Managerial Priorities in a Changing Economy

Edited by
James A. Cunningham and
Denis G. Harrington

BLACKHALL

IRISH MANAGEMENT 2.0

New Managerial Priorities in a Changing Economy

Edited by
James A. Cunningham and
Denis G. Harrington

BLACKHALL
Publishing

Blackhall Publishing
33 Carysfort Avenue
Blackrock
Co. Dublin
Ireland

e-mail: info@blackhallpublishing.com
www.blackhallpublishing.com

ISBN: 978-184218-159-1

A catalogue record for this book is available from the British Library.

Printed in Ireland by ColourBooks Ltd

J.C. – for Sammi

D.H. – for Julette, Jeanne, Ella and Euan

ENTERPRISE IRELAND WELCOME NOTE

Enterprise Ireland is the Irish government's lead agency responsible for the development and growth of the indigenous business sector. The mission of Enterprise Ireland is to accelerate the development of world-class Irish companies to achieve strong positions in global markets, resulting in increased national and regional prosperity.

In 2007 Enterprise Ireland published a new strategy for 2008–2010: *Transforming Irish Industry*. The objective of the strategy is to transform Irish companies into market-focused and innovation-driven businesses, capable of internationalising and maximising exports through leadership, innovation and growth.

Leadership, innovation and growth are the fundamental themes underpinning this strategy. Enterprise Ireland sees leadership and innovative capability in their client companies as absolutely critical to their success in international markets. The leadership and management within Irish companies are key ingredients and essential to growing companies that can compete on a global scale. For this reason, Enterprise Ireland provides support for the development of management and leadership capabilities through a range of programmes and services delivered by world-class institutions and aimed at supporting companies to radically develop their capacity to internationalise and drive their business growth.

This strategy will continue to underpin and grow a strong, sustainable and world-class indigenous business sector. Enterprise Ireland will support Irish companies to secure existing growth, capitalise on emerging opportunities and position for future growth.

ABOUT THE EDITORS

Dr James A. Cunningham is a senior lecturer in Strategic Management, executive MBA programme director, head of the Strategy Group and is a research cluster leader at the Centre for Innovation and Structural Change at the J.E. Cairnes Graduate School of Business and Economics, National University of Ireland (NUI), Galway. Prior to joining NUI Galway he held a lecturing position in the Michael Smurfit Graduate School of Business at University College Dublin. Before entering academia he worked as a strategy consultant.

He has published extensively and his publications include books, journal papers, book chapters, case studies and refereed conference papers. He has presented, given invited keynote presentations and chaired sessions at national and international conferences in addition to lecturing on executive programmes. He has held a visiting professorship at the Department of Management and Organisation at Penn State University. He has also worked as an advisor on commissioned projects for Forfás, Údarás na Gaeltachta and the American Chamber of Commerce, Ireland, and acts as a business strategy mentor for a variety of start-up businesses.

He has received a number of awards for his research, including conference best paper awards, and national and international case study writing awards. His main research interests focus on strategy, technology transfer and commercialisation. His research on technology transfer has been cited in the government's major policy document, *Strategy for Science, Technology and Innovation*, published in 2006, and his co-authored book, *Strategic Management of Technology Transfer: The New Challenge on Campus*, was recommended in *Business & Finance* (December 2006) as being 'part of the policy library of our entrepreneurs, venture capitalists and top managers in ICT and R&D oriented sectors.' His next book, *Strategy and Strategists*, will be published by Oxford University Press.

Dr Denis G. Harrington is head of the Department of Graduate Business at Waterford Institute of Technology (WIT). His research interests are in the areas of strategy implementation and management education and learning. He is a visiting professor at Reims Management School, France and has also given visiting lectures at the St Petersburg State University, the Academy of National Economy, Moscow and Imperial College London. He has contributed to the *Thunderbird International Business Review* and the *European Journal of Management*, amongst others.

Denis has facilitated a number of in-company workshops on strategy and leadership and has worked on several management assignments in Eastern Europe and within the Russian Federation. He is on the editorial board of the *Services Industries Journal* (UK), the *Irish Journal of Management* and the *Irish Business Journal*. He is also a council member of the MBA Association of Ireland and a member of the Academy of Management in the US.

Denis was a finalist in the International Academy of Business Case Writing Competition 2002 and winner of the John Molson International Case Competition 2003.

ACKNOWLEDGEMENTS

We would like to sincerely thank a number of people for helping us in the development and preparation of *Irish Management 2.0: New Managerial Priorities in a Changing Economy*. In particular, we are extremely grateful to the MBA Association of Ireland for their support and sponsorship of this book and for providing us with the opportunity to progress our ideas in this area. We extend our thanks to Denis McCarthy, former CEO of the MBA Association of Ireland, for his support for this project, for facilitating meetings and for his efforts in cementing commitment to the project within the wider business community. Our thanks also to President Greg Devlin of the MBA Association of Ireland, Vice President Anna Mooney and former President Gerard Kavanagh for their support.

As editors, we are extremely grateful to the case study and management reflection writers who contributed to the book. Without their collaboration, this book would simply not have been possible. In addition, we wish to acknowledge all our anonymous reviewers who provided constructive feedback to case authors. We are grateful to Thomas A. Stewart, editor of the *Harvard Business Review*, for writing an introductory article for the book on the significance of case studies.

Our discussions with many colleagues – academics and practitioners – and students has helped us to clarify the book's overall themes and also provided us with the opportunity to reflect on and evaluate our thinking on the idea of Management 2.0. We are especially indebted to: Professor Charles Snow, Penn State University, USA; Professor Liam Fahey, Babson College, USA; Professor Roy Green, Macquarie Graduate School of Management, Australia; Professor Philip McIlkenny, School of Management at the University of Ottawa, Canada; Professor Yahia H. Zoubir, Euromed Marseille, France; Professor Paul Stoneham, EAP-European School of Management; Professor Margaret Heffernan, Simmons School of Management, US; Dr Martin Fahy, CEO, FINSIA, Australia; Professor Thomas C. Lawton, Cranfield School of Management, UK; Dr Richard J. Schroth, CEO, Executive Insights Ltd, Maryland, US; Dr Thomas O'Toole, Waterford Institute of Technology; and Mr Eoin Daly, partner, McKinsey & Co. London.

We would also like to acknowledge colleagues in our own institutions for their support and contributions to this text, namely, Mr Ger Long and Ms Joan McDonald, Waterford Institute of Technology, and Mr Sam McCauley, chairman, Sam McCauley Group and CEO in residence, School of Business, Waterford Institute of Technology.

We would like to thank Gerard O'Connor, Elizabeth Brennan and the team at Blackhall Publishing for their helpfulness and patience with developing the manuscript.

Finally, and most importantly, we would like to thank our families without whose support and understanding this project would never have been completed.

CONTENTS

FOREWORD

We live in interesting times for Irish business. We are on the cusp of a new era, as our exceptional economic success story of the last decade gives way to a more demanding business environment.

This is a challenging period for Irish business, certainly, but it is one ripe with opportunity. Tough economic conditions have historically provided the genesis of new business thinking and practices. Innovation, creativity and organisational reengineering have been born out of organisational necessity to do more with less.

It is an opportune time, then, to examine the nature of Irish business success in the last two decades, and to look to the future and identify the challenges for Irish businesses, which is the purpose of this fine collection of case studies and management reflections, edited by Dr James A. Cunningham and Dr Denis G. Harrington.

Irish Management 2.0 tells the story of Irish business – accounts not of companies swimming in the slipstream of a Tiger economy, but of indigenous entrepreneurs, energetic and resourceful managers, courageous risk takers and organisational ambition and vision, in private and public sector organisations. Uniquely, the book combines management practitioner and academic contributions that encourage reflection, but that also describe the future universal management challenges that leaders, managers, entrepreneurs and organisations face in the next decade. The book is. a valuable and timely touchstone for business owners, leaders, managers and students of management alike.

Economic fair winds may no longer be at our back, but Ireland's new generation of dynamic, professional managers and leaders – Irish Management 2.0 – whose expertise has been honed by their international business experience as much as by our domestic economic boom, are better equipped than any previous generation to rise to the key challenge of international competitiveness; and, in doing so, to lead a fundamental management revolution in the manner in which organisations are managed.

We are proud to have many of the leaders, managers, entrepreneurs and organisations showcased in this collection as members of the MBA

Association of Ireland, a body that has been supporting and promoting continuing management education in Ireland for over forty-nine years.

We look forward with optimism to the next decade of change, and what innovations this exceptional generation of leaders, managers and entrepreneurs can bring to the story of Irish business.

Greg Devlin
President, MBA Association of Ireland

WHAT CASES TEACH

There are no right answers in business because the game is both open-ended and infinitely complex. An American football game ends after sixty minutes, a baseball game after nine innings (cricket seems interminable to Americans, but that's another story). However, in business there is always a next quarter. The bottom-line marks a moment in time, not an end. Furthermore, almost every decision is multidimensional. There are only two players, even in complicated games like chess, but businesses have many competitors, some of them not obvious, and have customers too, each with a mind of his or her own. Raising a price alters demand; but it might also provoke different responses from different competitors. It could induce new players to enter the game, and it could drive customers to seek out entirely different substitutes – if greens fees get too high, customers might go to the cinema instead.

Theoreticians speak about businesses and markets as 'complex adaptive systems'. For practical-minded people, that means it is really hard to learn business in a classroom. The university of the streets – the School of Hard Knocks – is as important as any formal education. Doing is learning. At the same time, however, there exists an important large and growing body of knowledge about business, and not just in 'hard' disciplines like finance and control. There are things we know about strategy, organisation, motivation, operations and customers; there are frameworks and tools of proven effectiveness.

The task of business education, therefore, is to reconcile two coinciding and conflicting truths: while every problem is new and different, it's stupid to waste resources reinventing the wheel.

This is why the best business schools study cases. Most professions create some kind of clinical training. Medical students begin by working with cadavers and textbooks, but are soon learning their profession by diagnosing and treating the ailments of real patients. Budding lawyers study statute books but, in Anglo-American countries, mostly dig into common law cases, studying argument, decision and appeal, while at the same time arguing cases in mock courts. Indeed, case-method education came to business via the law. Wallace P. Donham, the second dean of Harvard Business School (HBS), was a graduate of the university's law school and urged the HBS faculty to adapt case-method teaching to their own curriculum. By 1921, two years after Donham became dean, the faculty formally voted to do so, and the case method has been the foundation of HBS's curriculum ever since. By studying and discussing cases – real business problems that faced real companies, whose executives made decisions that had real consequences – students get as close to clinical experience as one can get in a classroom.

There are obvious differences between cases in law and in business. For one thing (a very important thing), the law gives great weight to precedent. Lawyers and judges, therefore, take pains to show that their argument is not new. Markets, by contrast, are largely indifferent to history. 'New' is the most powerful word in advertising. Business people are rewarded for prudence, but rarely for repeating the past – the biggest rewards come to those who think outside the box of precedent.

While there are differences, there is at least one central similarity: the purpose of the case is to instil a way of thinking, not to impart a set of facts. That is why cases work so well, not just for MBA candidates, but for executive education and corporate learning programmes as well. The majority of business people, after all, do not have MBAs. Probably even a minority of chief financial officers have a degree, and this is certainly true of most other functional heads – human resources, research and development, operations – as well as of chief executives. A book like this, therefore, should not be thought of as a student text. It is at least as important for readers outside an MBA programme. They – we – are the women and men running corporations and other organisations. They – we – need to learn the thought processes case-method teaching inculcates.

The most important of these concerns the habit of making decisions. Because business problems are always unique, information is never complete and delay is usually unwise, business people must learn to make up their minds and get on with it as best they can. During an academic year, students are forced to analyse, make and defend difficult decisions day after day at a pace faster than any they are likely to encounter in the real world, like tennis players chasing down the balls shot by a machine across the net. In the very best cases, as in the real world, it's not always immediately clear what the problem *is*. These stories force students to sort through a lot of information, some of it ambiguous or irrelevant, to find and define an important, hard-to-see problem.

The students are only pretending, but the temperature can be intense, as it can be in the real world. I once overheard a conversation in which a business school graduate described a class where a friend of hers said that one of the characters in a case study should be fired. The professor exploded. 'There's always someone who thinks the solution to a complicated problem is just to fire someone!' he cried. Then he turned on the student and ordered him out of the room: 'I don't want to see you for the rest of the day.' When class met next, the professor called on the student, sitting in the back of the room, and said, 'Jones, tell the class what it feels like to be fired.'

That extreme, rather horrible situation points out another consequence of case-based teaching: it forces one on to centre stage and into an unfamiliar role. The reader becomes a participant in the drama. In a classroom, a case seems to say, 'You're not a mere student, whose job is to sit and learn like a baby bird being fed by its mother; you're a captain of industry, responsible for millions of sales and thousands of people.' Executives, for their part, are forced out of their role. 'In real life', a case tells you, 'you're a product manager, fighting for your share of a limited budget. But here you have to put aside parochial concerns and think like the chief marketing officer.' That kind of role playing develops empathy, which is important, not just for managing people or for internal politicking, but also to help a person anticipate how suppliers, customers and competitors will think and behave.

Cases also help business people to learn to think with analogies. Executives use analogies far more often than they realise. A colleague once expressed her delight with retailers like Gap: 'They're supermarkets for clothes,' she said. Reasoning by analogy, hospitals today are improving health care by applying the principles of the Toyota Production System to their processes. Analogies are important because executives' decisions are made under conditions of uncertainty. Easy decisions – those that can be made by looking at the numbers on a spreadsheet – rarely make it to executives' offices, except for rubber-stamping. Executives make judgments about what's probably best. Analogies serve them in two ways. First, they're a rich source of alternative ideas: 'We can be the Tesco of telecoms, the Dell of banking, the Rolls Royce of retailers.' The more cases a person knows, the larger his library of possible futures. Secondly, analogies also help leaders to get objective distance. When war-gamers study battles of the past, they are freed from any bias that might affect their ability to be objective about the units they actually command today.

It's ironic that business, in popular culture, is seen as a dry world inhabited by cold people. In reality, it's full of fear, solicitude, surprise, disappointment, triumph – the stuff of every human drama. Cases capture those emotions and, moreover, reveal the ways people have tried to shape circumstances to their advantage. Although there are no right answers in business, there are right questions, approaches and attitudes, which improve the chances of getting a good answer.

Some years ago, on the first day of a two-day conference, I heard a speaker advocate a solution to a problem. The second day, another speaker urged a different solution to the same problem. When he asked for questions, a member of the audience rose up, pointed out the contradiction and, with an edge of outrage, said that he'd paid good money to come to this conference and wanted to know which approach was right. The speaker answered, 'You'll have to look at your own circumstances, and think for yourself.' That's so easy to say, so obvious, so simple. But it's so hard to do. Someone should write a case about it.

Thomas A. Steward
Editor and Managing Director, *Harvard Business Review*

PREFACE

As co-editors of *Irish Management 2.0: New Managerial Priorities in a Changing Economy,* our aim has been to illuminate the importance of quality and competent management in both public and private organisations – a cornerstone of sustainable economic success and competitiveness. The role of good quality management is often overlooked when examining our success at a national and company level. Significant investments have been made by the State and private organisations in developing Ireland's knowledge economy, but such investments are not always visible and tangible to society.

Yet, one of most essential ingredients required in delivering a knowledge economy is human capital in the form of managerial excellence. Other economies have the advantage of legacies of developing managerial excellence over centuries, with an innate global perspective. Ireland is a relative newcomer, but the combination of creativity, innovative instincts, educational attainment and a 'can do' attitude has meant that Ireland has developed a managerial class that is internationally competitive. A testament to this is the growing number of Irish managers attaining board positions in global companies.

We have seen a significant change in our economy over the last thirty years. Our economy will change significantly again over the coming decades. Economic change will force Irish managers to conceptually think differently about their businesses in global terms rather than in national, regional or local terms. One of the key weaknesses that concerns us currently is the lack of depth and breadth of managerial talent that is essential to sustain Ireland's knowledge-based economy and our national system of innovation. In time, this could become critical, as further investments are made by government and private sectors in the knowledge economy.

As our economy moves away from an over-reliance on construction over the coming years, the key challenge for all Irish-based businesses will lie in international competitiveness, the achievement of which necessitates sustainable national businesses that can scale globally. This in turn requires changes in managerial priorities for Irish management that are in tune with national and international economic and management changes.

These changes in management priorities include an increase in investment in management development within companies, and collaborative entrepreneurship and innovation within and outside of the firm with regional and international partners. They should aim to develop a knowledge base at firm level that can be leveraged for both economic and social ends.

Our approach as editors of this book has been to attempt to engage with management practice by fusing the perspectives of academics and practitioners through case studies and practitioner reflections. Our key overarching message is that the Irish economy needs to invest even more significantly in the development of managerial talent. This requires the same strategic approach as has been taken in developing our science, technology and engineering base. It means incentivising investments in meaningful management development in private and public organisations. It also means higher intensity engagements and collaborations between Irish managers and business school academics nationally and internationally.

We argue that there is a need for the development of a national Advanced Management Institute, the sole strategic focus of which would be on building the competencies and capabilities of Irish managers and fusing deeper collaborations between academia (both national and international) and management practice. Such developments would underpin managerial excellence, which is required in the evolution of our knowledge-based economy and essential to overcoming any deficits in the depth of managerial talent that Ireland currently faces.

We hope that you will enjoy reading the various sections of the book. We value your thoughts about the book and your comments will be most welcome. You can contact us at <james.cunningham@nuigalway.ie> or <dharrington@wit.ie>.

Dr James A. Cunningham and Dr Denis G. Harrington

INTRODUCTION

As we near the end of the first decade of the twenty-first century, we can see four significant structural changes in business that will impact on Irish management and on managerial priorities. Firstly, the fundamental character of organisations, management and managers will change. Technology companies like Google and Facebook are exemplars of this new management revolution, which we term 'Management 2.0'. It is likely that the hierarchical structure or the static nature of reporting relationships that we experience in our own contexts will dissipate and be replaced by structures and management excellence appropriate to market conditions. The ways in which companies manage resources and explore new opportunities will evolve significantly. Fluid collaborative entrepreneurship and innovation, focused on economic, social and knowledge acquisitions, are at the core of this management revolution.

The second and even more significant structural change is the rapid advances in science, such as nanotechnology, biomaterials, biomedical science, bioinformatics, semantic Web technologies, etc. Such advances present opportunities and complexities for society, business, government and managers. This rapid progress in science provides industries with convergent market and technology opportunities as well as industry specific market vertical opportunities, but, more significantly, requires management excellence to deliver products and services to the market.

The third structural change is in capital markets and the manner in which global companies are making capital investment decisions. What we are seeing is a duality of perspectives for company capital investment decisions, based on attractive trading conditions for manufacturing purposes, but also for knowledge development in the form of intellectual property exploration and exploitation. Such a change requires a pool of human talent oriented around exploration in the form of research and development and investment in innovation managers (scientists, engineers and technologists). It also requires management excellence to oversee knowledge development, horizontal innovation and manufacturing capabilities in single-site locations.

The final structural change we see is that it is possible to scale a company more rapidly in this century than in any other. Brands such as

MySpace, Bebo, Facebook, Google, eBay and Skype have scaled their business to a global level at a rate never seen before. Such scaling requires managerial excellence and a different conceptual approach to management and managing.

Irish Management 2.0: New Managerial Priorities in a Changing Economy is divided into three sections. The first section focuses on the evolution of the Irish economy and the changing nature of executive education. It highlights the changes in technology and management practice, and the challenges posed by Management 2.0. The second section of the book is a collection of case studies on a variety of businesses in the public and private sectors on the island of Ireland. It illustrates the varied challenges that Irish managers have dealt with and currently face. In drawing together this collection of case studies, it is our intention as editors that, in reading through them, you will reflect on the issues that were outlined in the first section, in addition to reflecting on your own experiences and contexts. The final section of the book brings together an eclectic mix of management reflections that identify some of the current management challenges and issues at the coalface.

Section I: Irish Management – Past, Present and Future

Chapter 1, 'Management Education: The Future Challenges', by Professor Patrick McNamee of the University of Ulster, traces the evolution of executive education in Ireland in the context of a developing economy. The author outlines the characteristics of management education that are timeless and those that seem likely to change. He concludes by noting the need for a national willingness on the part of management education to embrace change through new ideas, practices and perspectives.

Chapter 2, 'What Graduates Want: An International Perspective', by Professor Roy Green, dean of Macquarie Graduate School of Management in Australia, provides a global perspective on graduate business education and the business models for management education.

Chapter 3, 'Developing Management Capability in an Irish Context: Future Trends and Prospects', by Dr Denis G. Harrington, Waterford Institute of Technology (WIT), builds on the two previous chapters and argues that, in the future, managers will be challenged to rethink management competencies, capabilities and relationships and that Ireland must take advantage of this 'soft revolution'. In doing so, it is necessary to develop a new model of the practitioner-academic partnership to disseminate and spread leader knowledge, in addition to developing strategy and management practice capabilities.

Chapter 4, 'Management 2.0: Challenges and Implications', by Dr James A. Cunningham, National University of Ireland (NUI), Galway, follows on from Chapter 3 by focusing on the Management 2.0 challenges in achieving a culture of engagement and creativity in organisations. The implications of these challenges for managers, business schools, society and government are discussed. This chapter argues that the role of the manager must shift from that of doer to that of enabler in terms of creativity and socialisation. It concludes by outlining and discussing Management 2.0 approaches and collaborative organisational forms.

Section II: Case Studies

In this section of the book we have brought together a number of case studies on companies in private and public sector contexts, which illustrate the many and varied challenges experienced by management teams and stakeholders. We have deliberately chosen cases from a diverse range of industry sectors and that highlight some key managerial themes, which we believe are critical in a Management 2.0 context.

Chapter 5, 'CRH plc: Corporate-Level Strategy Redefined', is the award-winning case study written by Mr Mike Moroney, NUI Galway. CRH is one of Ireland's leading global companies competing in the worldwide building materials industry. Since its foundation in 1970, CRH has grown rapidly and, in doing so, has maintained an unrivalled financial performance. The CRH case highlights the role a small corporate parent can play in adding real value to single business units on a global scale.

Chapter 6, 'Lagan Technologies Ltd: Turning it Around', written by Dr Nola Hewitt-Dundas, Queen's University Belfast, describes how this Belfast-based software company, established in 1994 as a university spin-out, evolved and survived near bankruptcy in 1999. The case highlights the need to have a real understanding of market and position in addition to the necessity of having a strong management team to drive company performance.

The context switches to the public sector for Chapter 7, 'ESB International', written by Mr Chris O'Riordan and Dr Felicity Kelliher of WIT. The case traces the beginning of ESB International and demonstrates how, even in a public sector context with stakeholder constraints, visionary leadership, a clear strategic focus and the nurturing of a different culture can lead to growth and internationalisation. The balancing of risk against return is critical in a public sector context and is highlighted in this case study.

We continue with a public sector theme for our next case study in Chapter 8, 'An Post: Addressing Ireland's Mail Market', written by Mr Kevin Pyke, Dr Theo Lynn, Dr Malcolm Brady and Mr Paul Davis of Dublin City University (DCU) Business School. This case provides some interesting insights into the challenges and complexities involved in effecting major organisational change in a public sector organisation. In addition, the difficulties inherent in organisational renewal are a constant theme throughout the case.

Chapter 9, 'Vivas Health', by Dr Breda McCarthy of University College Cork, provides a fascinating view of market entry challenges in the Irish health insurance market. The case particularly highlights the importance of ongoing entrepreneurship in dealing with the market challenges and the importance of opportunity recognition in entering new competitive market spaces.

Chapter 10, 'Bulmers Original Cider: A Case in Strategic Repositioning', written by Dr Paul Ryan, Mr Mike Moroney and Mr Will Geoghegan of NUI Galway, explores the process of strategic repositioning in a corporate context. The case yet again highlights the importance of companies understanding what customers really want and buyer dynamics. This is an exemplar case of the execution of strategic repositioning within the marketplace, particularly in terms of people's perceptions of cider, through a clear focus on value built on heritage, craftsmanship and naturalness.

Chapter 11, our next case, moves to a small business context. The importance of developing a strategy that provides a platform for product development as well as reinforcing a market position is the focus of 'Cloon Keen Atelier: A Passion for Scent', by Ms Ann M. Torres, NUI Galway. Cloon Keen Atelier has range of products (candles, soaps, creams, lotions) based on scent. The case also highlights the challenges that small businesses face in marketing and scaling, online and offline.

U2 – one of Ireland's best-known global bands – is the focus of the case in Chapter 12, by Professor Thomas C. Lawton of Cranfield School of Management, with Dr James A. Cunningham and Dr Denis G. Harrington. 'U2: Keeping the Rhythm' traces the growth of U2 and highlights the many ingredients that are required for sustainable success. In the case of U2, their music, innovation regarding distribution and technology, a strong manager and, more latterly, political and humanitarian motivations have contributed to sustainable success.

Chapter 13, 'O2 Communications Ireland', by Mr Gordon Lynn, Dr Theo Lynn, Dr Malcolm Brady and Mr Paul Davis of DCU Business School provides an insight into the challenges that O2 face with the advent of even faster changes in mobile technology and associated business models. The case highlights the need for management teams to build a strong organisational posture and culture with embedded value and how this has to be balanced with organisational flexibility, which is essential to responding to new technology.

Chapter 14, the final case study, is entitled 'Managing Relationships for Innovation in the Food Industry' and is written by Dr Patrick Lynch and Dr Thomas O'Toole of WIT. This case takes a different focus than our previous cases as it concentrates on the complexity around inter-company innovation between two companies in the food sector. This case goes to the heart of management practice: the ability to maintain and develop relationships with multiple parties for various purposes. It also highlights the ever-broadening capabilities that managers at all levels need in order to deal with broad strategic and operational issues.

Section III: Management Reflections

The last decade of economic growth has seen Irish managers reaching new heights of managerial achievement in national and international arenas. However, the competitive demands placed on executives and the business community by current strategic challenges are many. Managers are expected to be strategic leaders who operate with a clear sense of direction and purpose. Equally, there is an expectation that they are operationally sound in and with any culture, whilst simultaneously being flexible and innovative to keep abreast of new developments. These demands on managers have heightened awareness of the importance of management capability and of the need to encourage and grow communities of good management practice. Indeed, the response to our call for submissions to this text is testimony to the interest within the managerial community for the development of knowledge networks to explore how ideas can be shared and 'practice communities' encouraged.

The modern business also requires managers to work effectively across different disciplines and to have an ability to navigate change throughout the organisation. Recent contributions confirm that the focus for value creation is shifting from product and financial markets to talent markets. As new innovations create challenges for companies, executives must have the strategic capability to identify and lead change effectively. To do so, individual managers require a range of strategic and analytical skills and a thorough knowledge of the organisation itself.

In the last decade we have witnessed dramatic economic change. Executives with leadership responsibilities in Irish businesses now have responsibility for acquiring and applying advanced knowledge and technology in innovative ways, which are appropriate to future organisational leadership. Such executives are encouraged to develop and extend their knowledge networks and focus organisational energies on nurturing the human capital so necessary for increased competitiveness.

As a recent European Foundation for Management Development (EFMD) report reminds us, never has it been so important for firms to make maximum use of available knowledge, learning and human talent, because innovation, speed and flexibility are more important than ever. The report also suggests that organisations need to become better at learning, that is, more effective at understanding and nurturing new capabilities and applying them successfully. Competences, as we are reminded, are increasingly viewed as a moving target, which heightens the importance of learning interventions. The report also highlights the requirement for critical reflective practices in organisations, practices that encourage knowledge communities and learners and an overall greater diffusion of ideas and energy in often business work environments.

Notwithstanding the above points, we argue that, while our economy has undergone dramatic transformation, in an Irish context, there has been little time to reflect and learn from each other about our strategies and operations, about our markets and value propositions, about our internal cultures and people and, of course, about our successes and failures. The purpose of this section is to capture some of these stories that focus attention on recent developments within Irish management practice from four main perspectives.

Chapter 15, 'Re-invention from Within: A New Mandate from Irish Management', by Mr George Bennett of the Irish Development Authority, considers the re-invention of Irish managers and management as our country transitioned to a knowledge-based economy over the past ten years. He reflects on the role of managers of Irish enterprises and, in particular, the proactive mentality that has engaged their work in leading transformations within their work spaces and lives. As is correctly argued in the account, the global environment in which multinationals operate has underlined the significance of learning and innovation in organisations and has prompted Irish managers to evolve and transition new practices to compete effectively and shape best operational and strategic business practice.

If we are to maintain and further develop our competitive status as a leading knowledge-based economy, then this contribution highlights the requirement for a comprehensive framework that will allow us to better understand existing management practices and stimulate discussion of new directions, and international management practices and research.

Chapter 16, in keeping with an international perspective, is entitled 'Software Sales Forecasting: How to Do it Well' and is written by Mr Stephen Allott, formerly of Trinamo Consulting. He outlines the importance of sales forecasting in a software context, which has universal practical lessons for managers. He gives an account of different types of forecasts, the reasons why forecasting matters and then outlines Trimano's approach to sales forecasting. As Stephen argues, the ability to do sales forecasting analytically and accurately is an essential management skill to possess in any company.

In Chapter 17, 'Female Entrepreneurs: How and Why They Succeed', Professor Margaret Heffernan of the Simmons Graduate School of Business, Boston focuses attention on a relatively untapped and underdeveloped source of entrepreneurship, namely female entrepreneurship. While numerous reports highlight that Ireland is highly supportive of entrepreneurs and entrepreneurial activity, they simultaneously highlight the importance of taking initiative and measures to build on current entrepreneurial momentum for the future. In particular, there is a growing emphasis on the need to optimise female entrepreneurial activity and promote greater visibility for female entrepreneurial role models in an Irish context.

Drawing on US research and experience, Professor Heffernan shows how women-owned businesses have grown at twice the rate of business as a whole and now employ more people than the global Fortune 500 combined. As she reminds us, every day in America, 420 new women-owned businesses are formed. She reflects on how we might encourage a greater focus on female entrepreneurs in Ireland and underlines the role and contribution that female entrepreneurs make to business and society in general.

It is encouraging to note that work is currently underway in this area. The FEIW initiative (Female Entrepreneurship in Ireland and Wales), an

Interreg IIIA-funded project that is being run by Dr Bill O' Gorman and Ms Margaret Tynan of the WIT Centre for Enterprise Development and Regional Economy (CEDRE), in partnership with the University of Wales, Aberystwyth, works to facilitate the growth and development of women-led businesses in the south-east of Ireland and south-west of Wales. The project research has led to the design and implementation of an enterprise training programme, specifically for women business owners in both regions.

These research-led initiatives strengthen the research and social networks to allow female entrepreneurs to gain access to resources and respond to the need to provide supports for the development of women-led business networks.

In Chapter 18, 'Building a Customer Responsive Organisation at BMW Group Ireland', Ms Lisa-Nicole Dunne, formerly of BMW Ireland, describes how BMW developed a more customer-responsive organisation through the roll out of a customer relationship management (CRM) system, which is an integral element of group strategy (understanding the customer is an issue focused on in Chapter 4). She outlines some of the implementation issues and identifies some of the key managerial lessons from the experience of BMW in Ireland.

In Chapter 19, 'Clustering on the Island of Ireland', Paul McCormack considers the emergence and role of collaborative networks and clusters in Ireland in empowering firms and professionals to improve their flexibility, innovation capabilities and performance in the global market. Paul has significant experience as cluster facilitator for two of the leading clusters in Ireland, the Environmental Technology Cluster (ETC) and the Emerging Technology Cluster (ETC). His account suggests that participation in networks and clusters evolves a 'culture of creativity', that in turn encourages reflection and thinking about the future. Clustering, as the writer points out, has delivered many successes internationally and, importantly, in an Irish context. Participant cluster organsiations reap the benefits of economies of scale, strength in numbers, credibility through membership, knowledge transfer, collaborations and joint ventures. There are also many 'intangible' benefits achieved through clustering, such as knowledge transfer, increased creativity, commercial confidence, innovation awareness and entrepreneurial activity. Paul suggests that engagement will provide companies with the necessary tools and access to the knowledge, skills, expertise and technologies to help achieve competitive success in increasingly competitive international markets.

In a public sector context, with the continued expenditure on public infrastructure projects under the National Development Plan, many projects cut across government departments, local authorities and legal jurisdictions. In private sector organisations, the rolling out of SAP human resources management systems, CRM systems, executive information systems (EIS) and management information systems (MIS), that are organisation wide in nature, means that organisations have to develop the capability to manage increased levels of complexity. This is the focus of Chapter 20, 'Managing Complexity in Business Integration Projects', by Pierre-Henri Baviera of PA Consulting Group. He argues that, with increased complexity, there is a requirement for different management methods and mindsets.

Finally, Chapter 21, 'Primary Health Care in Ireland: Change, Challenge, Opportunity', takes a health care management focus, addressing the issue of change within the primary health care sector in Ireland. Dr Mark Rowe, who is managing director of a large group practice in Waterford City, outlines some of the changes underway within the Irish primary health care sector and his ideas of how best management practice might inform management within this sector. As he remarks, given its increasing complexity, primary care must be treated as a business, whereby management principles are married to best medical practice.

SECTION I

IRISH MANAGEMENT: PAST, PRESENT AND FUTURE

CHAPTER 1

Management Education:
The Future Challenges

Patrick McNamee

*Department of Marketing, Entrepreneurship and Strategy,
University of Ulster*

Personal Introduction

Writing this chapter is an exciting project for me. It is so because this is the first time I have written a substantial document using exclusively the Web. This chapter is being written on the Web-based word processing software Writely (<http://www.writely.com>). The reason I am using Writely rather than a conventional word processing package is to signal the nature of this chapter, which aspires to capture the excitement of the opportunities being afforded to all through the Web. The second reason is that this Web-based genre of word processing, in my opinion, presages the future direction of all information technology and hence the future direction of management education in Ireland and elsewhere. The principal advantages of Writely are summarised below:

- It is free; it is supplied by Google (<http://www.google.com>) and can be obtained by anyone who has access to the Web.
- The Writely program is not downloaded and installed, or installed using a CD on my computer. Rather, it is held on Google's server, and users simply access it via the Web. After registering, users commence using it. Thus, it does not use any space on my computer.
- In addition, this document is not saved on my computer; it is saved continuously to a remote server that I may access at any time. Furthermore, should I wish to save it to my computer, I can save it as a Word document or in another specified format.
- This chapter can be accessed and amended simultaneously by up to fifty people. This means that, should I wish for contributions or comments from other people, I do not need to e-mail them this material as

an attachment. It is available live to those who I wish to have access to it and they can simultaneously work on it in real time. So, this document is currently being viewed by two other people who are deeply involved in this book project, namely the book's editors James A. Cunningham of NUI Galway and Denis G. Harrington of Waterford Institute of Technology. The three partners in this project – James, Denis and I – are currently in Galway, Waterford and Dublin, respectively. The distances between our locations are irrelevant as we are all connected to this chapter through the Web. Additionally, should any of us be out of the country – say, playing golf in Portugal – we can all still work on the project; all we need is access to the Web that can be provided, for example, by an Internet café. This means that to work on this chapter when I am outside my office I do not need to have my own computer or even to carry the chapter on a memory stick; all I need is access to the Web.

I find this process amazing and instructive. It is amazing that simply by being connected to the Web I can have such splendid communication. It is instructive because this type of Web-based distributed working will surely be replicated, as will be shown below, in many other facets of management and, of course, management education.

Finally, as an additional signal of the future and to give the chapter a contemporary flavour, all the references in this chapter will be in the form of Web addresses rather than being paper based. Indeed, every piece of research material used in this chapter has come from the Web.

Formal Introduction

On a wall in the Smurfit Business School in Dublin (<http://www.ucdbusiness.ie>) is a photograph of the first Master of Business Administration (MBA) graduates from the first MBA ever offered by an Irish university. Under the inspired leadership of Professor Michael McCormick, UCD had its first MBA graduates in 1966. This date marked a watershed in Irish management education and, accordingly, 1966 has been chosen as the starting date for the historical analysis carried out in this chapter. The sea change that has since taken place in Irish business and society has been reflected in the sea change in business education in Ireland in general and the MBA in particular. The MBA has grown from a single cohort of 12 graduates from a single school in 1966 to around 450 graduates from 7 Irish institutions in 2007, a remarkable transformation. This increase in number has been mirrored in the increase in the membership of the MBA Association of Ireland, from around 12 in 1967 – the year it was founded – to around 2,000 in 2007. Why this huge change in the MBA 'market' has occurred will now be examined. The following section considers the signals of future major change in Ireland in the role and nature of management education in general, and the MBA in particular.

Evolution: The Perpetual Driver of All Life, Industrial Development and Management Education

Prior to Ireland's first MBA the country was, largely, bereft of management education as it is known today. While it is true that there were certificated and short business courses in areas such as accounting, economics, personnel, time and motion, and other subjects, one key element of today's landscape of management education was missing. There were no post-experience postgraduate courses that focused on areas such as management, business strategy, leadership, change management, marketing, finance and accounting, entrepreneurship, innovation and human resource management. Also, the current pedagogical methods of the MBA – using real-life case studies to foster debate, discussion, analytical and presentation skills – were largely absent. It could be argued that the main reason for the lack of high-level management education was that there was no market for it, i.e. there was little or no demand from Irish business or the public sector for graduates with such qualifications.

This chapter uses a biological perspective and postulates that industrial evolution was the primary cause of the change in management education. The chapter further suggests possible patterns of management education for the future. It is asserted that, since the late 1960s, Ireland's successful industrial development has been, and will continue to be, an evolutionary process that mirrors evolution in nature, and that Ireland's associated management education has also been, and will continue to be, an evolutionary process.

At a basic level in evolutionary biology, it is assumed that an organism (say a plant) inhabits a host (say soil) and the organism interacts with the host in such a way as to bring benefits to both. For example, if a volcanic eruption ultimately leads to virgin soil (i.e. soil in which nothing has grown or is living) then, over time, eolian or water-borne seeds will land on the soil and from these seeds plants will grow. Over time, leaves from the plants will fall, interact with the soil and help increase the nutrition of the soil. The enriched soil will foster the growth of more plants

5

that, in turn, shed their leaves, further increasing the nutrition of the soil. Thus the initial interaction between the organism (the plants) and the host (the soil) develops into an interdependency in which both the organism and the host benefit. Over time, more and more organisms (species of plants) establish and then colonise the host, and ultimately compete with each other through evolution and natural selection – the survival of the fittest – for the limited nutrition provided by the soil. The most successful species become dominant and the least successful species ultimately disappear.

When this theory is applied to industrial evolution, it is assumed that a new firm (an organism) inhabits a new environment (a host) and interacts with it in such a way as to bring benefit to both in terms of wealth, profits, employment and infrastructure. In the case of Ireland, the country itself is the host and the many firms (many of them multinational corporations) who have set up in Ireland are the organisms. From 1966 to today, Ireland has proved to be a commercially nutritious and benign host to many of these firms, with the vast majority prospering and, as a consequence, becoming ever more committed to Ireland through increasing the size and scope of their operations.

The industrial base in Ireland that developed through this evolutionary process has, in turn, become a host to a new species of organisations that did not previously exist. These new species of organisations provided an increasing range of services for the developing industrial base. Services that evolved included international communications, infrastructure, transportation and, of course, the provision of skilled managers. Indeed, the country's ability to provide a pool of skilled managers in areas such as science, engineering and business has been essential to the continuing success of the country's firms. This evolutionary process in which the host – Ireland's businesses – provided the opportunities to develop new areas of business education, particularly the MBA, which in turn provided the industrial base with the key managerial skills it needed, meant there developed a mutual dependence between the two: the industrial base helped develop and sustain the management education system (i.e. the business schools), and the management education system helped sustain and develop the industrial base.

Today, Ireland's industrial base (the host) is transforming into a knowledge-based high-skilled entity and evolutionary pressures dictate that management education (the organism) must also transform (i.e. evolve) to cater simultaneously for industry's new needs, and also to help play its role in leading the changes.

Industrial Development in Ireland

Ireland's recent industrial development can be divided into two major phases – phase 1: volume of jobs and phase 2: high quality employment.

Phase 1: Volume of Jobs

Until the year 2000, Ireland's main debilitating and apparently insuperable economic problem was the very large number of unemployed people. Up to that time, Ireland's major industrial development strategy was to attract foreign direct investment (FDI) by offering, in addition to financial and tax incentives, the opportunity to avail of a large labour surplus and low unit costs. This phase, it is generally agreed, was successful, since many foreign companies established in Ireland and numbers employed increased from 1.3 million in 1996 to 2.1 million in 2006, with a corresponding drop in unemployment from 11.9 to 4.3 per cent (*IDA Annual Report* 2006: 6).

Phase 2: High Quality Employment

Social and economic development transformed Ireland's FDI ambitions into its current agenda of quality-based growth by which the economic agenda is driven by creating new areas of opportunity and raising living standards, causing new jobs to have the characteristics of being of higher quality, more satisfying and better paid. This transformation in the Irish national industrial development agenda reflects the transformation process of Irish-based multinationals that are in turn driven by the global competitive environment in which they operate (*IDA Annual Report* 2006).

As the evolution of management education is largely determined by the evolution of business, it is instructive to examine what has been the most recent universal evolutionary trend in business and how this force is likely to evolve in the future.

Web 1.0 and Industry Transformation

The dominance, usefulness and commercial benefits of using the Web at a business level and personal level are now established. The ways in which the Web – often called Web 1.0 – is used today, and how this has affected and will continue to affect business and, of course, management education, is now considered.

It is now, in 2008, possible to analyse the many effects on business that the Web has had and to distil the multitude of Web uses and successes into a small number of generic characteristics. This will provide a framework for examining how the Web has transformed business and management education.

It could be argued that the industrial transformation effects of Web 1.0 were caused by four related phenomena:

- *Open systems and universal connectivity*: prior to Web 1.0, electronic communication systems tended to be closed, i.e. proprietary software and hardware meant that independent users could not easily communicate with each other. Even in companies that used a single type of computer and software, electronic communication was often frustratingly difficult or indeed even impossible. Eventually, when computers became networked, communication between computers was still often difficult. The advent of Web 1.0 revolutionised this by providing, for the first time, genuinely open systems. Thus, irrespective of the location, scale or nature of any organisation – from the individual to the global corporation – Web 1.0 provided open systems in which global communication could be seamless.

- *The almost costless nature of information*: since the cost of using the Web is either free or almost free, the traditional costs of global communication have been reduced to almost zero. Consequently, the cost of exchanging very large amounts of information or data between companies or individuals, irrespective of its volume or location, is almost zero.

- *The speed of information exchange*: historically, the speed of data exchange – paper and electronic – was inversely proportional to the distance between the parties communicating. Information exchange is now almost instantaneous and, consequently, in terms of speed of communication, global location is irrelevant.

- *Increasing bandwidth*: the bandwidth of a communication system reflects its ability to handle complex communications. Today, broadband systems can transmit complex data such as text, drawings and video. As the information age develops, bandwidth is increasing rapidly and this is facilitating the development of businesses and entertainment, which rely on the communication of very large amounts of complex data.

Thus, Web 1.0 has utterly altered the ease, economics, nature, cost, speed and scope of information and, as a consequence, has had profound effects on how business is conducted in every industry.

Perhaps the most significant effect of the confluence of these forces was that, for the first time ever, it became possible to have very rich information (say, detailed technical specifications in the form of text, drawing, video, e-mail and telephone) which also had global reach (say, linking Dublin and China) (see <http://www.bcg.com>). The major effect of this new relationship between richness and reach was the deconstruction of the value chain. In practice, this meant that the once all-conquering value chains by which large companies took control of the entire production process – from procurement to after-sales service – often in a single location (e.g. many of America's largest integrated automobile companies were located in Detroit) was no longer necessarily the best type of structure for achieving the lowest costs in the industry, and hence the highest profits. In the value chain era the most profitable firms would tend to be the ones that achieved the lowest average costs in each element of their value chain, while in the Internet era the lowest cost firms are the ones that achieve the lowest actual cost in each element of the value chain, irrespective of where that activity is carried out or by whom.

One of the most visible Irish manifestations of this new type of strategy was Dell's (<http://www.dell.com>) decision to locate one of its major manufacturing facilities in Ireland. In Ireland, Dell is essentially a low-cost orchestrator company (see <http://www.bcg.com>), which orchestrates or coordinates low-cost inputs from suppliers throughout the world. Before Web 1.0, for economic and communication reasons, Ireland could not have been a commercially realistic location for Dell.

Web 1.0 and Management Education

Although the benefits of industry transformation are now clearly a feature of the Irish economy, its exploitation by management education, in Ireland anyway, has been less clear. While Irish management education has grown enormously in terms of number of courses, scope, variety and flexibility, its take-up of the opportunities offered by Web 1.0 has been limited. Indeed, it seems that most Irish management education institutions have used Web 1.0 to improve, augment or support their services rather than to transform the way they operate. Thus, most Irish providers of management education use the following legacy model.

.nysical and managerial:

- A major building or centre comprising classrooms, seminar rooms, an IT suite plus broadband access to the Web, a library, a dining area, staff rooms and parking facilities. The centre tends to be near a centre of population.
- The management structure tends to have the following hierarchical structure: a director, full-time academic staff, part-time academic staff and administrative support staff.

Web related; the Web tends to be used for the following purposes:

- Information and regulations for potential and actual students and other interested parties.
- Communication among staff and between students and the institution.
- Distance learning.
- Access for researching up-to-date electronic databases.

Thus, in Ireland, the Web tends to be a medium that *assists* management education to become better rather than one that operates as a catalyst for its *transformation*. However, today, the signals of impending transformation exist and are growing. These will be considered in the following section.

Management Education: the Opportunities Spawned by Industry Transformation

There seem to be three main contributions that Web 1.0 can make to management education, namely regarding availability, choice and cost.

Availability

Just as Writely is available to any person who has access to the Web, this should now be the case with management education, even though it tends not to be free. This means that any people, no matter how remote their locations from a business school, as long as they have access to the Web, can now, thanks to the reach and the richness of Web communication, participate in and succeed in a serious management educational qualification such as an MBA. A corollary of this universal availability is the increased number of students who now participate in management education. The reach of business schools was previously determined by the size of the eligible population in the vicinity of the business school.

Today, the reach of Web-based management education is global and hence the potential number of students has escalated to millions.

Choice

In addition to the expanded choice spawned by online offerings from individual business schools, there are now electronic federations of business schools that cooperate together to promote their interests through the leverage provided by the communal group identity. This has led to the development of navigator sites (see <http://www.bcg.com>), such as <http://www.rdi.co.uk> and <http://www.mba-online-program.com>, in which the participating institutions jointly offer an online MBA. The benefits of this approach to the collaborating institutions and the students who avail of it are considerable.

Cost

There are two major types of cost: the cost to the institution and the cost to the student. Clearly, for institutions offering online management education, the cost will be considerably less since it is infinitely scalable, and additional staff and facilities – classrooms, libraries, IT suites, dining facilities, staff rooms and parking spaces – are unnecessary. In a complementary fashion, the savings on cost and time for students working from home are immense.

It is clear that Web 1.0 has brought great benefits to all parties concerned with management education. Business schools can now have:

- Global reach to a global market with physical location of the institution and the students being irrelevant.
- A Web-based MBA at minimal cost.

And students can now have:

- An unprecedented degree of choice.
- Minimal travel costs.

The Future of Management Education in Ireland

Long-run forecasters of almost everything are almost always wrong and there is no reason to believe that the forecasts below will be any better. However, it may be useful to speculate about two major 'opposing' forces in management education, namely timeless characteristics that

...r change irrespective of industrial development and technology,
...ose new forces that must be embraced to develop management edu-
...tion as fully as possible.

Characteristics of Management Education that Seem to be Timeless

Irrespective of the long-run technological changes and the changes in
Ireland's industrial, economic and social structure, there are a number of
characteristics of the MBA, enumerated below, that seem so much part of
its fabric that it seems unlikely that they will change.

Core Content of the MBA

The core of the MBA is to provide experienced managers with:

- The multidisciplinary perspectives necessary to provide leadership
  and solve managerial problems.
- Those generic transferable skills that will make them more effective
  managers.

This core content is likely to remain the same.

Personal Contacts and Relationships

Most MBA graduates would agree that a key feature of their courses was
the friendships and business relationships that developed among students
and also between students and staff. Indeed, this face-to-face type of relationship is considered by many to be the key defining characteristic of the
MBA. Such an important characteristic must be retained and therefore it
seems likely that, in the future, irrespective of how it is delivered, an
esteemed MBA course will provide mechanisms to ensure that this feature is retained.

Verbal and Presentation Skills

As most management tasks tend to be verbal (one-to-one and addressing
and interacting with groups) rather than written, an MBA must continue to
provide opportunities for the development of these verbal and presentation
skills. Once again, distance learning does not provide for this so it is likely
that physical meetings of groups will be part of the MBA of the future.

Involvement of the Workplace

Successful MBA programmes tend to involve the students' workplaces in
the learning process. This is often achieved through work-based projects

and dissertations. The Web facilitates this approach. For example, Web-based electronic databases would greatly facilitate a student carrying out a project involving his or her firm's relative competitive position in its industry.

Characteristics of Management Education that Seem Likely to Change

The evolutionary hypothesis of the link between industrial development or transformation and development of management education postulated above will, almost certainly, continue in the future. It would appear that the benefits Web 1.0 has brought will continue to increase for business schools, teaching staff, students and society. More specifically, it is likely to be the case that:

- Business schools' infrastructure costs will decline as having large city centre buildings will become increasingly less important.
- The staff employed by business schools will become more distributed, and have, perhaps, many part-time contracts with different business schools. For example, a professor may be able to have a teaching contract with a number of schools rather than being tied to a single one. A further extension of this could be that individual professors become almost totally independent of all business schools and develop their own websites and servers, either on an individual basis or on a collective basis. This could lead to business schools eclectically picking the best available professors in the world and not necessarily in the country in which the school is based.
- Competition among business schools should increase. Thus, as the Web develops, there seems to be less and less reason to undertake a legacy MBA from a local business school. It may be superior – and perhaps cheaper – to undertake an online MBA from a foreign business school that has been ranked independently as superior. A further stimulus to competition among business schools may be an increase in new entrants into the business school markets – new entrants tempted in by the decrease in start-up costs.
- The structures of business schools and their course offerings will change to suit the contemporary wishes of students of business. In providing content and delivery in the forms that their users want, the most innovative institutions – which may not be business schools – are likely to be the most successful. Ultimately, those business schools that fail to adapt to this new environment will fail.

- The cost of business courses should decline in real terms. There are a number of reasons why this should happen: decrease in operating costs; increase in volume of students; increase in competition.
- The location of business schools will be no longer of crucial importance. Although it is obviously advantageous for a business school to be in a major business centre, location is likely to be less important in the future. Thus, champion institution Massachusetts Institute of Technology (MIT) in Boston, through its MIT OpenCourseWare (<http://ocw.mit.edu/OcwWeb>), is providing global access to its pedagogical expertise. This type of provision is likely to be replicated in Irish institutions and indeed, currently, the University of Ulster, through its Campus One website (<http://campusone.ulster.ac.uk>), is already providing such courses.
- Face-to-face contact and the attendant discussions among students and between students and staff will remain an essential ingredient of the MBA. So, it is likely that, in addition to the provision of superior distance learning, the MBA will still need to facilitate regional group meetings so that this interaction can take place.

Web 2.0 and Future Industry Transformation

Web 2.0 (for example, <http://www.wikipedia.org>) does not represent a change in technology, rather it represents the adaptation of Web 1.0 as a part of life rather than as a technology to help achieve certain goals – personal and business – more effectively. Web 2.0 is evolving in response to the characteristics belonging to the now more mature Web 1.0. Thus, instead of being regarded as a unique technology for communication, the Web has become, increasingly, an open platform for marketing, supply chain management, education, and internal and external communication. In the process of this evolution, critical masses of unforeseen knowledge have arisen. Thus, previously unconnected areas of expertise – which could be as simple as a number of people who have, say, a great collection of 1960s music – have, through sharing on the Web, transformed into globally shared knowledge. So it can be argued that, in the area of digital music, the Web has aggregated millions of small digital islands of music into large 'land masses' of music. These land masses of music are now so large that they may exceed the size – in terms of catalogue breadth and number of people sharing – of large commercial music providers. The mathematics illustrate this: if 2.5 million people are online at any time and each person has just 40 music tracks available for sharing, this means that 100 million tracks can be shared at any one time. Perhaps the best-known examples of these peer-to-peer music-sharing sites are <http://www.napster.com>, <http://www.limewire.com> and <http://www.kazaa.com>.

Music was used to illustrate the nature of Web 2.0 but the trend towards online peer-to-peer sharing communities is very large and growing. A number of today's best-known ones and their services are listed below:

Auctions: <http://www.ebay.com>
Telephone: <http://www.skype.com>
Encyclopaedia: <http://www.wikipedia.com>
Tee shirts: <http://www.threadless.com>
Social contact: <http://www.myspace.com>
Social contact: <http://www.facebook.com>
Video exchange: <http://www.youtube.com>
Estate agency: <http://www.trulia.com>

A major effect of these Web 2.0 peer-to-peer sharing sites is that the distinction between the creator and the customer has altered enormously, as the customer has become a creator and the creator has become a customer. Thus, in the example of music sharing, the person sharing his or her 1960s music is a creator. However, when this same person is downloading music from another creator's site, he or she is a consumer.

Although most of the above examples are social rather than industrial examples of Web 2.0, industrial examples involving companies such as Deutsche Bank, IBM and Toyota have emerged (Evans 2007).

Web 2.0 and Future Management Education

Although not yet a feature of management education in general and the MBA in particular, it would appear that the management education community, i.e. the business schools, their staff and the students, is structurally suitable for the development of Web 2.0 peer-to-peer initiatives. Thus, there are many thousands of management students (consumers) in the world who would be natural sharers. Information that they would, presumably, wish to share would include essays, case studies, case analyses, dissertations, in-company projects, notes on management topics, examination answers, etc. In addition, it is likely that the more progressive professors in business management institutions would also wish to participate in this and as yet other unforeseen Web 2.0 initiatives. The connection of the many thousands of MBA students' digital islands of knowledge would indeed lead to a substantial land mass of information.

Irish Industry and Management Education

The host-organism interdependency between management education and business is likely to continue and, if the Irish economy moves strongly in the direction advocated by government – towards a knowledge-driven, high value-added economy, based on difficult-to-obtain skills and knowledge rather than unit costs – the MBA, and other types of management education, will evolve in a similar fashion.

A second facet of future Irish industrial development is that it will probably be incorrect to view national industrial development as Irish. Increasingly, industrial development is global rather than regional and, in recognising this, Ireland's future management education must benchmark its performance with that of its global peers, and then weave international benchmarks of firm practice and performance into the content of its courses so that graduates' contributions to their firms' performances will reflect world rather than regional best practice.

Conclusion

This chapter commenced with and ended with references to the Web as a force, which has and will continue to transform business and society, and management education. Perhaps because Ireland has only a recent history of substantial industrial development, the society seems predisposed to accept new global best ideas and best practices. This national willingness to embrace the future positively has garnered huge economic rewards for Ireland and Ireland's economic future. The future of management education in Ireland will surely be even more successful if the current willingness to change evolves into a thirst for change.

References

Evans, P. (2007), *The Python in the Garden*, available from: http://www. bcg.com/impact_expertise/publications/files/435ThePythonintheGard enMay07.pdf.

Industrial Development Agency (IDA) (2006), 'Ireland, Knowledge is in Our Nature', *IDA Annual Report*, available at: <http://www.idaireland. com>.

CHAPTER 2

What Graduates Want:
An International Perspective

Roy Green

Macquarie Graduate School of Management,
Macquarie University, Australia

Introduction

What do students need and what do they get from graduate business education? As the world is changing faster than the curriculum can be revised, it is perhaps unavoidable that this alignment, so often sought by business schools, cannot always be achieved.

Yet experience shows that results can be matched to expectations. This may not be due simply to keeping the curriculum up to date, but to an emphasis on critical self-reflection and the opportunity being provided for students to question accepted thinking. While this is less likely in specialised master's programmes and short courses that tend to focus on a narrow set of techniques or knowledge, it should be central to the broader management philosophy of the MBA.

The Bad Press

Why then has the MBA had such a bad press in the recent past, not just in Australia but globally? In my view – based on observations as a dean in both Australia and Ireland – this is because expectations were set too high and were consequently bound to be dashed, especially in the case of the intensive, high-fee full-time programmes for US college graduates. In his book *Managers, Not MBAs* (2004), Henry Mintzberg points out that, whatever the surrounding hype, the MBA cannot make managers out of young people in their early twenties with limited or no experience in organisations, and no one should pretend otherwise.

However, even mature post-experience MBAs, as we find at the Macquarie Graduate School of Management (MGSM), are under pressure to address many more problems than those envisaged in the traditional MBA structure. For example, following a number of corporate scandals, business schools around the world are being asked to make ethics an integral part of the curriculum. Similarly, with global warming and the threat of food and energy shortages, there is a growing and understandable demand to include issues relating to environmental sustainability.

To add to the clamour, academics writing in the *Harvard Business Review* over a year ago called on business schools to abandon allegedly futile attempts at social science rigour in favour of more relevant models, such as those of medical schools with teachers as clinicians. While superficially persuasive, and indeed a timely counter to the self-indulgence found in some business journals, this argument forgets that medical training is nothing without scientific rigour.

Future of the MBA?

Where does this leave the future of the MBA? Management gurus tell us in the scarcely grammatical but supremely confident prose of the airport bookstall that we should 'think outside the box' and 'pick the low hanging fruit'. Yet we know that a truly world-class MBA enables the students to analyse, decode and systematise what is inside the box, and to set their sights on the highest, seemingly unreachable fruit – and then to have the great satisfaction of being the ones to pick it.

This prospect was anticipated not only by the founders of 'management science', as it was once known, but also more prominently in the 1960s by former University of California President Clark Kerr in his pioneering work *The Uses of the University*. Kerr wrote that, 'The university today finds itself in a quite novel position in society.... We are just now perceiving that the university's invisible product – knowledge – may be the most powerful single element in our culture, affecting the rise and fall of professions, and even of social classes, of regions, and even of nations' (1963: 66).

For those aspiring to the leadership of firms and organisations, the general management MBA remains the most valuable and relevant degree qualification. But this does not mean that all MBAs are the same, even if we confine our consideration to the highest quality programmes. Some institutions, like MIT, Columbia and Tuck, retain a traditional focus on the key functional areas of management, such as finance, marketing, strategy, operations, human resources and organisational behaviour, with an opportunity to specialise in elective courses.

Others such as Stanford have recently pursued a more innovative approach to the curriculum, with an emphasis on 'customisation' and 'flexibility' in the programme, whereby students are mentored through chosen career pathways. Still others, such as Babson and IMD, favour a more 'integrative' model, which requires students to apply their knowledge in real-world interdisciplinary projects, sometimes as the capstone for the degree.

Yale has taken this approach further in its new MBA curriculum, and, according to the Yale School of Management MBA brochure for 2007, is 'breaking down the traditional management disciplines just as the contemporary organisations blur the distinctions among management functions'. In doing so, Yale builds on a strong foundation of business and social science research on the changing nature of organisations, as good teaching should.

In the same brochure Joel Podolny, dean at Yale School of Management, points out that:

> Today, managerial careers cross the boundaries of function, organisation and industry, as well as cultural and political borders. Even managers in large organisations must be entrepreneurial in the sense that their success depends on their ability to synthesise disparate information, analyse competing functional priorities, and draw together and coordinate resources and individuals in a context that is often fluid and decentralised.

MGSM too is undertaking a review of its MBA curriculum, taking account of not only these international trends, but also the local, professionally driven environment for management education. Led by the chair of the MGSM board, Sydney investment banker Dr Bill Beerworth, and Macquarie University's Provost Judyth Sachs, this review will also examine cross-fertilisation with other disciplines on campus, such as law, medicine and engineering, and will explore the potential of external networks and alliances. These networks will comprise not just other business schools, but also media organisations and industry associations that can increasingly take advantage of our role as 'content providers'.

Of course, we recognise that the MBA is just a part of the rich spectrum of management education, and is increasingly supplemented by corporate customised and open enrolment executive programmes. In this context, it is pleasing to note that three Australian business schools have recently been included by the London *Financial Times* in the world's top forty-five schools for executive education, with MGSM being ranked 'number one' in Australia. This is quite an achievement, given the much greater resources available to our international competitors.

While the US business schools are able to rely to a greater or lesser degree on the largesse of private benefactors and the Asian schools are able to access substantial state funding, Australian schools, as well as most of the European institutions, have the benefit of neither. This may not be a problem for large 'integrated' schools with undergraduate students and a range of master's programmes, but, for autonomous graduate business schools, the realisation that MBA fee income alone is insufficient to ensure viability has come as something of a shock.

New Business Models for Management Education

As a result, new business models have emerged. In the UK, for example, Cranfield has streamlined its MBA programme with a reduction in the number of electives from seventy-three to eleven, and reinvented itself as a provider of corporate customised programmes. Even earlier, Peter Lorange, the recently retired dean of IMD, Switzerland, anticipated these trends with a highly selective full-time MBA programme as a 'flagship' and quality marker for its strategic shift to customised programmes, which now account for 90 per cent of IMD's revenue and contribute significantly to recent infrastructure renewal.

Meanwhile, the elite US schools continue to upgrade their already lavish facilities. Paul Danos, dean of Tuck, is proud of his fine new teaching extension, but laments that his school has an endowment of 'only' $300 million. Indeed, a recent straw poll has suggested that at least fifty of the top sixty schools in the US had built new facilities in the last decade. In Ireland too, as part of its remarkable economic and social transformation, business schools have developed rapidly – with two featuring in *Financial Times* rankings. I am personally delighted that my former school, the National University of Ireland, Galway, has an excellent new facility, funded through a mix of private philanthropy, competitive research funding and state grants.

Pleasing though it is to attract funding for physical infrastructure, the main international accrediting bodies, the North American-based Association to Advance Collegiate Schools of Business (AACSB) and the European Foundation for Management Development (EFMD), remain resolutely committed to the quality of the student experience and its outcomes in the form of a set of defined 'graduate attributes' of students and their expanded opportunities for career advancement. This encompasses increasing attention to processes for 'assurance of learning' within the business school curriculum so that quality is embodied formally, not just in the school's brand promise, but in the practice and delivery of the product.

The importance of clear and comprehensible learning outcomes has been highlighted in the just-published report of the Organisation for Economic Cooperation and Development (OECD), *Tertiary Education for the Knowledge Society*. This report notes: 'the widespread recognition that tertiary education is a major driver of economic competitiveness in an increasingly knowledge-driven global economy.... The imperative for countries is to raise higher-level employment skills, to sustain a globally competitive research base and to improve knowledge dissemination to the benefit of society'(2008: 11).

However, this approach must be interpreted in the light of evidence from a recent innovation benchmarking study, conducted jointly in 2004–5 by MIT's Industrial Performance Center and Judge Business School's Centre for Business Research at Cambridge. Instead of making assumptions about business expectations, the study asked 3,500 firms in the UK and US what they actually wanted from higher education, including business schools. The response was that learning and interaction should not be simply instrumental but contribute to personal self-fulfilment, knowledge generation and above all the capacity, in the words of management theorist Peter Drucker, to 'think things through'.

Conclusion

The strategy at MGSM is both an adaptation to these existing trends and an attempt to anticipate new ones. In this sense, it mirrors the approach of many comparable business schools all over the world, which are striving to combine rigour with relevance, and thinking inside the box as well as outside it. A perceptive study, *The Future of Business Schools in the UK* (2006), by the Advanced Institute of Management Research made an attempt to categorise the different strategies of business schools by relating their aspirations to the boundaries set by capabilities and resources.

The typology proposed in the study grouped business schools into those aspiring to be professional schools, those in the liberal arts tradition, those grounded in social science research and, finally, those contributing to the development of a knowledge economy. While these categories might, and probably will, overlap, the point of the exercise was to highlight the need for 'deans and advisory boards... to make strategic decisions in response to the challenges they face; strategic decisions that support the models business schools choose to employ. However, the complexity and challenge of implementing any change in the profile of a business school must not be underestimated'(2006: 20).

MGSM's aspirations resonate with each of these categories but, ultimately, like most graduate business schools, it lives or dies by the quality of its orientation to professional practice, grounded in both the theory of key discipline areas and the experience brought into the classroom by lecturers, practitioners and the students themselves. While business schools, operating as they do in a diverse and demanding market, will inevitably configure their strategies differently, the common thread is a commitment to the quality of the student experience and to students' success as graduates both in their organisations and in the wider community.

MGSM has thought long and hard about its strategy in terms of writer Tom Friedman's 'flat world', characterised, as Friedman describes, by interconnectedness through new technologies and the mobility of people and resources. However, we also recognise with Richard Florida that 'the world is spiky', in the sense that some localities and regions achieve competitive advantage in this flat world through the deployment of superior knowledge and ingenuity. Surrounded as we are in our locality by a cluster of global technology companies, as well as being positioned in a leading destination for investment, migration and tourism, MGSM has defined a strategy with five main components. These are:

- To review and develop the MBA curriculum with increased flexibility provided by a constellation of specialised master's programmes spinning out of the core modules and an emphasis on 'graduate attributes'.
- To pursue globalisation not simply through student and faculty exchange with other schools, but also through the development of global partnerships and alliances, including joint degree programmes.
- To build open enrolment and customised executive programmes both as a source of revenue and as a 'brand identity' and means of achieving deeper client relationships with partner organisations.
- To expand research and research training with a major emphasis on the quality of outputs and the evolution of centres of research excellence with vibrant and attractive doctoral student programmes.
- To develop the school's engagement with business and the community through public events, alumni activity and fundraising for key priorities, whether 'bricks and mortar' or endowed chairs.

We may conclude that the future of the MBA is more sustainable now than it has been in the past, but that it is evolving into a different programme – subtly in some places, more radically in others – with changes brought about by globalisation and technology in increasingly knowledge-based societies. It is up to business schools not only to reflect and influence these changes but to also prepare the graduates who will lead them. Again, as Peter Drucker constantly avowed, 'the best way to predict the future is to create it.'

References

Advanced Institute of Management Research (AIM) (2006), *The Future of Business Schools in the UK: Finding a Path to Success*, London: AIM Research.

Bennis, W. and O'Toole, J. (2005), 'How Business Schools Lost their Way', *Harvard Business Review*, 83(5), 96–104.

Kerr, C. (1963), *The Uses of the University*, Cambridge Mass.: Harvard University Press.

Mintzberg, H. (2004), *Managers not MBAs: A Hard Look at the Soft Practice of Managing and Management Development*, San Francisco: Berrett-Koehler Publishers.

Organisation for Economic Cooperation and Development (OECD) (2008), *Tertiary Education for the Knowledge Society*, OECD Thematic Review of Tertiary Education, Paris: OECD.

CHAPTER 3

Developing Management Capability in an Irish Context – Future Trends and Prospects

Denis G. Harrington[1]

School of Business, Waterford Institute of Technology

Introduction

In a lead article in 1988, *The Economist* magazine concluded that the Irish economy was in a catastrophic state, suggesting that Ireland had tried to erect a welfare state on continental European lines in an economy that was too poor to support one. The nation's debt ratio in the 1980s had reached as high as 130 per cent of the gross domestic product (GDP), and unemployment grew to 18 per cent. Industrial unrest was growing, infrastructural problems loomed large and what little trade the country had was over-reliant on the sluggish UK economy. By the middle of the 1980s, economic stagnation was ongoing for five consecutive years and fears were growing over national insolvency. This prompted *The Economist* magazine to lead with the title 'Poorest of the Rich' on its cover and devote a significant commentary to the overall state of the Irish economy. However, only nine years later, in 1997, Ireland featured again on *The Economist*'s cover as Europe's shining light, growing and transforming from a sleepy European backwater into a vibrant economy that in some years grew by as much as 10 per cent. Ireland became the richest country in the European Union (EU) next to Luxembourg, with a per capita GDP higher than that of Germany, France and Britain. The turnaround prompted Friedman, an award-winning *New York Times* columnist, to devote a section to Ireland in his best-selling text, *The World Is Flat*

[1]The author gratefully acknowledges the insights and contributions of the following colleagues in developing this work: Dr Felicity Kelliher, Waterford Institute of Technology; Professor Thomas C. Lawton, Cranfield School of Management, Cranfield University, UK.; Prof. Liam Fahey, Babson College; as well as my fellow editor Dr James A. Cunningham, NUI Galway.

25

(2005). In his book and in a subsequent article in the *New York Times* (2005a), Friedman makes the following key point that Ireland's economic turnaround tells us a lot about Europe today: 'all the innovation is happening on the periphery by those countries embracing globalisation in their own ways – Ireland, Britain, Scandinavia and Eastern Europe – while those following the French-German social model are suffering high unemployment and low growth.'

The Irish economic transformation was purposeful and strategic. The country's industrial policies during that period sought to prioritise community interests over those of individuals and heightened the awareness of the importance of attracting foreign direct investment (FDI). In fact, the country became a magnet for inward investment flows that underpinned a radical restructuring of its industrial base, leading to rapid growth in both imports and exports. The government also invested heavily in developing and nurturing human capital, allowing a focus on upgrading education to develop and nurture young Irish students and managers for the future. In fact, Ireland's total investment in knowledge (including investment in public and private spending on higher education) increased by an average annual rate of over 10 per cent in the past decade compared with averages of around 3 per cent by the EU and the OECD (see *IMD World Competitiveness Yearbook 2007*, <http://www.imd.ch>). The recent IMD report has also shown the education system in Ireland to be one of the best in the world with just less than one million people in full-time education. The system in Ireland produces over 35,000 graduates every year, and, since 1992, there has been an increase of 35 per cent in students studying the third-level engineering and technology courses.

In this sense, one could suggest that it has been the strong support of human capital development and the leveraging of this that has helped to transform business and industry in Ireland over the past decade. Ireland has embraced the need for initiatives that support the development of knowledge equity and capital, and the overall evolution into an information society. Comparisons internationally show that, as a country, Ireland fares well on technological development and adoption, especially given its relatively late industrialisation (O'Higgins 2002). These factors have been significant in the overall development of the economy and strategic positioning of Ireland on the global scale. As the Industrial Development Agency (IDA) suggests, the government's economic policies have been consistently directed towards the creation of a stable economic environment through a focus on knowledge development and diffusion that is supportive of the ideas and requirements of business in the context of the country's economic growth rates; these, up until recently, being among the highest of the OECD countries (see < http://www.idaireland. com>).

Equally, our view and our argument in this book suggest that this period of economic growth across all sectors of the Irish economy has led to a deepening of Irish management experience in managing success and sustainability. As stated earlier, other economies have legacy advantages in the development of managerial capabilities over time with an innate global perspective. Ireland is a relative newcomer, but the country's creativity, attitude and educational qualifications have collectively meant that Ireland has developed a managerial class that is competitive in the global context. Irish managers and the firms in which they operate now exist in an increasingly networked global economy. Presently, as Ireland transits to further compete in the knowledge era, organisations in the country face fast-paced technological, regulatory, environmental, demographic and business cultural change that will impact their ability to remain agile, relevant and viable. This is a key issue for the government and agencies, and also for the wider business community, and will challenge our current thinking on competitiveness in the Irish context. As the government report to the Inter-Departmental Committee on Science, Technology and Innovation on building our knowledge economy emphasised:

> Sustainable economic growth will be dependent on the success of knowledge-driven companies being able to access high skills and new technological developments. Increased R&D performance is essential to develop Ireland as a location for high-tech and knowledge-based industries, to embed the existing multinationals here and to create the 'new' indigenous industries of the future. (2004: 22)

However, many reports have highlighted – and are highlighting – the tensions going forward. The International Monetary Fund (IMF) notes how growth has become increasingly unbalanced in recent years, with heavy reliance on building investment, sharp increases in house prices and rapid credit growth, especially in property-related sectors. At the same time, competitiveness has eroded, reflecting the combination of faster wage growth in Ireland compared to its trading partners, declining productivity growth and the appreciation of the euro against the US dollar. It also concluded that Ireland's small, open economy is vulnerable to external shocks (see <http://www.imf.org>). The aim of this book is to contribute to the debate on how Ireland positions itself for further growth going forward, and how the country responds to some of the challenges that are being outlined by economic and business commentators within the country and further afield.

Quality of Management and Leadership Pivotal to National Performance

In an earlier chapter, our colleague Professor Patrick McNamee charted Ireland's economic development across two key phases: (1) the volume of jobs and the requirement to attract FDI; and (2) the current focus on the development of quality-based growth and the exploitation of ideas and knowledge to create and support new pockets of opportunities.

Professor McNamee also examined the transformation from Web 1.0 to Web 2.0 through the new opportunities presented by the *adaptation* of Web 1.0 in opening the avenues and platforms for marketing, supply chain management, education, and internal and external communication. This evolution presents masses of unforeseen knowledge to businesses, managers and management educators. The main challenge is to encourage an engagement with this new dynamic and stimulate the current cadre of experienced executives to explore new ideas and thinking to further develop their capability sets and exploit the opportunities presented by Web 2.0. Indeed, Ireland's pursuit of a *knowledge economy* requires a honing of its business leadership skills and management capabilities in order to successfully compete on the global stage going forward, a point made forcefully in the Enterprise Strategy Group report *Ahead of the Curve* (2004), which identifies management capability as one of the essential conditions of sustainable progress. There is room for improvement here in the Irish context. In a recent global survey by the World Economic Forum, Ireland's quality of management schools ranked fifteenth, product sophistication twentieth, value chain breadth twentieth and capacity for innovation twenty-fourth, indicating that, among the more developed economies, Ireland lags behind in key areas (World Economic Forum 2008). Within the public sector, a recent study credits the small business sector with aiding economic growth to date, but sees future challenges for management in facilitating greater delegation, delivering higher quality service, often at lower cost, and designing mechanisms to deliver greater transparency and accountability (OECD 2008).

This point has also been made by international commentators in the area, most recently by Hooijberg *et al.* (2007), whose text on the changing nature of leadership in the knowledge era focuses on the need for organisations to facilitate debate on how senior team members create organisations where leadership is developed, knowledge is created and disseminated, meaning is shaped and shared, and vision cascades to all corners of the organisation. All these have heightened awareness of the importance of developing and nurturing managerial capability to support knowledge development and dissemination in organisational contexts. Indeed, management activity also has positive externalities. The conventional economic viewpoint is that the manager, by efficient allocation of resources, generates profit that benefits shareholders and also employees. However, increasingly, there is recognition that managers take part in inter-organisational and regional activities that benefit stakeholders (Mawson 2007). In the south-east region, small businesses and regional development bodies such as enterprise boards and regional assemblies benefit from the input of management of multinational and major indigenous businesses. Small businesses in Ireland have been shown to have benefited from links with and managerial experience served with multinational firms (Arora *et al.* 2001). In terms of management capability, this has been shown, in a small sample study, to lead to improved management education, improved skills in the conduct of international business, and skills in the management of modern distribution systems (McKeon *et al.* 2004).

In view of the above, there is now wide recognition of the fact that knowledge acquisition, sharing and effective management are prerequisites for competitive advantage in a wide range of markets (O'Regan and Ghobadian 2004). The quality of management and leadership is widely regarded as being pivotal to organisational and national performance. This point was made recently by Minister Micheál Martin when he remarked in a speech at the Young Entrepreneur of the Year Awards in 2006 on the increasing complexity of the management task and also on the nature of the skills required to compete in knowledge-based industries. In this context he suggested that 'management capability is now recognised as the most important long-term determinant of success for any company, whether that is at CEO, senior management or board level'. Similarly, Forfás suggest that 'as Ireland repositions itself towards high value-added manufacturing and as the distinction between manufacturing activities and service activities becomes increasingly blurred, management skills become increasingly important' (2007: 5). The Enterprise Strategy Group report (2004) stated that indigenous firms in particular require external assistance in developing their management capabilities and expertise. In the UK there have also been calls to focus attention on better understanding of managerial capability and the potential that managers and leaders have for influencing organisational and national performance (e.g. see Tamkin *et al.* 2003; Burgoyne *et al.* 2004; Tamkin and Denvir 2006). Specifically, the UK Council for Excellence in Management and Leadership stated in their 2002 report that 'good management and leadership is pivotal to investment, productivity, delivery of service and quality of performance across both the public and the private sectors' (5).

Aligning Management Styles and Paradigms to the New Economy

For many companies, increasing the management capability is often relegated as a priority because of more pressing short-term business survival and growth issues. Organisations increasingly view learning as a strategic competency (Richter 1998; Crossan *et al.* 1999); at the same time, they are struggling to change their cultures and processes so that they can capitalise on what people know. Pedler *et al.* suggest that, whilst the information age and the knowledge era put a premium on learning and knowledge creation, blockages to the sharing and transfer of knowledge abound in organisations (2004). As Ghoshal *et al.* comment, 'It is time to expose the old, disabling assumptions and replace them with a different, more realistic set that calls on managers to act out a positive role that can release the vast potential still trapped in the old model' (1999: 9). The writers emphasise the need to replace paternalistic exploitation with employability and value creation in the pursuit of sustainable competitive advantage.

However, the concept of the knowledge economy has changed the paradigm of management in Ireland. The essence of management in the past was stewardship. This focused on preserving order in organisational life. There was emphasis on stability rather than change. The manager was an administrator. Today, new skills are required. These include supply chain management (IDA Ireland 2008), leveraging intellectual capital (Brennan 1999), change management and management of network relationships (McCarthy *et al.* 2003). The new model of management capability in a changed manufacturing and service landscape will involve the manager as innovator and leader within a global competitive arena (Forfás 2008). Innovation in particular, while in danger of becoming an overused mantra, challenges management towards developing new capabilities such as new performance management, longer term thinking, new leadership styles and changes in processes and organisational culture (Hordon 2007).

In this changed context, the major challenge for all organisations, irrespective of size, is the ongoing adaptation of core management paradigms and styles to deal with new knowledge economy trends. This challenge is a major one for the services sector, where value proposition and business models are built on intangible rather than tangible aspects (Iles and Yolles 2002). Consequently, having the people with the right management talent and expertise, who have the capability to deploy multi-business models and manage the resource bank, is critical to sustainable competitive advantage. The managerial role is no longer set within the confines of one organisation but rather straddles the boundaries of a complex nexus of organisations. The manager impacts upon this complexity by virtue of decision making. The manager is not entirely independent. Decisions are a product of previous decisions and also of the potential and actual reactions of other management actors on the network. In this setting, the ability of the manager to cope with constant change impacts on the sense of self. Management development takes place both formally and informally through membership of such networks, as managers learn to integrate the experiences of others with whom they can identify into their own organisations. Within the context of a network, greater investment in management education is likely to pay off in terms of knowledge absorbed and given by an educated manager. The educated manager possesses a high level of human capital that results in a higher incidence of learning from others (Bergin and Kearney 2004).

Future economic development in Ireland depends to a large extent on management's ability to stimulate and develop innovation (OECD 2008). The extent to which a business exploits such innovation opportunities depends on the capabilities resident within the business (Teece *et al.* 1997). Management capability fosters innovation by tapping into experience and 'network effects' as shown in a recent EU-wide study. Specifically, the research showed that social capital at macroeconomic level in regions leads to innovation (Semih and ter Weel 2008). Such social capital formation depends on government intervention (Herreros 2008) and improved regional development emanates from a complex mix of social capital, a commitment to life-long learning and the management of a sense of place (Osborne *et al.* 2007). From a social capital perspective, management capability may be seen, not as something cultivated within the narrow confines of organisational life, but rather as the product of a region. This has implications for business. Certain regions where government-facilitated social capital exists may have greater management capability, or greater capability to grow extant capability. Secondly, management capability may be accessed on a temporary basis, perhaps in the form of inter-organisational cooperation in the form of project management groups. Finally, management capability brought by organisations new to regions may stimulate regional development due to learning effects and linkages with academic and public bodies (Harrington and Kearney 2008). In their report on management and leadership capability in the UK context, Burgoyne *et al.* remarked that, 'Management and leadership capability in the UK (and elsewhere) is substantial and the quality of the capability is difficult to assess. The overall conclusion is that ... there is an opportunity to gain further advantage from its enhancement' (2004: 79).

Developing Capability and the Evolution to Management 2.0 Practices

As outlined earlier, Ireland underwent a significant economic transformation and our success has now encouraged a new set of questions. The abundance of new perspectives and ideas emanating from our companies and business schools is challenging and reshaping the existing practices and business models. We are challenged to rethink the management competencies and capabilities that will shape business success in the next decade and beyond. The development of such management capability will take place in a dynamic context where the relationships between work and worker, leader and team, colleague and colleague will all be subject to re-evaluation and redefinition. The old paradigm will be challenged and will evolve to respond to the demands placed on it from growing numbers of knowledge workers. Storey, in the review of key trends in the area, summarised this as follows: 'Traditional organisations and associated behaviours have outlived their usefulness. Management must seriously question and challenge the ways of thinking that worked in the past ... the old management paradigm of planning, organising and control will be replaced by one of vision, values and empowerment' (2004: 29).

As Ireland continues to transform itself to take advantage of the 'soft revolution' in which knowledge is evolving as the main driver of economic growth, power will shift from business owners and managers to teams of knowledge co-workers. New skills and capabilities will be required to orchestrate distributed forms of leadership that will be increasingly apparent in a large number of organisations. We are, as is suggested in this text, encouraging critical reflection on our experiences and learning over the past ten to fifteen years in an effort to imagine the next evolution in the thinking and practice of management. This should not be a challenging exercise, especially – as Gary Hamel, professor of Strategy at London Business School, correctly remarks – since it is hardly surprising that most thinkers have a difficult time imagining how management might be re-invented in the decades to come, given how little management practices have changed over the past several decades (2007). Consider some examples: we have wider spans of control but the layers are still prevalent in most organisations; we may have passed power on to our middle management teams but they are still largely the 'sense makers' and 'signal givers' in most organisations; most of the key decisions are still made at the top of organisations; and, while executives may feel empowered in organisations, they are still expected to support executive decisions. Storey similarly reports a number of evident problems with current approaches when he shows (drawing from the Work Foundation's 2003 report) that in a survey of 221 firms, while the 'vast majority of senior executives espoused the value of leadership capability as a core organisational priority, in practice they just do not seem to get around to doing much about it at the highest level in the organisation' (2004: 7).

This will change as organisations and their management teams are challenged with the new expectations and demands of knowledge workers. In the search for *difference* and in their efforts to remain relevant in a complex, sophisticated marketplace, a new form of engagement will be necessary to make sense of the masses of unforeseen knowledge (referred to in Chapter 1) available to businesses and their management teams. There will be a focus on the skills and knowledge needed to exploit and not just access key information to support executive decision making, and knowledge teams will excel not just by possessing traditional skills and tools but by demonstrating a degree of agility in dealing with technology and people, and by staying meaningfully connected to others in a diverse and changing world (see more on these ideas at <http://www.strategy-business.com>; and Malknight and Keys 2007). My colleague and co-editor Dr James A. Cunningham also reinforces this argument in the next chapter when he posits that the challenge now is to provide real clarity of purpose for the employee with the role of the manager, evolving into that of a coach, who takes a holistic perspective in managing all the ingredients and environments to inspire exceptional individual performance in a team-orientated context. Our position and argument is that the role of the manager will extend beyond the planning, leading, organising and controlling functions to that of enabling; that is, managers in this new environment will be *enablers* as opposed to *doers*. Leaders will enable teams of knowledge workers to build competence to execute key strategic decisions.

This argument is consistent with Hamel's thinking (2007*a*) where again he suggests that, in the new economy, the individuals and organisations that create wealth are those that upend long-held industry conventions and challenge the old assumptions. They re-imagine their marketplace and provide customers with products and services that could scarcely have been imagined a few years earlier. In doing so, they render the existing business models obsolete. In this new environment, where the new power derives from 'softer', more creative sources, the key threat to continued success is not inefficiency but *irrelevancy*. Organisations that are not engaging their workforce in meaningful ways to instil this new sense of competitiveness are already on the road to insignificance. This applies as much to individuals as to the firms in which they work. The late Peter Drucker remarked in a significant contribution to the *Harvard Business Review* as early as 1999 that: 'In the new knowledge economy, each of us becomes our own CEO. Doing the analysis is not enough ... knowing our strengths, our method of work and our values is the starting point, but the key is to *act* on this knowledge' (1999: 66).

New Organisations: Places of Engagement and Creativity

In responding to some of these challenges, and in particular in facilitating a new form of engagement that will allow a more distributed form of organisational leadership, there will be a requirement for what Dess and Pickens (2000) describe as a 'loosening up of the organisation' to encourage creativity and adaptation without losing strategic focus or spinning out of control. In this book we argue that organisations need to transform themselves to become 'places of engagement and creativity' where dialogue is valued and individuals are encouraged to continually re-imagine 'space and place'. In organisations that transition to create and exploit socialisation and creativity capabilities, leaders at various points in the firm become *strategy and management practice carriers*. This we refer to as the process of evolution to Management Practice 2.0, emphasising a form of emotional and behavioural leadership that will use real engagement as a form of strategic thinking. In practice, this point was made by Jack Welch when he remarked: 'The pace of events is going to be so fast that people aren't going to wait for the next level of approvals. There is going to have to be far more delegation. There is going to have to be far more participation. The leader must become an ever more engaging coach, an ever more engaging person' (Garten 2001: 111).

So, what are our responses as business leaders, thinkers and educators to the changes underway in the wider business context? The important issue for thought-leaders and educators is to explore future directions in ways that are inclusive of current thinking but at the same time aware of the requirement to suggest themes for discussion that help us to challenge long-held conventions and old assumptions. In this context, we would like to explore some ideas drawing on our ongoing work in Ireland and overseas in addressing some of the challenges previously outlined.

Moving forward, it is significant that we promote and build awareness of the relationship between management capabilities at all levels and organisational performance. In this context, the critical importance and contribution of education, training and ongoing professional practice development needs to be highlighted. This will ensure that our teams of knowledge workers are equipped with the necessary skills and knowledge to undertake their work effectively. As outlined in the earlier sections of this account, particular emphasis should be placed on the non-technical management domains, namely communication, leadership and areas associated with innovation and creativity. To underpin this focus on capability building, we highlight the requirement for studies of leadership capability and practice to develop an empirical basis for evaluating what is actually being done to encourage and develop the nation's management talent and improve the overall performance.

In disseminating the knowledge of these and other activities, we also suggest the need for a greater examination of practitioner–academic relationships and partnerships to promote a network of shared learning and experiences amongst our management community. This will also be used to manage collaboration and foster creativity and innovation across all sectors of the economy.

Developing New Models of the Practitioner–Academic Partnership

In order to ensure relevance in a dynamic business environment, there is need for greater consideration of the methods and approaches of engaging leading practitioners at the frontline of Irish business evolution within the system of knowledge dissemination. In Ireland, we have particular issues in that we do not have the sustained history of knowledge dissemination, and, due to the rapid pace of change in our economy, the story will be outdated by the time it is clear enough to codify (Kelliher *et al.* 2007). Educational institutions have an opportunity to position themselves as unique sites of knowledge generation and diffusion in this environment, and they encourage a new kind of engagement with students and executives.

As we know, and as is reported elsewhere, there is a developing interest in linking academic ideas and knowledge to practice (Sizer 2001; Starkey and Tempest 2005; Augier and March 2007). Bennis and O'Toole (2005) have argued that business school faculties must simply rediscover the practice of business, and that academia needs business cooperation in order to discover what goes on managerially in companies (Starkey and Tempest 2005). Watson has reinforced this perspective by contending that management education should lead to three distinct characteristics: skills of intellectual analysis, interpersonal skills and a body of knowledge about organisations (1993). Indeed, in his account in Chapter 2, our colleague Professor Roy Green pointed out that some international business schools have pursued a more innovative approach to the curriculum with an emphasis on 'customisation' and 'flexibility', whereby students are mentored through chosen career pathways. What all these writers have in common is their emphasis on the need to infuse the business curriculum with multidisciplinary, real-world, practical and ethical ideas, and questions and analyses reflecting the complex and challenging world that business leaders face.

Again, in response to this requirement and the overall need for greater interaction and a form of dynamic collaboration between third-level institutions and corporate leaders in modern Ireland, we suggest a requirement for practitioner–academic partnerships to cultivate a practice-based perspective in leadership education and training (see Kelliher *et al.* 2007). This is a live and ongoing project at the School of Business at Waterford Institute of Technology where we are developing a model for a practitioner–academic partnership in disseminating and spreading *leader knowledge*. The leader-knowledge dissemination model aims to promote the cycle of theoretical action and practical conceptualisation among students through their interaction with business leaders. The proposed model promotes the skills of intellectual analysis, interpersonal prowess and deep knowledge about organisations, as advised by

Watson (1993), and seeks to develop each skill in management education, rather than focusing solely on knowledge attainment, prevalent in the traditional business education environment. Through the introduction of a new CEO in Residence Programme we are evaluating the potential for co-created knowledge to facilitate the development of management capabilities among business and management students within the School of Business at Waterford Institute of Technology. We also suggest that it will carry wider significance and relevance for business leaders and educators in Ireland and also internationally.

Conclusion: The Journey of Discovery and Evolution

Overall, these responses and initiatives will help stimulate a new form of engagement and confidence to embrace the challenges that lie ahead. This is significant because, as O'Higgins reminds us in a contribution to the *Academy of Management Executive* in 2002, even where there is a national-level social consensus on the importance of developing managerial knowledge and capabilities, such consensus must be translated into 'co-operative modern workplace practices to ensure gains in productivity and innovation for competitiveness' (117). The complex, changing and turbulent world characterising organisations today, staffed by increasingly diverse and knowledgeable people, can no longer be pulled together by bureaucratic authority. The enterprises that flourish and that continue to be competitive are those where every organisational member will have the necessary tools not only to run his or her immediate work area, but also to see how that function connects to the rest of the organisation (Raelin 2006).

Many will argue that we have been here before, debating and discussing the fads and fashions of different management practices or paradigms. Others will highlight the apparent tensions in achieving the bigger ideas of the last decade and still more will offer illuminating critical evaluations of some of the ideas and concepts presented in this text. All are welcome and add to the network of knowledge that culminates in the editing of a text such as this one. In saying this, I am aware that our ideas build on the thinking espoused by the late Sumantra Ghoshal who, at the close of the last century, observed a very different management philosophy emerging and one that he suggested would become dominant – the purpose, process, people philosophy. Perhaps we are still on that journey, on the evolution to a more engaging management philosophy, whereby, as Ghoshal suggests, we move beyond strategy to purpose, beyond structure to process and beyond systems to people. Specifically, he wrote about a shift in the basic doctrine of shareholder capitalism, so that:

> If people are adding the most value then people will increasingly have to be seen as investors, not as employees. Shareholders invest money and expect a return on their money and expect capital growth. People will be seen in the same way. So they will invest their human capital in the company, will expect a return on it, and expect growth of that capital.' (1999:19)

We hope that in our work and collaborations in the development of this project, and in participating and observing the practice of management, that we will help to further stimulate the growth of human capital development in Ireland and to contribute to the debate on future thinking on management education and practice. For, in the end, as Handy reminds us in his book *The New Alchemists*, 'There is much that we don't know about alchemy, even after a concentrated year of talking to some outstanding practitioners. We can only learn by watching and observing others ... the best that we can do is to make it fashionable to try, for fashion is still the most powerful agent of change in every field, including that of business and organisation' (1999: 238).

References

Arora, A., Gambardella, A. and Torrisi, S. (2001), 'In the Footsteps of Silicon Valley? Indian and Irish Software in the International Division of Labour', SIEPR discussion paper 00-41, Stanford Institute for Economic Policy Research, Stanford, CA.

Augier, M. and March, J.G. (2007), 'The Pursuit of Relevance in Management Education', *California Management Review*, 49(3), 129–146.

Bennis, W. and O'Toole, J. (2005), 'How Business Schools Lost Their Way', *Harvard Business Review*, 83(5), 96–104.

Bergin, A. and Kearney, I. (2004), 'Human Capital, the Labour Market and Productivity Growth in Ireland', ESRI working paper No.158.

Brennan, N. (1999), 'Reporting and Managing Intellectual Capital: Evidence from Ireland', OECD Symposium on Measuring and Reporting of Intellectual Capital, Amsterdam, June 9–11.

Burgoyne, J., Hirsh, W. and Williams, S. (2004), 'The Development of Management and Leadership Capability and Its Contribution to Performance: The Evidence, Prospects and the Research Need',

Research Report RR560, Department for Education and Skills, Lancaster University, UK.

Commission of the European Communities (CEC) (1996), 'The First Action Plan for Innovation in Europe – Innovation for Growth and Employment', COM (96) 589 Final, Brussels.

Council for Excellence in Management and Leadership (2002), *Managers and Leaders Raising Our Game*, final report of the Council for Excellence in Management and Leadership, London, UK.

Crossan, M.M., Lane, H.W. and White, R.E. (1999), 'An Organizational Learning Framework: From Intuition to Institution', *The Academy of Management Review*, 24(3), 522–37.

Dess, G.G. and Pickens, J.C. (2000), 'Changing Roles – Leadership in the 21st Century', *Organisational Dynamics*, 28(3), 18–34.

Drucker, P. (1999), 'Managing Oneself', *Harvard Business Review*, March–April, 77(2), 65–74.

Enterprise Strategy Group (2004), *Ahead of the Curve*, Enterprise Strategy Group, available at: <http://www.forfas.ie>.

Expert Group on Future Skills Needs (2005), *SME Management Development in Ireland*, Dublin.

Forfás (2008), *The Report of the High-Level Group on Manufacturing*, available from: <http://www.forfas.ie>.

Forfás (2007), *Research and Development Performance in the Business Sector Ireland 2005–6*, Dublin: Forfás Publications.

Friedman, T.L. (2005), *The World Is Flat*, New York: Random House.

Friedman, T.L. (2005a), 'The End of the Rainbow', *New York Times*, 29 June 2005.

Garten, J.E. (2001), *The Mind of the CEO*, New York: Basic Books.

Ghoshal, S., Bartlett, C.A. and Moran, P. (1999), 'A New Manifesto for Management', *MIT Sloan Management Review*, Spring, 40(3), 9–20.

Government of Ireland (2004), *Building Ireland's Knowledge Economy: Report to the Inter-Departmental Committee on Science, Technology and Innovation*, available at: <http://www.entemp.ie/>.

Grant, R.M. (1991), *Contemporary Strategy Analysis: Concepts, Techniques, and Applications*, Oxford: Blackwell.

Hamel, G. (2007), 'What Google, Whole Foods Do Best', available at: <http://money.cnn.com>.

Hamel, G. (2007*a*), *The Future of Management*, Massachusetts: Harvard Business Press.

Handy, C. (1999), *The New Alchemists*, London: Random House Group.

Harrington, D. and Kearney, A. (2008), 'Management Innovation in an Irish Context', Working Paper, School of Business, WIT.

Herreros, F. (2008), *The Problem of Forming Social Capital: Why Trust?*, New York: Palgrave.

Hooijberg, R., Hunt, J. *et al.* (2007), *Being There Even When You Are Not – Leading through Strategy, Structures, and Systems*, UK: Elsevier.

Hordon, D. (2007), 'Innovation and Creativity', IMI Paper, available at: <http://www.imi.ie/uploads/innovation_04_07_web_002.pdf>.

Iles, P. and Yolles, M. (2002), 'Across the Great Divide: HRD, Technology Translation, and Knowledge Migration in Bridging the Knowledge Gap between SMEs and Universities', *Human Resource Development International*, 5(1), 23–53.

IMD (2007), *World Competitiveness Yearbook*, Switzerland, May.

Industrial Development Agency (IDA) Ireland (2008), 'Supply Chain Management', available at: <http//www.idaireland.com>.

Kelliher, F., Harrington, D. and Galavan, R. (2007), 'Spreading Leader Knowledge: A Proposal for Practitioner-Academic Partnership in Disseminating Leader Knowledge', *Conference Proceedings of the Irish Academy of Management*, Best Paper Award, September 2007.

Malknight, T. and Keys, T. (2007), 'Surfing the Storm: Translating Long-Term Global Trends into Today's Decisions', IMD No. 145, April, available at: <http://www.imd.ch>.

Mawson, J. (2007), 'Regional Governance in England: Past Experience and Future Directions', *International Journal of Public Sector Management*, 20(61), 548–86.

McCarthy, A., Garavan, T. and O'Toole, T. (2003), 'HRD: Working at the Boundaries and Interfaces of Organisations', *Journal of European Industrial Training*, 27(2), 58–72.

McKeon, H., Johnston, K. and Henry, C. (2004), 'Multinational Companies as a Source of Entrepreneurial Learning: Examples from the IT Sector in Ireland', *Education and Training*, 46(8), 433–43.

Nielsen, B. (2000), 'Strategic Knowledge Management: a Research Agenda', working paper 2, Copenhagen Business School.

Nolan, D. (2008), 'Ireland Ahead on Finance but Behind on People Skills', Irish Management Institute, available at: <http://www.imi.ie>.

O'Higgins, E. (2002), 'Government and the Creation of the Celtic Tiger: Can Management Maintain the Momentum?' *Academy of Management Executive*, 16(3), 104–20.

O'Regan, N. and Ghobadian, A. (2004), 'The Importance of Capabilities for Strategic Direction and Performance', *Management Decision*, 42(1–2), 292–312.

Organisation for Economic Cooperation and Development (OECD) (2008), *Economic Survey of Ireland 2008*, 16 April, OECD.

Osborne, M., Sankey, K. and Wilson, B. (2007), *Social Capital, Lifelong Learning and the Management of Place*, London: Routledge.

Pedler, M., Burgoyne, J., and Boydell, T. (2004), *A Manager's Guide to Leadership*, London: McGraw-Hill Business.

Raelin, J. (2006), 'Does Action Learning Promote Collaborative Leadership?', *The Academy of Management Learning and Education*, 5(2), 152–69.

Richter, I. (1998), 'Individual and Organizational Learning at the Executive Level', *Management Learning*, 29(3), 299–316.

Semih, A. and ter Weel, B. (2008), 'Social Capital, Innovation and Growth: Evidence from Europe', Institute for Study of Labour, IZA paper 3341, February 2008.

Shaw, E., O'Loughlin, A. and McFadzean, E. (2005), 'Corporate Entrepreneurship and Innovation Part 2: A Role and Process Based Approach', *European Journal of Innovation Management*, 8(4), 393–408.

Sizer, J. (2001), 'Research and the Knowledge Age', *Tertiary Education and Management*, 7(3), 227–42.

Starkey, K. and Tempest, S. (2005), 'The Future of the Business School: Knowledge Challenges and Opportunities', *Human Relations*, 58(1), 61–83.

Storey, J. (2004), 'Signs of Change: Damned Rascals and Beyond', in J. Storey (ed.), *Leadership in Organisations: Current Issues and Key Trends,* London: Routledge.

Tamkin, P. and Denvir, A. (2006), *Strengthening the UK Evidence Base on Management and Leadership Capability*, IES Report 2117, Brighton: Institute for Employment Studies UK.

Tamkin, P., Hirsh, W. and Tyers, C. (2003), 'Chore to Champions: The Making of Better People Managers', IES Report 389, Brighton: Institute for Employment Studies UK.

Teece, D., Pisano, G. and Schuen, A. (1997), 'Dynamic Capabilities and Strategic Management', *Strategic Management Journal*, 18(7), 509–30.

Watson, S.R. (1993), 'The Place for Universities in Management Education', *Journal of General Management*, 19(2), 14–42.

World Economic Forum (WEF) (2008), *The Global Competitiveness Report*, available at: <http//:www.gcr.weforum.org>.

Work Foundation (2003), *Developing Leaders*, London: Work Foundation.

CHAPTER 4

Management 2.0: Challenges and Implications

James A. Cunningham[1]

J.E. Cairnes School of Business and Economics,
National University of Ireland, Galway

'I must create a System or be enslaved by another Man's
I will not Reason and Compare; my business is to Create.'

William Blake (1757–1827)

Introduction

In advertising the new Audi A6, Audi claim to have more patents filed for this model than that of NASA. The approach by music executives to invest in new talent for global markets changed when the Arctic Monkeys, a Yorkshire-based band, succeeded in the monetisation of their music and gained popularity by using social networking. Radiohead have gone even further by releasing one of their albums online. Their fans pay whatever price they feel it is worth. Even Google have launched a satellite channel, *Current TV*, which potentially could change the business model for the sources and production of TV programmes. Countries such as Macedonia are offering foreign direct investment (FDI) companies an array of financial incentives to locate in Skopje, which includes 0 per cent corporation tax for ten years and 10 per cent thereafter, 5 per cent personal income tax for five years and 10 per cent thereafter, and no value added tax (VAT) and customs duties for

[1] The author gratefully acknowledges the insights and contributions of the following colleagues in developing this work: Prof. Charles Snow, Penn State University; Dr Martin Fahy, CEO, FINSIA, Australia; Mr Eoin Daly, partner, McKinsey and Co., London; Mr Stephen Allot, chairman, Trinamo, London; Dr Richard Schroth, CEO, Executive Insights Maryland, USA; as well as my fellow editor Dr Denis G. Harrington, Waterford Institute of Technology.

export production. Other countries like India and China are attempting to be attractive from manufacturing and research and development (R&D) perspectives simultaneously. The pace of change is relentless, not only within the industries and firms but also within societies. Ideas and business models that were considered unimaginable are now the norm in many industries. In addition, the new power players in international financial markets have enabled the growth of both hedge funds and private equity firms by providing greater liquidity. In particular, Asia's central banks and oil-rich producers will have an even greater influence over international financial markets based on their growing capital size. In tandem with this development come the changes in governance structures. In this structurally changing context, the four key tasks of managers, that is, planning, leading, organising and controlling, seem unchanged and timeless at one level, but have become more sophisticated in daily organisational life. But do they remain the core tasks for managers in the 21st century? In this chapter, the managerial challenges and Management 2.0 are outlined; the implications for managers, business schools, society and government are discussed; and the Management 2.0 organisations are described.

Management 2.0: Managerial Challenges

The challenges that face managers are significant against a backdrop where employees and society are becoming increasingly sceptical about a range of issues and where personal intellectual property is being valued and monetized more through the advent of social networking. New organisational structures are emerging that ensure that organisations are using the concept of social networking to source ad hoc expertise to fulfil certain tasks for a period of time, which are transactional in their orientation. Collaborative innovation and entrepreneurship within and outside firms are becoming the norm. Consequently, aided by advances in Web technologies, an increasing number of people are working for a variety of companies, making the concept of the portfolio worker a reality for a growing percentage of the workers. The appeal of convergent markets and technologies is growing apace where, for example, food producers are collaborating with pharmaceutical companies in developing products that have health benefits and may be preventative in nature. New products being developed around convergent technologies in information and communications technology (ICT) and biomedical market arenas are potentially leading to changes in the current business models for the delivery of health care to users, and this will potentially lead to more patient DIY diagnosis and monitoring. The pace of offshoring of activities to lower cost locations continues to be seen in only 1 per cent of companies strategically assessing the rationale for undertaking such an activity (Ghemawat 2007), leaving county multinational corporation managers dealing with a death watch challenge. Governments and policy makers are being challenged to provide supportive economic and societal conditions that enhance organisational and industrial competitiveness from exploitation (manufacturing) and exploration (R&D) perspectives. The demand for accessible public services is growing apace as citizens are becoming more vocal about deficits in service offerings. Even the whole notion of government being the architect and the provider of public services is coming under increasing scrutiny in different jurisdictions. The lines between activities that are good public activities are beginning to blur significantly for citizens, politicians and civil servants alike. Yet, irrespective of the context, there are four key managerial challenges – strategic challenge, continuous change challenge, temporal context challenge and trade-off challenge – that organisations and managers face in a changing economy. How they are addressed in the Management 2.0 context is outlined in Table 4.1.

Strategic Challenge

Given the changes in markets, industry and sectors, the single largest challenge for businesses is having real clarity about what their core business activity, value propositions and future orientation are. Simply put, it is the perennial question for any organisation: what businesses or activities are you in? Irrespective of the size, scale and reach of an organisation, having a collective managerial and organisational view of its purpose is essential to serving the customer's perceptual and actual needs, attracts the best human talent and drives individual, team and organisational performance. It also encompasses developing and refining authentic value propositions that transcend organisational essence, purpose and strategy and is translated with competitive impact into the marketplace. Given the increasing disaggregating of value chains and evolving collaborative organisational structures, and customers being more informed and demanding, having real clarity about purpose is essential and it affords the management team the possibility to build a core organisational posture that is simultaneously strong and flexible. This enables the organisation to sustain itself through multiple forms of competitive challenges without losing its focus on achieving

Table 4.1: Management 2.0 Managerial Challenges

Managerial Challenge	Management 2.0
Strategic challenge • Clarity about essence, purpose, strategy and core business activities.	• Communicating organisational essence, purpose and strategy clearly to all individuals. • Developing core organisational posture – secure and flexible. • Agile strategy process. • Understanding of real value of strategy. • New governance structures.
Continuous change challenge • Innovate or die. • Fit with customer expectations, stated purpose, strategy and defined value propositions.	• Identification of successful management and strategy practice bundles. • Experiential understanding of customers that is holistic in nature. • Futurology. • Analysis of competitors' CEOs, patterns of behaviour, actions and decision making.
Temporal context challenge • Emotional connections with stakeholders.	• Metaphors grounded in journeys rather than destinations.
Trade-off challenge • Customer offering. • Long- and short-term performance. • Risk and reward levels. • Manager and individual plays.	• Clear communication of boundaries of customer offering. • An achieving strategic role of board members. • Profit and CSR measures reporting. • Increased personalisation of performance with additional measures linked to overall guiding principles. • Manager as performance coach/enabler.

core activity objectives. But even in a Management 2.0 context it goes deeper than just purpose – it is about defining the essence of the organisation.

In a Management 2.0 context this means that all individuals and stakeholders involved in an organisation have an understanding in clear and unambiguous terms of the essence, purpose and the strategy of the business. Moreover, individuals and stakeholders understand the purpose and their role in delivering the organisational strategy on a day-to-day basis, and that the risk and reward of achieving it is personalised for each employee, and this is attributable to value propositions. Organisational essence and purpose will become an important part of shaping organisational culture as organisations deploy more business models to support product and service offerings, which are aligned with the organisational strategy. Furthermore, from the core anchor of organisational essence, organisations can engage in collaborative innovation and entrepreneurship inside and outside the firm. In the case of Ryanair, all stakeholders, internal and external, have a clear and unambiguous understanding of its essence, purpose and strategy. Such clarity gives Ryanair a core organisational posture, affording them a flexibility of response to competitive challenges. Public sector entities dealing with the strategic challenge can even prove to be more challenging and potentially fruitless given the complexities and the interrelationship of activities. Nonetheless, it requires public sector entities to clearly state and communicate their organisational purpose and strategy. Take the example of the Health Service Executive (HSE); multiple views have emerged as to the essence, purpose and strategy of the HSE, simultaneously heightening expectations and discontent.

Secondly, dealing with the strategic challenge in a Management 2.0 context requires managers to understand and develop an agile strategy process (from crafting to implementation), which is enabled by a social process that rapidly converts creativity and entrepreneurship into actions that are aligned to purpose and uniqueness. Having a meaningful and active socialisation process around organisational strategy processes is essential in building a core organisational posture and moulding core organisational understanding of essence, purpose, strategy and key competitive challenges. An active and meaningful socialisation process connects with the inner life of employees (Amabile and Kramer 2007), reduces internal organisational filters and enhances managerial and organisational credibility. Traditionally, this social process may be confined within the organisation but in a Management 2.0 context it means developing a socialisation process that encompasses competitors, customers, research institutions, government bodies and other industries, using the principles of social networking. The process is collaborative at its core. Web 2.0 has the potential to provide the enabling tools to achieve elements of the socialisation processes external to the organisation, which serve the essence, purpose and strategy of the organisation. Such an agile strategy process allows for the deployment of business models that have commonality across core activity areas but are customised depending on the market or individual customer context.

Finally, dealing with the strategic challenges in a Management 2.0 environment requires that managers see, understand and buy into the real value of strategy, which can be difficult given the tactical and daily operational focus and the temporal nature of organisational life. The structural changes of the sources of capital and the shift in power to Asian central banks and oil-rich countries may force managers and organisations to think about organising their operations differently, to seek new forms of collaboration within and outside the firm and to develop more sophisticated governance structures.

Continuous Change Challenge

The continuous change challenge is all too familiar for managers and employees alike. Managerial and performance expectations are growing exponentially quarter on quarter, with many of the constraints that inhibit performance remaining constant. New formal and informal routines and processes are devised to deal with these performance expectations. The mantra 'innovate or die' is rolled out by managers and organisations as a means of coping with a continuous change challenge, but its effectiveness on organisational employees seems to lessen with time. The managerial expectation is that there is real sustainable fit between customers and organisational posited value propositions and the manner in which goods or services are delivered to consumers. In simple terms, why should anyone buy anything from your business now, in one year's time, in five years' time or in ten years' time? Will their usage and purchasing patterns change? In essence, the real continuous change challenge is to ensure sustainable real ongoing alignment between stated purpose, strategy, defined authentic value propositions (i.e. uniqueness of product or service) and customer expectations (i.e. perceptual and actual).

Dealing with this challenge in a Management 2.0 context requires managers and organisations to develop effective management systems that are clearly aligned bundles of management and strategy practices, and to understand and improve on an ongoing basis the linkages that exist between stated business strategy, process, performance outcomes and learning. In simple terms, this is about achieving 100 per cent operational effectiveness on a consistent basis. Furthermore, the management system required to manage the exploration (research and development) part of an organisation differs from the exploitation (manufacturing) parts. Experience and learning curve effects come into play, but also the manager's willingness to reflect on all types of performance. In international rugby, it is normal for individual players to get a DVD after each match capturing their positive and negative performances on the pitch. Coaches can then use these to improve the individual technical aspects of a player's game which ultimately contributes to the overall team performance. How many managers can claim that they can identify bundles of management and strategy practices on daily or weekly basis that contribute to the success of their companies? Therefore, management system failures and successes need to be marked and really understood within the organisation so as to achieve operational effectiveness on a consistent basis, broadening the role of a manager to that of a coach.

Secondly, managers need to gain a real understanding of what it is that makes the firm offering unique and relevant to customers. This means that managers and organisations need to invest more time and resources in really understanding the customer. The reality is that customers do exaggerate their needs and preferences. In a Management 2.0 context, this means understanding the customers in a holistic way, not just in terms of the product or service that your company is selling. For managers, it means experiential immersion in understanding of customers through working and living with them for periods of time in different cultural and transactional contexts. Through this experiential approach, a manager can gain a greater insight into the authentic uniqueness and relevance of his or her company's product and services and into whether his or her stated essence, purpose, strategy and value propositions connect with the customers and are meeting real market problems in different transactional and cultural contexts. In addition, managers see new opportunities where they could potentially begin to disaggregate their value chain and develop new streams from the existing activities. Such an experiential focus also allows the managers and the organisations to deal with or to develop strategies around horizontal innovation (see Miles *et al.* 2005).

The final element of dealing with continuous change challenge is devoting organisational time and effort to thinking conceptually about the future industry or market sector's competitive and customer landscapes. This reflection should encompass gaining a deeper understanding of competitors, not in terms of product or service offering alone, but in terms of their management team, board and CEO. This is important as the more uncertain the environments become, the more probable that human beings, particularly top team managers, will repeat consistent management practice patterns of behaviour, actions and decision making.

Understanding these managerial patterns in competitor organisations affords a new level of understanding of both the competitive environment and the real capabilities of competitors from a short-, medium- and long-term perspective. In essence, it is developing this cool running effect that captures movements internally and externally, leading to mastery of organisational and competitive context, which can ultimately lead to market dominance.

Consequently, in a Management 2.0 context, understanding management and strategy practice bundles that intersect with strategic and operation practices, an experiential-based perspective of customers coupled with competitor analysis and an understanding of competitor managerial behaviour patterns, provides managers with an ability to cope effectively with the continuous change challenge at an organisational and individual level. This provides the organisation with clear quantification for the evolution of credible uniqueness and relevance in terms of each transaction with customers for their products or services through clearly stated value propositions. For some commentators, Google symbolises this ability to harness continuous and relentless change, which can then lead to an exponential growth in customer usage and demand.

Temporal Context Challenge

How often have we looked at old photographs and cringed to see the haircuts and the clothes, or, when new models of cars come into the market, do we see the old model in a different light. In other words, the context changes and so do our perceptions. The natural human focus tends to be on the short term, the here and now, and it is hard to envisage the future. For managers, the fusing of past, present and future in an accessible manner that creates an emotional connection with stakeholders in a temporal context is a significant challenge, particularly given the real scepticism that pervades society, organisations and employees.

To cope with this challenge, the Management 2.0 context fuses the past, present and future by focusing on the metaphors and language that are used to describe the organisational essence and purpose. Due to increased individual uncertainty, the human focus is on the present, a situation that is heightened by the growing fragmentation of society. Therefore, focusing in a metaphorical sense on journeys rather than places appeals to the temporal human focus. Grounding metaphors in journeys not only provides flexibility in terms of actions and approaches, but also provides interesting challenges for the organisation and individuals. This approach does not negate the fact that quantitative measures are essential, but the metaphor of the journey draws the individual focus and attention to real open-ended challenges and further opportunities. Therefore, reaching the profit and sales targets will not hold people's long-term attention or provide a real long-term challenge. The development of overarching organisational strategy scripts, grounded in essence and purpose, that encompass the temporality of all stakeholders is one means of overcoming this temporal context challenge. Doing so should create a common sustainable understanding of organisational essence and purpose. For Vodafone it is 'How are you?', for Tesco it is 'Every little helps' and for Coca-Cola it is 'Making every drop count'. Moreover, the language and metaphorical linkage between stated essence purpose, strategy, value propositions and lived daily reality for employees is critical in dealing with temporal context challenge. Take, for example, Toyota, one the world's most successful car manufacturers. Toyota's organisational strategy script is 'The best built cars in the world' and its organisational purpose is based on quality (the Toyota Way), which is a journey that is simple, emotional and clear. Katsuaki Watanabe, CEO of Toyota, puts it succinctly: 'The Toyota Way has been and will continue to be the standard for everyone who works for Toyota all over the world. Our guiding principles define Toyota's mission and values, but the Toyota Way defines how we work. To me, it's like the air we breathe' (2007: 80). Using quality as a key metric for being number one is less temporal than sales or market share. This simplicity of approach to quality means it transcends all organisational levels. It manifests itself at operational and production level where workers can pull the andon cord to stop production. In doing so, the rhetoric from the CEO has not only organisational-wide reality but also market-wide reality. It creates a compelling common mindshare that has impact beyond the organisational boundary. It is best summed up by Watanabe:

> I don't know how many years it's going to take us, but I want Toyota to come up the with the dream car – a vehicle that makes the air cleaner than it is, a vehicle that cannot injure people, a vehicle that prevents accidents from happening, a vehicle that can make people healthier the longer they drive it, a vehicle that can excite, entertain, and evoke the emotions of its occupants, a vehicle than can drive around the world on just one tank of gas. That's what I dream about. (2007: 82)

Choosing a compelling and authentic journey-based metaphor for your context that takes into account stakeholder mindshare really challenges CEOs and managers to define the essence and purpose of the business.

Trade-off Challenge

Increasing analytical focus and scrutiny is centred on the appropriate business model that organisations need to adopt to be sustainable over a lengthy period of time. Volatility in the financial markets in the latter quarter of 2007 and first two quarters of 2008 highlights that growth and organisational performance at all costs can have implications for the manner in which industries, organisations and individual managers approach the trade-off challenge. Managers face a number of trade-off challenges.

The first challenge is with their customers with respect to the products or services they are willing to place in the market using online and offline transactional and distribution channels with varying price points. The main challenges in deciding what way to serve the strategic customer typically are internal, depending on the political strength of managers and departments. For many managers, their strategic customer is the next managerial grade or a competing department or strategic business unit and not the end buyer of the product or service. In a Management 2.0 context, the boundaries are clearly laid in terms of dealing with the customer trade-off challenge, as is the case currently with Ryanair customers who know exactly what they will get and expect when travelling with this airline. Managers functioning within the Management 2.0 model need to set clear service and product expectation levels with customers. In a public sector environment, having such clarity about what services will and will not be provided will become essential in setting customer expectations. Take the announcement in January 2008 by Gordon Brown, prime minister of the UK, of a more personalised National Health Service (NHS) for end users, based on choice. This evolution in purpose will challenge existing structures and management systems within the NHS and clearly shows to citizens where the user trade-offs will exist.

The second trade-off challenge is with stakeholders in terms of short- and long-term growth prospects and the leveraging of capabilities to deliver quarter-on-quarter growth in profitability and net margins. Some studies have shown that, at board level, directors abdicate their strategy obligations, bringing into question the real efficiency of capital markets (see McNulty and Pettigrew 1999). In dealing with this trade-off in a Management 2.0 context, the long-term performance orientation will ultimately matter more from a risk and investor perspective. The fundamental structural changes in international capital markets may further change this investor perspective. Moreover, long-term performance will also encompass many aspects of corporate social responsibility (CSR) and involve collaborative innovation and entrepreneurship for non-economic purposes. Critical to this will be the role of directors and non-executive directors in determining the essence, purpose and strategy agenda for the company. Abdication of this responsibility will no longer be a tenable position to take for corporate boards. Furthermore, in a Management 2.0 context, companies' activity measuring will include various aspects of CSR performance data. Such data will be reported and validated more comprehensively and authenticated independently in the same manner as financial data, and CSR performance will coalesce with the existing performance measures and in time could even be individualised per employee.

The third trade-off challenge is with employees, particularly at the risk and reward levels. A symptom of the realignment of this trade-off is the changes in private pension schemes for newly appointed workers in many companies, which fundamentally impact, in psychological terms, the employee and employer contract. In a Management 2.0 context, increased risk-taking is divested to individual managers in terms of the configuration of resources to achieve required performances, with a greater sharing of the rewards. Nevertheless, the risk and the reward levels will become even more personalised and include more measures to ensure that managers will operate towards a number of simple principles. This means reorienting existing performance management systems from activity management systems to real and meaningful performance management systems that underpin organisational management systems.

This brings us to the final trade-off challenge: the manager versus the individual. At its basic level, everyone in an organisation is competing with each other for varying outcomes and recognition. Such competition is desirable to ensure organisational performance and that the best skills and talents of individuals are used to maximum effect. In a Management 2.0 context, harnessing the collective team effort over the individual manager is the real trade-off challenge. For managers, it will mean providing real clarity of essence and purpose, which encompasses such activities as quantification of effort, the visualisation of tasks and objectives and the use of metaphors to describe a journey rather than a destination. Consequently, in practical terms, the role of the manager evolves into that of a coach, like in competitive team sports, who takes a holistic perspective of the employee, organisational management systems, competitive conditions, etc, which require the management and coaching of exceptional individual performance in a team-orientated context. In doing so, the focus will be on team performance and increased levels of consistent individual performance, but managing the inner life of employees will become more common in companies. An extension of this coaching role is for managers to create an organisational enabling platform for employees to develop in an individual and collective way.

From Doing to Enabling: Creativity and Socialisation

In dealing with the four challenges in a Management 2.0 context, the role of the manager extends beyond the planning, leading, organising and controlling functions, which are core to the management function, to becoming that of an enabler rather than a doer. The metaphor of a coach encapsulates this enabling capacity that 2.0 managers need to develop. This enabling capability focuses on individuals and processes, and builds on the four functions of management that supports the organisational management systems. Enabling at a team or individual level means that the manager is focused on ensuring the best dynamic between essence, purpose, strategy, people, processes and performance outcomes. This dynamic within organisational management systems is constantly being retuned to gain higher organisational performances. Moving from doing to enabling requires 2.0 management teams to build an organisational enabling platform on two capabilities – creativity and socialisation (see Figure 4.1).

Figure 4.1: Management 2.0 Managers – From Doing to Enabling

The creativity focus is on ensuring consistent optimisation of the dynamic between essence, purpose, strategy, people, processes and outcomes, and socialisation facilitates this optimisation within and outside the organisation. In simple terms, this may mean reinforcing the core essence, purpose, strategy and value propositions of the business among employees and communicating clearly how this relates to their personal activities. In practical terms it means 2.0 managers creating organisational space for the expression of individual creativity that is focused on the organisation core essence and purpose. Creating this creativity space may mean, for example, allocating a percentage of employees time towards personal projects or holding innovation days where employees put forward new ideas on a range of organisational activities. This personal creativity should also extend to the execution of the ideas. Therefore the enabling (coaching and facilitation) capabilities of 2.0 managers are essential in building and harnessing personal creativity within the firm.

Socialisation capabilities are essential to 2.0 managers irrespective of the context, be it in the boardroom, with senior managers, subordinates or internal and external customers. The socialisation process broadens the managerial capability, but also means that managers become carriers of management and strategy practices within organisational management systems. This enabling capability of 2.0 managers means that they can be potentially deployed in any part of the business. In addition, further honing of their creativity and socialisation capacities means they can create organisational core postures that are both secure and flexible within the organisational management system, irrespective of organisational context. It is akin to uprooting a tree in one part of the garden and planting it in another part of the garden, knowing it will grow and flourish in addition to enhancing its surroundings. These 2.0 managers are strategy and management practice carriers within the organisational management system as they bring with them practice bundles that deliver and enhance individual and team performance, innovation and creativity activities. The building of organisational platforms based on creativity and socialisation and the enabling roles of managers affords strong connectivity between the hands and minds of the organisation (Mintzberg 1987). In doing so, this unleashes the personal innovative capacity and entrepreneurial behaviours of individuals for exploration (R&D) and exploitation purposes. Having a management team that is creative, flexible, thinks differently and is willing to experiment with partners inside and outside the firm will become an integral element of organisational competitiveness and provide a context for management teams to excel.

In order to enable, 2.0 managers need to have mastery of detail, a point that Mintzberg raises in his article 'Crafting Strategy', published in the *Harvard Business Review* (1987). This mastery of detail is required in real depth from a personal, managerial and organisational perspective. How many managers have this real mastery of detail in their own contexts? In some respects this seems impossible, given the complexity of organisational life. Yet organisations are awash with enablers like customer relationship management systems. Mastery of detail minimises risk, gives greater clarity to decision making and ultimately provides managers and organisations with a posture that is strong and flexible. It is akin to a student going into an exam with little preparation competing against students who have studied for the exam. Managers need mastery of detail to make well-informed decisions and this detail is not just confined to the organisation itself but to the competitive context, customer base and to society. It also requires an ability to synthesise complexity to a high level that customers, competitors, employees and other stakeholders can really understand and relate to, which signifies authentic uniqueness through clearly articulated value propositions. This also requires simplicity of thought and perspective in framing decision making and action around the transaction between company and customer, and by asking the simple question: why should anyone buy anything from you? It also means reaching a commonality of understanding of organisational essence and purpose around core activities, using a metaphorical language of journey that engages stakeholders.

Implications for Managers, Business Schools, Society and Government

The evolution into Management 2.0, against a backdrop of overarching structural changes in the character of organisations, management systems and global capital markets, and rapid advances in science, has implications for managers, for business schools, for society and for government.

Implications for Managers

For 2.0 managers of the 21st century the legacy effect of decades of management thought is a significant and yet stifling burden to bear, given the real individual and organisational uncertainties that need to be faced. In facing up to these challenges and uncertainties, the first requirement that 2.0 managers need is that they know themselves. Given the increasing levels of organisational 'noise', managers have less time to reflect on getting to know their real strengths and weaknesses. Experientially, this means exceptional managers not only develop strengths and deal with their deficits but also attempt to gain fit between individual capability and appropriate context. Therefore, having honest, impartial assessment of their individual capabilities is essential for 2.0 managers and having a personal social network outside an organisational setting will become even more essential for managers as they reflect honestly on their individual capabilities. The competitive context that 2.0 managers find themselves working in requires greater periods of personal reflection and renewal. Increasing managerial intensity means that these periods are rare but essential if 2.0 managers are to enhance their sphere of influence. Such personal reflection and renewal as an ongoing process may focus on personal essence and purpose, and/or enabling capabilities.

The most significant implication of Management 2.0 for managers relates to their ability to learn and experiment. Managers and organisations can become more conservative in their approach and perspective as time goes on. The ability to learn and to be open to new ideas internally and externally will be an essential characteristic of 2.0 managers, and this is linked to personal reflection, renewal and self-awareness. Coupled with learning is the ability of 2.0 managers to experiment within their context on multiple fronts, be it with processes, product and services offerings, reporting relationships, recruitment of staff, etc. Experimentation and flexibility in a Management 2.0 context is essential to the development and refinement of difference, and is linked to unique value propositions.

Coupled with learning and experiment implications of Management 2.0 is the change in managerial mindset and conceptualisation of organisations and competitive contexts. This will be driven to some extent by the current convergence trends in technology and markets but also by 2.0 managers totally reconceptualising the competitive arenas grounded in organisational essence and purpose. For example, Coca-Cola has totally redefined conceptualisation of the beverage marketplace and Tesco's conceptualisation of competitive arenas is built around increasing customer loyalty. This also means reconceptualising the organisational management system, the psychological contract with employees and how organisational market dominance can be ultimately achieved. In summary, the new managerial priorities are centred on personal renewal and reflection, learning and experimentation, and reconceptualisation of competitive arenas grounded in organisational essence and purpose.

Implications for Business Schools

Management 2.0 provides business schools with some significant challenges and opportunities, which will have a knock-on effect on their roles and missions. One of the key challenges for business schools is how to adequately prepare pre-experience students to become potential managers of the future. Is exposure to all aspects of business an essential prerequisite? Should it be more experiential? Should it be different? The answer is 'yes' to all of these questions. Future 2.0 managers should have an understanding of business in all its aspects and this should be enhanced in terms of exposure to management practice and maybe not in the traditional sense of work placement. So, for example, students may get the opportunity to shadow operational managers, business unit managers, CEOs, board directors and entrepreneurs for periods of time. Such teaching approaches around the Lego as Serious Play (LSP) programme may become the norm for pre- and post-experience student cohorts to develop coaching, creativity and socialisation skills and capabilities. In addition, it should be different in the sense that the curriculum should encompass such subjects as philosophy, sociology, business history, biomedical technology, etc. It may seem 'hardly revolutionary', but if all of these aspects – business subjects, experiential management practice and other discipline subjects – are fused into a three- or four-year broad undergraduate business degree, this could provide a more meaningful preparatory ground for 2.0 managers of the future and provide them with the capacity to consistently enable, reflect and renew. For this to occur, it takes courage and leadership within business schools, a real understanding of the knowledge, skills and values that 2.0 managers require in different industries and organisational settings, and investment in resources and support from companies and practising managers.

For post-experience students, Management 2.0 will see new approaches used to support managers at different levels in varying contexts. There is no doubt that the MBA will remain as the flagship programme for business schools, but it will evolve further in terms of content, pedagogical approach and in delivery. New programmes will be developed for the post-MBA market that support and enhance managerial performance. The post-MBA product offerings could range from short executive courses, doctor of business administration (DBA) programmes or ongoing mentoring and coaching offerings. In many ways such offerings in this market space will attempt to elongate the 'MBA experience' of mobility, knowledge acquisition, openness, support and purpose.

The engagement models of business schools are fundamentally challenged by structural changes and by Management 2.0. Business schools, if institutionally integrated and managed appropriately, can enhance institutional reputations, assist institutional commercialisation and technology transfer agendas and play an active role in regional and national competitiveness. The challenge for business schools is to find new engagement models beyond the status quo. This might mean creating an environment or intellectual space within business schools where the confluence of ideas are shared among organisations, practising managers, academics and students across a range of discipline areas.

The challenges faced by 2.0 managers have implications for academics, which will bring into question the credibility, relevance and value of academics to management practice. Approaching the last quarter of 2007, the debate about academic rigour and management relevance continued with a special section on art and design in management education in the *Academy of Management Learning and Education* journal and an editors' forum on research with relevance to practice in the *Academy of Management*. Therefore, the task for academics is to appreciate that their contributions to practice are essential and are needed by organisations. The challenge for the academic is to experiment with new distribution mechanisms that are oriented to practising managers. The professional and academic attainment of human capital within business faculties will become important to meaningfully fusing theory and practice.

The danger, as Bennis and O'Toole (2005) highlight, is that what we may have in time is a concentration of academics in business schools who have no substantive managerial experience and that these academics will be responsible for designing, developing and delivering management programmes, in addition to carrying out research on organisations and managers. In addition, this has implications for the recruiting focus of business academics and the manner and the type of rewards for business faculties. More fundamentally, the process and the manner in which doctoral students complete their studies comes into question. The traditional dissertation model requires, depending on the methodological approach, only minor contact with management practice relative to the overall work effort required to complete a doctoral dissertation. New doctoral models for pre-experience candidates may mean the fusing of traditional doctoral models with the DBA designed model for practising managers. Such an approach would have implications for the advancement of theory and practice and the manner in which such advances are communicated to practising managers. In essence, it means that the academic and manager move beyond mutual misapprehension and see the value of each perspective to enhancing managerial, employee and organisational performance. This requires collaboration, courage, imagination and willingness to take action in terms of experimenting with new engagement models that truly bridge the theory-practice divide and are mutually beneficial.

Implications for Society

The benefits to society of adopting Management 2.0 will be felt at individual, community and national level. For individuals, it may lead to greater fulfilment, increased levels of ambition, purpose and passion, which can pervade personal lives, family units and communities. Given that creativity is at the heart of Management 2.0, benefits to society could flow in terms of living and community space design, advancements in the delivery of public services and ultimately in the products and services and the manner in which society consumes. In addition, measures with respect to business performance around CSR will be measurable and reported in tandem with profitability, enhancing the value attributed to managers and business within the society.

As society becomes more aware of the nuances of the knowledge economy, the perceptions about the role of management and managers will change. Communities and societies will be focusing on the inventory managerial talent within their region or country, and this will be an issue as important as justice, health and environmental issues. Investing and developing this inventory of managerial talent will become a key conditional factor in attracting and sustaining economic development regionally and nationally. This inventory of managerial talent in time could not be predominantly indigenous and this could have broader societal issues. In time, these managerial talents may be leveraged further for non-economic purposes but in the community across a range of activities and organisations.

Implications for Government

If a government is pursuing, like the Irish government, a knowledge-based economy agenda, then significant ongoing investment in management education is an absolute necessity at secondary and tertiary levels. In addition, further investment at primary level is required so that basic skills, knowledge and socialisation skills are embedded in formative years. Furthermore, it means that governments develop and implement specific policies designed to stimulate world class excellence in management education and research, which is essential to supporting the knowledge-based economy. In an Irish context, this means further investment in human capital in business schools in Ireland, increased levels of multi-disciplinary research and deeper collaborations within and between business and academia. To become a technology-making country in a knowledge-based economy requires significant ongoing investment in management capability alongside investments in science, technology and innovation.

Management 2.0 challenges policy makers to incentivise and support organisational exploration and exploitation capabilities of companies and their associated management systems. The exploration incentivisation is built on developing true world class research capabilities within public research institutions through investment but also incentivising the collaboration between companies and research organizations, not only from a funding perspective but also from tax, IP and legal perspectives. It also means supporting, in terms of policy, the development and nurturing of management systems within organisations for both exploration (R&D) and exploitation purposes. This requires policy makers to take risks.

Management 2.0: Approaches and Organisations

The organisational structures that we are accustomed to now will dissipate slowly with time, in addition to the way that organisations and managers view markets, industries and competition. The nucleus of the Management 2.0 approach is based on collaboration and cooperation through the building of external and internal communities. With increased levels of societal and organisational complexity and growing demand for personalisation of product and service offerings, the reality will be that no one firm will be able to deal with these increasing challenges on their own. Therefore collaboration, new organisational collaborative forms and communities are core elements of any Management 2.0 context.

Miles *et al.* (2005), in their book *Collaborative Entrepreneurship*, provide an insight into how organisations will be structured around collaborative communities, thereby being continuously innovative and responsible to horizontal innovation threats for economic gain. A contemporary example that provides some first tangible signs of this new collaborative organisational form is IBM's building of Blade (<http://www. blade.org>). Building on the ideas of Miles *et al.* (2005), organisational paradigms in a Management 2.0 context will centre around collaboration and cooperation within and between firms and industries.

Consequently, firms will experience even more intense inter-organisational activities with competitors or with new stakeholders in collaborative arenas. These collaborative organisational forms may be formed naturally, given the commonalities that competitors see in addressing market problems and the realisation that it may be impossible for one firm to achieve this and technology market making on its own. More importantly, these collaborative environments endow architects of them with significant advantages. First, through collaborative organisational forms the best human talent is being deployed for common exploitation by all participants and members for economic and non-economic gain. Second, it potentially hollows out direct competitors through participation in these new collaborative organisational forms. Third, it provides customers with more advanced and personalised offerings, aligned with individual firm efforts around uniqueness and differentiation. Fourth, it means that firms have the capability through participation in these collaborative organisational forms to deal with any competitive and market eventualities. Fifth, it reduces the individual organisation's risks taken in pursuing exploration activities. Sixth, it also provides companies with the ability to plug any product offering gaps they possess. Last, it provides firms with the capabilities of intellectual exploration and exploitation.

It is likely that firms will be involved in multiple collaborative organisational forms in different regions of the world and for different purposes. The communities that are built around these collaborative organisational forms are drawn from competing organisations, out of industry players and knowledge creators (private research organisations, universities, etc.). These communities would be akin to communities that software companies like Microsoft, Linux and IBM build to ensure the proliferation and development of their software offerings. These communities are focused simultaneously on the exploration and exploitation of knowledge for both the collaborative organisational forms and the individual companies' competitive ends. Irrespective of collaborative organisational forms, the ownership of IP and knowledge would remain with the originator, but would be pooled on a commercial basis for exploitation purposes. Such collaborative organisational forms reduce risks for all parties involved, while providing a platform for increased levels of experimentation and learning for all participants with economic gain orientation. Moreover, these collaborative organisational forms will provide both a structured and a flexible environment where learning can take place with respect to successful management and strategy practices that allow companies to cross-pollinate management and strategy practices within the collaborative organisational form and their own company for exploration and exploitative purposes.

This is where the enabling capabilities of 2.0 managers become vital in building up the external and the internal communities around collaborative innovation and entrepreneurship. In time, the competition for market capital could be between different collaborative organisational forms based on their collective exploratory innovative capacities and individual organisational exploitative capabilities. The orientation of the flow of capital could switch focus towards these collaborative organisational forms and would lessen the capital available at firm level as these collaborative organisational forms generate and raise capital.

So what would organisational life be like in Management 2.0 companies? One of the single most significant features of Management 2.0 organisational life is increasing levels of organisational flexibility and the unleashing of individual creativity – particularly in the deploying of all resources, decision making, reporting relationships and organisational structures. Management 2.0 organisations have the capability to quickly change the configuration of its human talent and allied reporting relationship and structures. Also, in time, the perceived importance of internal communities supersedes that of departments or business units; however, increased flexibility allows that skilled and specialised human talent can be easily deployed and leveraged to meet collaborative organisational community requirements or for firm exploitative (near market) purposes. The potential reality for employees is that their specialised skills can be deployed in several organisational forms within and outside the firm or for the rollout of different business models in any given year. At the heart of these communities is learning and experimentation, and such flexibility is achievable given the commonality of understanding of organisational purpose, the enabling capacity of 2.0 managers and employees, and learning capacity of employees that allow them to be management and strategy practice carriers between organisational and collaborative community management systems. Also, multiple forms of innovation become a daily reality for companies and 2.0 managers with lead user innovation. This is where companies work with a group of customers for new product development purposes, and open source innovation approaches become company-wide as the focus is on deepening the difference of individual firms (Figure 4.2).

In terms of creativity, in Management 2.0 organisations the personal creativity and entrepreneurship – opportunity recognition – of individuals

Figure 4.2: Management 2.0 Organisations

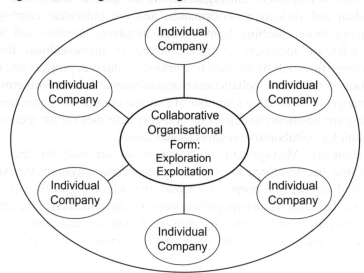

is released and utilised for company and collaborative organisational form purposes. This unleashing of personal creativity and entrepreneurship will have implications for the innovative capacity of firms in terms of exploration and exploitation. Such a leveraging of this creativity has endless possibilities for individuals, companies and society. Consequently, 2.0 managers' focus will be on developing this individual capability as well as their collaborative skills. Releasing personal creativity and entrepreneurship and generating more perceived and actual flexibility are essential for sustaining the company and collaborative form competitiveness. Furthermore, for Management 2.0 organisations to maintain sustainable competitiveness, 2.0 managers must have management capabilities for intellectual exploration and exploitation.

In Management 2.0 organisations the reconceptualisation of control means that it is embedded in the essence and purpose of the organisation and is reinforced to all stakeholders in guiding principles, providing a core organisational posture that enables overall organisational flexibility in coping with competitive conditions. Consequently, the organisational culture and value systems of individual organisations are aligned with the collaborative organisational forms, reinforcing the integrity of the company and the collaborative organisational forms. Managing the inner life of employees and individualised performance management systems will become the important tools in maintaining flexibility and control.

Therefore, Management 2.0 organisations are able to assess real-time individual and collective performance, and the individual employees experience more coaching from internal managers, mentors and from those who are members of the collaborative organisational forms. Employees' time will be devoted to working on internal projects and participation in these new collaborative organisational forms. Furthermore, 2.0 managers will manage a number of external contractors under crowdsourcing arrangements to deliver on non-core activities for the individual firms and for collaborative organisational forms.

In summary, Management 2.0 organisations are built on three key tenets: first, the development of effective management systems for exploration and exploitation purposes; second, the unleashing of the personal creativity, innovation and entrepreneurship of each individual in the organisation, thereby changing the physchological contract; and third, the creation of a stimulating, fun, challenging and meaningful work environment.

Concluding Thoughts

In the year 2025, the way you live your life will be different. You will only receive news that you are interested in, and your e-mails will probably come on a convergence communications device that also monitors your health and well-being. You will be managing portfolio workers under crowdsourcing organisational structures. You will have a second life which will be providing you with additional income. The old adage, that the only constant in business life is competition, will still apply as organisations will see an increase in the disaggregation of business models, the introduction of new market segments and an increased emphasis on the importance of the managers at all levels to ensure organisational strategies are achieved. A new business lexicon will be in vogue to describe competitors, competitiveness, performance and management life. The socialisation process required to ensure 2.0 managers can maintain constant organisational performance will have to become even more personalised and sophisticated in terms of both hard and soft skills at the early stages of their careers.

Unleashing personal creativity and entrepreneurship capacity at levels that organisations have not experienced to date, whereby intellectual managerial and coaching skills of managers are aligned with organisational essence and purpose, requires the real expansion of the characteristics of 2.0 managers to encompass being entrepreneurs, innovators, strategists and leaders (see Figure 4.3). I believe that this combination of

Figure 4.3: 2.0 Managers – From Doing to Enabling

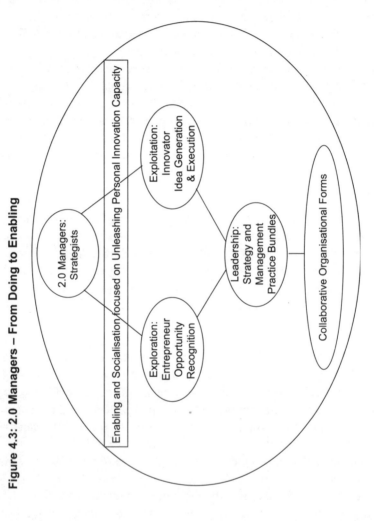

embedded characteristics, behaviours and capabilities are at the core of being a 2.0 manager. Such managers must be strategists who channel personal creativity and entrepreneurship to find sources of difference and maintain threshold competitiveness. For intellectual property exploration, 2.0 managers will adopt the characteristics and behaviours of entrepreneurs seeking new opportunities and learning, in terms of practice, products and processes based on a real understanding of the market, customers and organisational capabilities. In terms of market and technology exploitation of intellectual property, 2.0 managers will adopt the capabilities and behaviours of innovators for technology-making purposes. Furthermore, 2.0 managers will need to demonstrate leadership capabilities for intellectual exploration and exploitation purposes.

From my perspective, Irish managers are well placed to deal with the challenges described. However this requires increased levels of investment by multiple stakeholders to ensure the development of the breadth and depth of managerial talent and practice that allows indigenous Irish companies to grow and to ensure that large FDI companies deal effectively with the challenge of activities relocating to low-cost countries. This requires a targeted focus in academic and organisational contexts over and above the existing efforts. The real danger for Ireland is that the services side of the Irish economy will dissipate because of the lack of breadth and depth of managerial talent used to leverage investment in science, technology and engineering for home and international markets. Overall, the Irish economy management system development has been orientated towards exploitation whereas the management system to support exploration is in its infancy. Nevertheless, I believe there are two core capabilities and priority areas that 2.0 managers and firms need – creativity and socialisation – and Irish managers have these in abundance. This is evidenced in multinational company (MNC) environments where Irish management teams continue to punch above their weight against international peer groups in terms of achieving enhanced mandates for Irish operations. This creativity is seen again more broadly in increased levels of entrepreneurship throughout the Irish economy. Furthermore, Irish managers' socialisation skills are distinctive and sought after. Irish managers can and do deliver organisational performance and prove this daily in home and international firms and markets.

Looking forward, a real challenge for Irish society is to develop coherent national and local policy responses to specifically support the nurturing and development of Irish management talent and management systems. In other countries, being ordinary is about being ambitious;

having ambitions for your company and country is the norm. As President Sarkozy of France notes in his book *Testimony*:

I have been convinced since I was very young that you have to make your own future – otherwise you're condemned to accept whatever comes you way. It's no secret that I don't miss childhood. I was impatient to become an adult and to become free. This desire for independence made me determined to live the present with the energy of someone who knows that the promise of the future does not come automatically. (2007: xxvii)

There is no reason why Irish companies, management teams and employees cannot achieve global ambitions and business success. There is no reason why international business journalists, commentators, international think tanks, policy makers and academics will not look at Irish managers in the same light as the Japanese or the American managers and as exemplars of Management 2.0. There is no reason not to see more Irish companies being quoted on Dow Jones, NASDAQ or FTSE 100. There is no reason why Irish managers cannot take the lead in developing Management 2.0 organisations and managers. The Management 2.0 challenges, approaches and collaborative organisational forms and the enabling capabilities required of managers positionally and naturally favour Irish management. From an economic perspective, in the last decade Ireland has made the transition to economic adulthood. To sustain this momentum in a changing economic climate, Irish firms need to continue to be competitive, professionally managed and global. The real question and test for Irish managers, both individually and collectively, is how ambitious, passionate, willing and persistent they are in embracing Management 2.0 and new management paradigms. How willing are they to experiment and build collaborative organisational forms? How willing are policy makers and business schools to take risks and support a new generation of Irish managerial talent? How willing are Irish managers to unleash the personal creative and entrepreneurship capacity within their firms? How willing are Irish managers to experiment with and develop their own management systems for exploration and exploitation purposes for technology and market making on a global stage? As Mohammad Ali once said, 'Impossible is nothing.'

References

Amabile, T.A. and Kramer, S.J. (2007), 'Inner Work Life: Understanding the Subtext of Business Performance', *Harvard Business Review*, May, 72–84.

Bennis, W.G. and O' Toole, J. (2005), 'How Business Schools Lost Their Way', *Harvard Business Review*, 83(5), 96–104.

Ghemawat, P. (2007), 'Managing Difference', *Harvard Business Review*, 85(3), 58–68.

McNulty, T. and Pettigrew, A.M. (1999), 'Strategists on the Board', *Organization Studies*, 20(1), 463–85.

Miles, R.E., Miles, G. and Snow, C.C. (2005), *Collaborative Entrepreneurship: How Communities of Networked Firms Use Continuous Innovation to Create Economic Wealth*, Stanford, CA: Stanford University Press.

Mintzberg, H. (1987), 'Crafting Strategy', *Harvard Business Review*, July–August, 66–75.

Miles, R.E., Snow, C.C. and Miles, G. (2000), 'The Future.org', *Long Range Planning*, 33(3), 300–21.

Sarkozy, Nicholas (2007), *Testimony: France, Europe and the World in the Twenty-first Century*, New York: Harper Perennial.

Watanabe, K. (2007), 'Lessons from Toyota's Long Drive', *Harvard Business Review*, July–August, 74–83.

Further Reading

Academy of Management Journal (2007), 50(4), 739–82.

Academy of Management Learning and Education (2006), 5(4), 484–523.

Bryan, L.L. and Joyce, C.I. (2007), *Mobilizing Minds: Creating Wealth from Talent in the 21st-Century Organization*, New York: McGraw-Hill.

Chesbrough, H. (2003), *Open Innovation: The New Imperative for Creating and Profiting from Technology*, Boston: Harvard Business School Press.

Florida, R. (2002), *The Rise of the Creative Class: And How It's Transforming Work, Leisure, Community and Everyday Life*, New York: Basic Books.

Link, A.N. and Siegel, D.S. (2007), *Innovation, Entrepreneurship, and Technological Change*, Oxford: Oxford University Press.

Wren, D., Halbesleben, J.R.B., and Buckley, M.R. (2007), 'The Theory-Application Balance in Management Pedagogy: A Longitudinal Update', *Academy of Management Learning and Education*, 6(4), 484–92.

SECTION II

CASE STUDIES

CHAPTER 5

CRH plc: Corporate-Level Strategy Redefined

Mike Moroney[1]

J.E. Cairnes School of Business and Economics,
National University of Ireland, Galway

In March 2007, CRH announced financial results for 2006, celebrating thirty-six years of unrivalled growth and performance since the formation of the group in 1970. During that period, CRH had metamorphosed from a local player supplying the small, peripheral Irish construction market to one of the top five building materials companies in the world, with global operations and a market capitalisation of €16.6 billion at the end of 2006. One hundred euro invested in CRH shares in 1970 would have yielded more than €70,000 thirty-six years later – a total annual shareholder return of more than 20 per cent. Moreover, the group's performance was achieved in a notoriously hostile industry environment. CRH's accomplishments in no small way reflected the central role of its small corporate headquarters, in particular its strategy of acquisition-led expansion.

The Building Materials Industry

The industry involves the manufacture and distribution ('merchanting' and DIY) of primary materials (e.g. cement, aggregates, asphalt, ready-mixed concrete, lime and magnesia), heavyside building products (e.g. concrete, bricks, insulation, glass and security products) and lightside building products (e.g. plumbing, heating, electrical and lighting products). The sectors served are new construction work (residential, industrial, commercial and public works) and RMI (repair, maintenance and improvement). In general, building materials and products are

[1] The author wishes to acknowledge CRH for its support while researching and compiling this case study. The information in this case study relates to the position of CRH up to 2007. This case is intended as a basis for class discussion and not as an illustration of good or bad practice.

standard, similar across markets and largely stable over time. Production processes are also standard. Technology is non-proprietary and, for some products, relatively unsophisticated.

Characteristics

The building materials industry is a cyclical, commodity business, characterised in most markets by maturity and fragmentation. Cyclicality reflects the considerable capital investment involved, long lead times and 'lumpy' additions to capacity. Industry cycles are longer in duration and larger in amplitude than general economic cycles. However, their timing varies between countries. Building materials and products are largely commodities with little differences depending on supplier, who compete mainly on the basis of price. Construction is a mature sector in the Western world, reflecting stable economic activity and populations. The average growth in construction activity is less than half the rate of economic growth, while RMI accounts for upwards of half total output. By contrast, in newly emerging areas of the world (Asia, Eastern Europe and Latin America) and in Western countries at an earlier stage of economic development (such as Ireland, Finland and Portugal), construction is buoyant. On the other hand, cyclicality in such markets is more pronounced.

Traditionally, the building materials industry has been highly fragmented. Production is often linked to the location of reserves, of varying value, leading to a proliferation of facilities and low barriers to entry. In addition, building materials and products are, by and large, characterised by a high weight-to-value ratio. As a result, high transport costs rapidly outweigh scale economies and determine the radius of economic activity and competition, which in many cases can be 150 kilometres or less. Furthermore, markets have tended to be local in nature due to differences in building regulations, construction practices and product standards. Finally, success is often determined by factors such as personal service, local contacts, close operational control and the ability to react to change. As a result, the industry has developed as a large number of small- and medium-sized firms, often family-owned and run.

Recent Trends

Since the mid-1990s, a number of structural trends emerged, in part prompted by sustained low levels of activity. In certain markets, supply side concentration and significant corporate activity occurred, resulting

Table 5.1: UK Building Materials Market Concentration (2005)

Primary materials/ heavyside products	Largest player market share (%)	Top three market share (%)
Cement	42	84
Aggregates	25	65
Asphalt	28	64
Ready-mixed concrete	23	62
Concrete blocks	32	81
Merchanting	20	65

Note: Merchanting concentration ratio is for the top four producers.
Source: Estimates derived from Merrill Lynch.

in the disappearance of a number of previously well-known industry names. This was most pronounced in UK markets for primary materials, 'heavyside' products and merchanting (see Table 5.1). At the same time, a number of large, international building materials companies had emerged over time, typically using the base of a strong local market position and/or product competence as a springboard to expand into other regions and areas of activity.

There was also evidence that local differences between geographic markets were eroding. Driven by institutional factors, such as at EU level, a harmonisation of building regulations, product standards and tendering procedures was occurring. This was reinforced by convergence in building practices across markets, resulting from mobility of workers and the increasingly multinational character of contracting and building materials firms. In addition, the industry's customer base was consolidating, customers' needs were homogenising and they were becoming more demanding. Nonetheless, the underlying logic of fragmentation continued to prevail in many markets. In general, products and distribution were less concentrated than primary materials. Also, construction markets globally remained fragmented, in particular the large US market with a value of $700 billion.

Profile of CRH

Headquartered in Dublin, Ireland, by 2006 CRH employed 80,000 people in over 1,000 subsidiaries in more than 3,000 locations in 26 countries. The group enjoyed a major presence in mature markets in Europe and North America and a growing foothold in emerging regions, including Eastern Europe and Latin America. CRH's prominence had been

Table 5.2: CRH Growth since Formation

	1970	1980	1990	2000	2005
Sales (€ billion)	26*	0.4	1.7	8.9	14.5
Countries	2	5	7	19	25

In million
Source: CRH

recognised by many industry awards over the thirty-six years since its foundation for financial reporting, investor relations, and excellence and innovation in environmental and safety practices.

History, Growth and Development

CRH was formed in 1970 following the merger of Irish Cement and Roadstone/Wood, an Irish building materials company. Since then, the group has undergone major growth (see Table 5.2) through three major phases of development described in the following sections. In general, change was evolutionary, involving a managed, learning process of building, augmenting and layering competences.

Organic Market Penetration in Ireland (from 1970)

During the 1970s, Irish construction enjoyed a boom on the back of a modernising economy. The newly merged CRH capitalised on this favourable environment through its vertically integrated and leading positions in virtually all domestic markets for heavyside building materials and products.

Acquisition-Led Overseas Expansion (from the late 1970s)

In the late 1970s, with a view to spreading risks and opportunities more broadly, CRH made a strategic decision to invest in familiar business sectors overseas, through add-on acquisitions of medium-sized (often family-owned) businesses. Early expansion in the UK and the Netherlands was followed by further acquisitions in mainland Europe. In 1977, Don Godson (later chief executive, 1994–2000) went to the US with 'a telephone and a cheque book'. By 2006, the Americas accounted for more than half of the group's turnover and profits. The presence of CRH in emerging regions gathered pace from the mid-1990s. The group also expanded in a limited, but highly rewarding, way into new product areas, including merchanting and DIY, security fencing, clay brick products and glass fabrication (in the US).

Product Focus and Larger Acquisitions (from the late 1990s)

During the 1990s, the previous regional structure of CRH evolved to a more product-based organisation to bring greater focus to business development and sharing best practice. At the same time, anticipating greater industry consolidation, the group began to supplement traditional mid-sized deal flow with larger acquisitions.

Strategy

CRH's strategic vision is 'to be a responsible international leader in building materials delivering superior performance and growth'. This strategy is 'to seek new geographic platforms in its core businesses and to take advantage of complementary product opportunities in order to achieve strategic balance and to establish multiple platforms from which to deliver performance and growth' (CRH 2005: 1–2). Growth is achieved:

- Through investing in new capacity.
- From developing new products and markets.
- By acquiring and growing mid-sized companies, augmented from time to time with larger deals (see <http://www.crh.com/chrcorp/about/characteristics>).

Products and Markets

Over the years to 2006, the core businesses of CRH included primary materials, heavyside building products and specialist distribution (through builders' merchants and DIY stores). There were two notable characteristics of CRH's product/market portfolio. The first was leadership (Table 5.3). Reflecting industry fragmentation, the group focused on securing and maintaining leading positions in local or regional markets and in product segments or niches. Also unique was CRH's deliberate geographic, product and segment balance (Figure 5.1), which smoothed the effects of varying economic conditions and provided greater opportunities for growth. (CRH outperformed peers in the industry downturns of the early 1980s, 1990s and 2000s.)

Two markets stood out in CRH's portfolio. The main drivers of growth since the early 1990s, US operations earn above average returns and demonstrate remarkably low volatility. Analysts' estimates of 40 per cent return on net assets (RONA) for the group's Irish operations reflected CRH's 60 per cent share of the cement market on the total island of Ireland, buoyant Irish construction, a low rate of manufacturing

Table 5.3: CRH Leadership Positions (2006)

Materials		Products		Distribution	
Europe					
Aggregates	No. 1 Fin, Irl	*Concrete Products*	No. 1 Eur	*Merchanting*	No. 1 NL
Asphalt	No. 1 Irl	*precast*	No. 1 Ben, Den		No. 1 Swi
Cement	No. 1 Fin, Irl	*paving*	No. 1 Ben, Ger, Fra, Slo		No. 1 NW Ger
	No. 2 Por, Swi	*Clay Bricks*	No. 2 UK		No. 1 Aus
	No. 3 Pol	*quality facing*	No. 1 NL		No. 1 Fr (3 reg)
Ready-mix	No. 1 Fin, Irl	*Building Products*			No. 2 Ile de Fr
	No. 2 Por, Swi	*Fencing/Security*	No. 1 Eur	*DIY*	No. 1 NL (franchise)
		Daylight/Ventil	No. 1 Ben, Ger		No. 1 Por (50:50 JV)
		Construct Access	No. 2 Eur		
		Insulation (EPS)	No. 1 Irl, NL, Pol, Nordics		
Americas					
Aggregates	No. 4 US	*Concrete Products*		*Roofing and Siding*	Top 3 US
Asphalt	No. 1 US	*masonry/paving*	No. 1 US	*Interior Products*	Top 6 US
Ready-mix	Top 10 US	*paving/patio*	No. 1 Can	151 branches primarily in metro	
Leading market positions		*mixes*	No. 2 US	regions on both coasts and in the	
throughout operations		*precast*	No. 1 US	Northern Tier states	
Strong regional aggregate		*Clay Bricks*	No. 1 NE US		
Reserves		*Glass (arch. fab.)*	No. 1 US		

Source: CRH

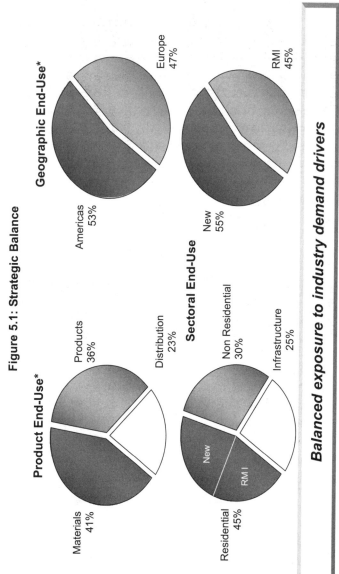

Figure 5.1: Strategic Balance

Product End-Use*

Products 36%

Distribution 23%

Materials 41%

Geographic End-Use*

Europe 47%

Americas 53%

Sectoral End-Use

RMI 45%

New 55%

Non Residential 30%

Infrastructure 25%

New

RMI

Residential 45%

Balanced exposure to industry demand drivers

* Based on current annualised sales, March 2007.

corporation tax (12.5 per cent) and heavily depreciated assets (Goodbody Stockbrokers 2003).

Management and Organisation

Unlike its peers, CRH operated a federal structure, comprising a small central headquarters and four regionally focused product divisions (Figure 5.2). To capitalise on local market knowledge, a high degree of individual responsibility was devolved to operational managers, within group guidelines and controls. According to Jack Golden, human resources (HR) director, 'while the local operating units have operational autonomy, they do not have independence.'

CRH adopted a rigorous approach to project evaluation, approval and review. The twin requirements of performance and growth were continually reinforced, with entities having to earn the right to grow. Planning was formalised and interactive, centring on the rolling five-year strategic plan, year one of which constituted the budget. Stretch targets were established for financial and operational output measures. Performance measurement was timely, formal and rigorous. This allowed early critical review of under-performance, to identify reasons, provide assistance, put in place corrective measures and enable senior management to draw broader lessons. However, ongoing cross-subsidisation was not contemplated. If necessary, CRH implemented a management change to support the recovery of performance to satisfactory levels. This could include a strategic review to consider the most appropriate disposition for the business, going forward.

Continuous improvement was relentless, as demonstrated by ongoing programmes of benchmarking and best practice. In addition, products and processes were continually re-engineered to yield greater returns, primarily through greater efficiencies (but also from selective expansion into related products and regional markets). Ongoing development investment (consistently well in excess of the level of depreciation (Goodbody Stockbrokers 2005)) incorporated new plant, capacity extensions and major upgrades.

Over time, CRH's pool of managers had increased, as a result of continuing growth and a relentless stream of acquisitions. Nonetheless, in 2006 the core group of key corporate, group and operational managers only numbered 350. Managers were drawn from internally developed operating managers, experienced finance and development professionals, and owner-entrepreneurs from acquired companies, providing a healthy mix and depth of skills.

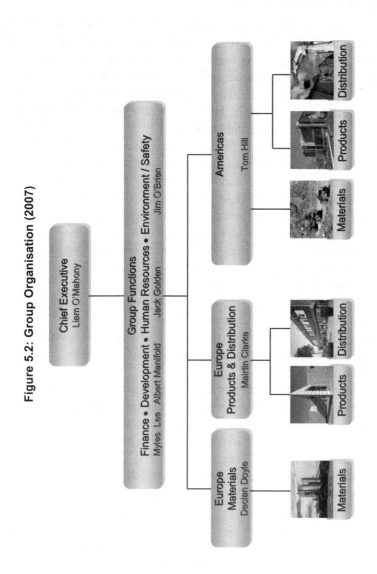

Figure 5.2: Group Organisation (2007)

Notwithstanding the strong pace of growth, CRH's management was characterised by experience, stability and continuity. In thirty-six years, there have been only five chief executives, all of whom (like a majority of senior managers) were Irish. Having joined the group, few managers left. There were several reasons for this constancy. Continuing success was clearly a factor, reinforced by the market-driven, performance-related remuneration policy of CRH, which aimed at creating shareholder value. (This comprised variable compensation, share options for key managers and employee share participation schemes.) In addition, a range of formal and informal mechanisms promoted integration. Finally, low turnover, rotation and promotion from within resulted in a wealth of in-house industry knowledge and expertise.

Finances

CRH had a strong and consistent track record of financial performance (see Table 5.4). 2006 represented the twenty-third consecutive year of dividend increase, while the group had experienced only two relatively short periods of declining earnings per share (in the early 1980s and early 1990s). Moreover, the group's peak-to-trough performance during industry downturns demonstrated an improving trend over time (Goodbody Stockbrokers 2003). CRH's level and consistency of performance was also superior to that of its peers internationally (Figure 5.3). CRH enjoyed a premium of 2 per cent (i.e. one-sixth) in the bell-weather return on capital employed ratio (notwithstanding that the group's operating margin matched the industry average).

CRH was noted in financial markets for its finance function, which was characterised by extensive business knowledge and operational contribution, as well as diligence, conservatism and prudence. The two hallmarks of the financial management of CRH were a strong focus on return on capital and cash generation. Operations were required to earn 15 per cent RONA on an ongoing basis. Newly acquired businesses often found such

Table 5.4: CRH Average Growth Rates (%)

	5 years	10 years
Sales revenue	10	19
Earnings per share	9	16
Cash earnings per share	7	17
Net dividend	13	14

Source: CRH Annual Report 2005

Figure 5.3: CRH Comparative Financial Ratios: (a) Returns and (b) Solvency

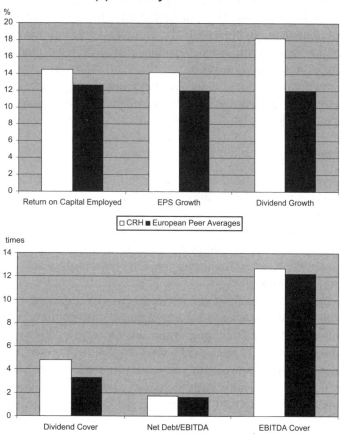

financial rigour challenging. A cash generative mentality pervaded all operations and was central to the group's evaluation and control processes. Cash earnings were consistently around two-thirds higher than reported earnings per share (EPS), a major factor enabling CRH to fund its acquisition-led expansion overseas without compromising its financial principles.

Corporate-Level Strategy at CRH

Consistent with its federalist philosophy, CRH's corporate headquarters was small, with a limited range of central functions. Less than 100 people were employed in Dublin. Counting support staff in the four divisions, around 200 people were engaged in headquarters-type activities. Traditionally, finance and business development were the only central functions. In the recent past, internal audit had grown in line with external compliance requirements. Also, the group development team acted as a catalyst for renewal on cross-divisional deals, strategic planning and opportunities in emerging regions.

Notwithstanding small size and limited scope, headquarters drove the development and integration of CRH through a variety of formal and informal mechanisms.

Formal Mechanisms

The strategic stance of CRH was explicit, enduring and continually reinforced. Over time, the broad thrust of the group's strategy had become progressively more articulated and refined under successive chief executives. Strategy was reinforced by rigorous measurement, evaluation and control processes, and by the value-added business contribution and advice of the finance function, ensuring early intervention and appropriate corrective measures.

CRH operated a group-wide management development system to develop the critical experience base of managers, particularly when they are mobile and in their twenties and thirties. Over time, this system had become more formal and structured because, unlike in the past, managers were unlikely to get the requisite exposure to a wide range of CRH's operations unsystematically. A key element was the management database, on which the core 350 managers in the group had been formally profiled.

There were a variety of formal development programmes for managers, many of which involved inputs and presentations on strategy from senior management, including the chief executive. The management seminar was held in Dublin in late March each year in advance of the Annual General Meeting (AGM) of CRH plc in May. This event provided an opportunity for 130 senior managers to discuss strategy, based on a dedicated theme. Careful selection ensured that around 40 per cent of participating managers each year were first-time attendees. The development forum was run annually for a cross-section of experienced and relatively new development personnel, and was a very valuable training and best practice sharing and development activity. A leadership development programme (LDP 1) was run in each division in the winter. (As building materials are weather dependent, winter is downtime in many regions of the group.) Aiming to give a periscopic view, this programme covered strategy, personal development and networking. This was followed two years later by LDP 2, which was group-wide.

The business leadership programme (BLP) involved the four divisions and corporate headquarters, with the aim of preparing experienced managers for senior leadership roles. (It was supplemented by other programmes for developing specific competences, for example, negotiating skills for operating companies.) BLP involved four sessions over twelve months, with work-based assignments between sessions, and covered psychometric testing, mentor support and individually tailored development plans. The annual Euroforum with employees was initially established as a Section 13 agreement in response to the EU Information and Consultation Directive. Over time, a HR forum was established in conjunction with the Euroforum to tackle issues proactively, such as developing future HR competences for the group.

At division level, integrated product management had become progressively strengthened over time, especially in the US. Divisionally coordinated, ongoing best practice activities involved meetings of small teams of experts at local, regional and international levels, facilitated by technical advisors. These resulted in highly innovative ideas and exchanges of products, which 'push forward the frontiers of excellence and "sharing the learning" … we all have to continually get smarter in what we do, reducing costs and offering better quality and service to our customers' (CRH 2005: 7). There were around seven best practice programmes in each of the four product-based divisions. Best practice was supplemented by benchmarking exercises and the development of common systems platforms (the latter particularly in the US).

Finally, communications and coaching opportunities were exploited to the maximum. CRH's excellence in external relations was mirrored internally utilising communications technologies. The use of e-mail and bulletin boards was common, while regular editions of the internal news magazine *Contact* were read avidly by managers and employees alike. All formal integrative mechanisms involved *de facto* coaching, for both team and individuals. Such fora were used as opportunities to restate key messages, from reinforcing the 'right to grow' mantra at strategic level, to the minutiae of operational best practice.

Informal Mechanisms

Notwithstanding the foregoing, 'the culture of performance and achievement which pervades CRH is its key strength' (*CRH Annual Report 2005*: 7). This restless culture was nurtured and sustained constantly.

CRH continually reinforced its core values in formal statements of strategy, in external and internal communications and through corporate folklore. (Managers in Poland referred to 'RONA the bitch'!) More subtle mechanisms also existed, including leading by example and clear norms of acceptable behaviour (such as the ethos of 'owning up' in financial reporting).

Strong informal networks existed among managers, even between far-flung regions of the group's activities. These emerged from frequent manager rotation within and between divisions and from management development programmes, benchmarking and best practice activities (which provided ready fora for interaction). In addition, a social dimension accompanied formal events (involving dinner and, occasionally, golf). This contributed to a family atmosphere, such as at the annual get-together of senior managers at the AGM of CRH plc in Dublin every May. The AGM itself was an important ceremonial occasion, and served as an induction for new managers, all of whom attended in their first year in the group.

Other informal mechanisms underpinned integration. Hierarchy and job descriptions were highly flexible. Harry Sheridan, the former long-serving finance director, also held operational responsibility for the emerging region of Latin America in the 1990s. Jack Golden, the HR director, was involved in a wide range of group issues pertaining to France, based on his previous experience as country manager there for another multinational. At operational level, informal mentoring, hands-on assistance and individual coaching are common within and across entities.

Acquisitions

Acquisitions were the most visible aspect of corporate-level strategy. From 1978 to 2006, CRH completed around 620 deals, spending over €13.5 billion, over 90 per cent in the period since 1995 (see Table 5.5). The group's acquisition performance was extolled widely. A leading global investment bank commented: 'CRH has the best track record of its peer group … of growing returns through acquisitions' (Goldman Sachs 2005: 3). It was estimated that acquisitions accounted for 70 per cent of CRH's profit growth (with organic growth contributing one quarter, and currency movements the remainder) (Goodbody Stockbrokers 2005).

Traditionally, CRH's acquisitions were add-on in nature. However, in the period since 1995, over half of expenditure has been on larger deals, of which materials businesses accounted for more than 70 per cent. By

Table 5.5: Profile of CRH Acquisitions

	1978–1990	1991–1995	1996–2000	2001–2006	1996–2006	1978–2006
Add-on deals						
Number	74	60	171	288	459	593
Value (€ million)	526	594	1761	3288	6049	7170
Average value (€ million)	7.1	9.9	10.3	14.9	13.2	12.1
*Value/cap. Employed**	*10.1%*	*14.6%*	*15.4%*	*10.0%*	*11.3%*	*N/A*
Medium-sized deals						
Number			9	13	22	22
Value (€ million)			2641	3721	6362	6362
Average value (€ million)			293	286	289	289
Value/cap. Employed			*23.1*	*6.3*	*10.3%*	*10.3%*
Sectoral breakdown						
Americas materials			1347	1822	3169	3169
Americas prods./distrib.			0	270	270	270
Europe materials			744	633	1377	1377
Europe prods./distrib.			550	996	1546	1546
Total deals						
Number	74	60	180	301	481	615
Value (€ million)	526	594	4402	8009	12411	13532
Average value (€ million)	7.1	9.9	24.5	26.6	25.8	22.0
Value/cap. Employed	*10.0%*	*14.6%*	*38.5%*	*16.3%*	*21.6%*	*N/A*

Capital employed is with respect to prior year.
Source: CRH, author estimates.

the end of 2006, the group had completed twenty-two such purchases, with no single deal amounting to more than 10 per cent of its capital base (Figure 5.4). In general, CRH acquired purchase prices that were a low 6.8 times operating profits (Goldman Sachs 2005: 2) (although multiples for larger deals were somewhat higher). In part, this reflected 'the group's commitment to completing transactions only at prices that will contribute to long-term value creation for its shareholders' (*CRH Annual Report* 2005: 6). Moreover, CRH was adept at generating superior returns from deals. From an estimated level of 10 per cent on purchase, in general RONA rose to 12 per cent within the first year and to the benchmark level of 15 per cent within two to three years (Goodbody Stockbrokers 2005: 10). Finally, as a result of its strong financial position, CRH had considerable 'fire-power' to finance a continuing high level of acquisition spend (Goodbody Stockbrokers 2005).

Acquisition Process

Rigorous, comprehensive and inclusive, the acquisition strategy of CRH was singular in conception and execution and had 'proven very difficult to replicate' (Merrill Lynch 2005: 12). Much of the management time at all levels was consumed by acquisitions. For the initial identification phase, CRH had fourteen development teams spread across the group seeking opportunities and maintaining contact with an extensive database of potential targets accumulated over more than twenty-five years. At any one time, a considerable number of acquisitions were under active consideration, ensuring a steady deal flow. Each purchase gave rise to further opportunities, in other (occasionally new) product lines in other geographic areas.

Courtship involved a patient and often long approach of familiarisation and coaching. CRH took time to assess suitability and strategic fit, and to know the management and their evolving needs. Much effort was spent appraising the target of CRH's strategy, management, values and expectations, including up-front clarity on post-acquisition priorities. It was not unusual for CRH to walk away from a deal, on grounds of timing, price or compatibility. Sometimes, acquisitions were completed at a later date.

To aid negotiation, CRH codified in a classified, proprietary document the best practice, knowledge and processes involved in making an acquisition, gleaned from many years of experience. This was full of collected wisdom, including recommended letters of introduction, follow-up procedures and practical advice on deal making. An experienced operational

Figure 5.4: CRH Acquisitions 1991–2006

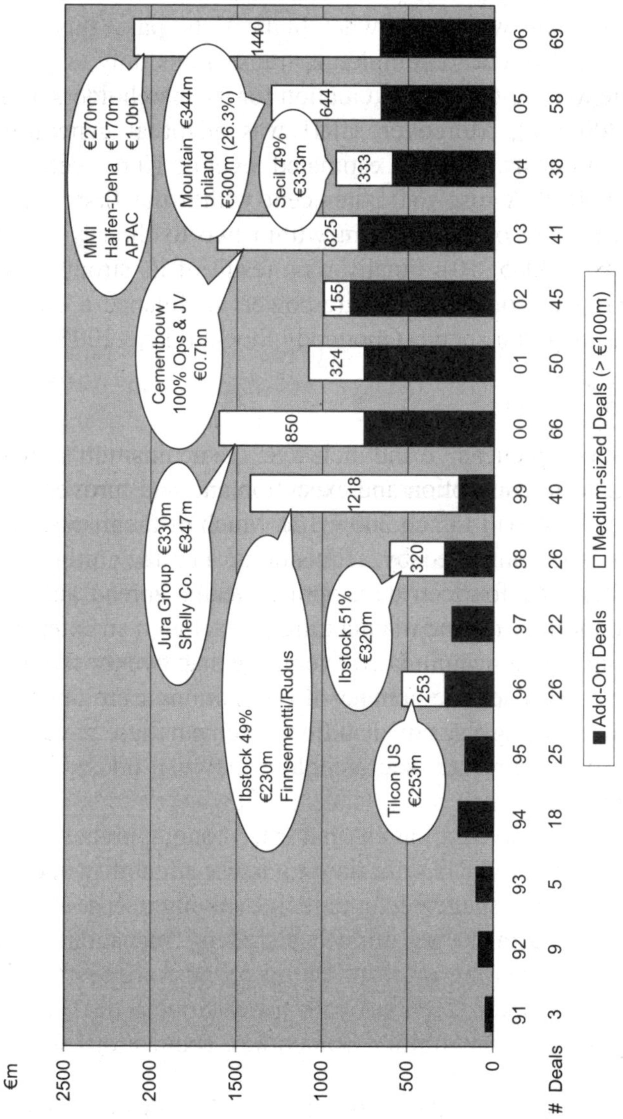

€m

	91	92	93	94	95	96	97	98	99	00	01	02	03	04	05	06
# Deals	3	9	5	18	25	26	22	26	40	66	50	45	41	38	58	69

Legend: ■ Add-On Deals □ Medium-sized Deals (> €100m)

Tilcon US €253m; Ibstock 51% €320m; Ibstock 49% €230m Finnsementti/Rudus; Jura Group €330m Shelly Co. €347m; Cementbouw 100% Ops & JV €0.7bn; Mountain €344m Uniland €300m (26.3%); Secil 49% €333m; MMI €270m Halfen-Deha €170m APAC €1.0bn

Values: 253, 320, 1218, 850, 324, 155, 825, 333, 644, 1440

manager guided each acquisition team. At the appropriate time, a senior level 'ambassador' was introduced to close the deal.

Before completion, each deal underwent rigorous evaluation, including qualitative operational review, due diligence, strict cash flow testing and board approval. Traditionally, CRH's acquisitions shared many common characteristics:

- They were medium-sized, private, often family-run businesses.
- They were geographic or product market leaders, with potential to enhance existing group operations or fill a gap.
- Deals were carefully structured and often involved initial stakes with options to increase in new regions or product areas.
- Owner-managers were retained to ensure continuity and maintain human capital.

Post-acquisition integration to boost returns was rapid and well practised. Group financial, management information systems (MIS) and control systems were implemented immediately. Revenue and cost synergies were captured, often followed over time by targeted capital investment. Benchmarking and best practice programmes were also put in place. For a period, the newly acquired entities operated under the guidance of a related existing CRH business, while the 'right to grow' mantra was exhorted informally through the hierarchy. After three years, a formal look-back review was carried out.

Although similar in principle, the acquisition process for larger deals was somewhat different. Higher level (corporate or division) involvement and greater public availability of information on targets facilitate truncated courtship and rapid completion. While, for the most part, CRH engaged in negotiated deals, tendered bids were not uncommon and the group did not rule out hostile or disputed acquisitions. Integration was assessed on a case-by-case basis. In a new region or product area, experienced CRH managers might have been brought in to run the business for a period, with the situation determining the skills and experience required.

Outlook

The first half of 2007 provided not only challenges but also opportunities, which CRH was in a position to exploit. On a broad canvas, rising energy prices, high debt levels, stubborn global imbalances and regional geo-political instability added uncertainty to the economic backdrop. However, global economic growth continued to be robust and emerging markets remained prospective, while the building materials industry continued to provide opportunities for consolidation. Although housing was slowing in both the US and Ireland, its overall impact on CRH was around 10 per cent of sales, and was offset by growth in other sectors of activity.

With improved prospects for the group's materials businesses on both sides of the Atlantic, the benefits of CRH's strategic balance were manifest. In terms of development, there was evidence that the market for acquisitions was tightening. Over recent years, the average value of add-on acquisitions in the sector had fallen (Goodbody Stockbrokers 2005) whereas, for large deals, the prices had risen and returns were lower. At the same time, the stock market looked to the group for a 'benchmark level' of acquisition spend of €1 billion annually (Merrill Lynch 2005: 13).

As Liam O'Mahony and his management team celebrated thirty-six years of achievement in 2007, CRH could look to the future with the confidence borne of outstanding business success and robust financial health. But high shareholder expectations and the demands of a hostile industry environment bred constant vigilance. Specifically, could the corporate strategy and acquisition model that had served the group so well over the years be sustained?

References

CRH (2005), *Contact* (internal magazine), issue 14.

CRH (2005), *Annual Report*, available at: <http://www.crh.ie>.

Goldman Sachs (2005), 'CRH', October.

Goodbody Stockbrokers (2005), 'CRH: Still to play its "Trump Card"', July.

Goodbody Stockbrokers (2003), 'CRH: The Foundation Stone of Value', July.

Merrill Lynch (2005), 'Adding Value or Hot Air?' 25 October.

CHAPTER 6

Lagan Technologies Ltd:
Turning It Around

Nola Hewitt-Dundas[1]

School of Management, Queen's University, Belfast

Introduction

Lagan Technologies[2] is a privately owned software development company based in Belfast, with offices in Newbury, Washington DC and Chicago. The company provides software solutions to governments in Europe and the US designed to assist them in becoming more citizen and business centric. From 1999, the core business of Lagan has been to provide customer relationship management (CRM) solutions to local governments. However, since 2005 the company offers its clients a broader enterprise case management (ECM) capability. This case charts the development of Lagan over thirteen years, from its inception in September 1994 to the start of 2007. Three periods are identified: the first is from Lagan's incorporation as a university spin-out struggling to clearly define its market to approaching the point of bankruptcy in 1999; the second stage sees its entry into the local government market in the early 2000s; and the third stage encompasses more recent attempts by the company to diversify its product and market portfolio into human (social) services and its securing venture capital investment in 2006 of £8.3 million. Lagan is currently listed in the Microsoft Tech Track 100 annual league as one of the UK's fastest growing private technology companies. Sales revenue has grown by approximately 65 per cent per annum since

---

[1] The author wishes to acknowledge Lagan Technologies' cooperation in the production of this case study. The case was compiled from published sources and has not been verified by Lagan Technologies. It relates to the position of the company up to 2007. This case is intended to be used as a basis for class discussion and not as an illustration of good or bad practice.

[2] Hereafter referred to as Lagan.

2002 to over £15 million by 2006–7, with the company being awarded major government contracts in the UK and North America.

Early Stage: 1994–1999

Lagan as a Software Service Provider

The early stage of Lagan's development dates from its inception in 1994 to 1999. This period, as the company outlines, saw it developing as very much a services company but trying to be a product company. Principally, it was undertaking services for a range of blue-chip companies including ICL, IBM, Fujitsu, TeleWest and General Cable. These services were predominantly focused on mediation services including interactive voice response and call centre and computer telephony services which, while providing a source of revenue, were not generating any long-term capability. Some effort was also being made to develop a SSL product (secure sockets layer, a communications protocol and the predecessor to the more common transport layer security – TLS); however, the company never commercialised this product.

Even at this early stage in the company's development, Lagan recognised the importance of selling into international export markets. In 1998, it participated in a trade mission to the US, organised by the local council and the business development agency in Northern Ireland. As a result of this, the company secured a £150,000 deal with a US software company and one of their founding directors, John Montgomery, stated that 'as a result of the mission we have a foot in the door. We have been trying to get into the US market for over a year and this was a major breakthrough for us' (*Belfast News Letter* 1998).

Despite this emphasis on the provision of services to the software sector, the company was relatively profitable for the first four to five years. The technical director remarks that, during the first year of operations, he recounted unease in the company because it had only eleven months of cash flow. In hindsight, he now realises that, while the company was financially comfortable, there was also the recognition that the business model had limitations in allowing the company to expand (*Gulf News* 1999).

Targeting the Mobile Telecommunications Market

During the early stage of company development, Lagan also pursued a second strategy focused on the mobile telecommunications sector. In 1999, it was announced that Lagan had formed a Middle East partnership with Abu Dhabi-based Gulf Business Machines (GBM) to provide a new

Java call centre. The call centre was designed to handle telephone banking telecommunications and to reduce the workload of call centre agents, therefore increasing the capacity of the centres. Strategically, this appeared to fit with the other activities being undertaken by Lagan at that time which included call routing, service activation and deactivation, and account enquiries in both telecommunication companies and banks throughout Europe and the Middle East (*Gulf News* 1999). Although Lagan pursued this market sector for some time, ultimately, as chief technical officer David Moody stated at a public seminar in 2007, 'GSM didn't work for us. It is a hard market to be in and we did not differentiate ourselves at all, and we didn't have a chance.'

Developmental Stage: 1999/2000–2006

By the end of the early stage of development, the company was in difficulties both strategically and financially (see Figure 6.1). In 1999, turnover was £844,295 and the company was making a loss of £30,503 before tax. The profit margin was, therefore, 3.61 per cent with a return on capital employed of 38.29 per cent. At this point, a new chairman, John Lillywhite, was appointed to the board of directors.

New Chairman Appointed

John Lillywhite came to Lagan with extensive experience and contacts in the telecoms and banking sectors, having worked for ICL throughout the world. In 1990, ICL helped to set up another small software spin-out from Queen's University Belfast, Kainos, with an investment of £50,000 and John Lillywhite sitting on the board. ICL, however, decided to rationalise its holdings and sold 31 per cent of its holdings. This share of the business was acquired by Lillywhite and he was made chairman. Kainos is currently valued at around £15 million to £20 million. John Lillywhite was appointed as the chairman to the board of directors at Lagan in 1999, when the company 'was teetering on bankruptcy' (Chairman's Network[3]).

Software Product Developed: Frontline[4]

Looking back, the other key development for Lagan during 1999 was the development of their CRM product, Frontline. Frontline was built based

---

[3] Chairman's Network – Where Technology Leaders Connect, see <http://www.chairmansnetwork.com>.

[4] The product names Frontline and Frontlink are no longer used by Lagan.

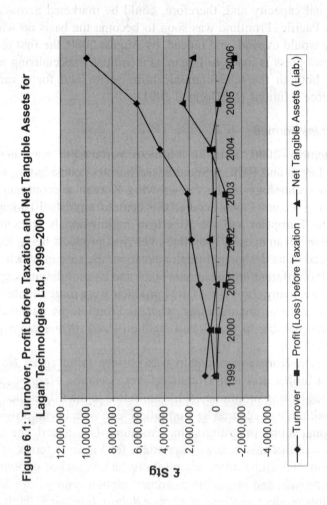

Figure 6.1: Turnover, Profit before Taxation and Net Tangible Assets for Lagan Technologies Ltd, 1999–2006

on Java-based technology, allowing it to be used on a range of operating systems including Linux, the main rival to Microsoft Windows. Frontline enabled the companies to provide a 24-hour response service to customers, irrespective of whether they communicated by telephone, fax, e-mail or the Internet. From the outset, Frontline was designed with a multilingual capacity and, therefore, could be marketed across Europe and Asia Pacific. Frontline was soon to become the basis on which the company would expand, and indeed, by August 2000, the first reference in the news press is made to Lagan as a company specialising in CRM products both in the telecommunications sector and for a variety of e-commerce solutions (McDonnell 2001).

Partnerships Formed

By September 2000, a major business partnership was announced between Lagan and BCK, a Seoul-based business consultancy, to introduce new technology to the fast-growing Korean telecommunications and banking sectors. Lagan secured this contract amidst stiff competition among the European and the American multinationals with the main competitive advantages of Frontline over rival products being identified as the speed of its design and implementation, the ease in which it could be scaled to different organisational sizes and its multilingual capability. Furthermore, many competitor CRM products were more suitable to very large multinational organisations, whereas Frontline was adaptable and particularly suitable to small- and medium-sized organisations (*Belfast Telegraph* 2000).

The South Korean partnership was closely followed in November 2000 by a further deal with ComputerFleet, Australia's largest specialist in managed leasing programmes. Lagan shared in the £10 million private finance initiative as secured by ComputerFleet, with Lagan providing an international rental programme for Frontline. Des Speed, the CEO of Lagan, stated that this deal was important for Lagan in terms of market penetration: 'Frontline gives organisations an unmatched opportunity to establish reliable and profitable customer relations and we are delighted to carry this product into new markets' (*Belfast Telegraph* 2000).

In addition to the Australian deal with ComputerFleet, in November 2000 Lagan also won part of a multi-million pound contract with Guernsey Telecoms, supplying customer care, order handling and billing solutions (Smyth 2000). It shared the contract with consortium partners Usha Communications and Eftia. Besides this, Lagan also had a software reseller agreement with IBM, which is regarded by CEO Des Speed as 'a unique agreement for companies in our product range. Our product will now go into IBM's sales books and its sales representatives will have a strong incentive to ship the product' (Smyth 2000).

Signs of Recovery and Optimism

In just over a year, the company had moved from 'teetering on bank-ruptcy' (Chairman's Network) to securing a number of significant contracts. This was reflected in January 2001 with Lagan being ranked forty-third in the Deloitte & Touche Technology Fast 50 Awards, which recognises and ranks those companies throughout Ireland that have reported rapid growth over the previous three years.

In the company, optimism was expressed in a newspaper report (McGann and Castano 2000) that the company was close to securing between £2 million and £4 million ($2.9 million to $5.8 million) in second-round funding. It was, however, going to be approximately eight-een months later before this became a reality, and on a much smaller scale. Another expression of optimism in the company was the move in November 2000 to new premises. This comprised a 10,000 sq. ft office space with the company announcing that it planned to double its workforce to 100 within a year, i.e. by the end of 2001. Again, this employment target was to take more time to achieve than anticipated, with employment at the end of 2001 being around fifty employees.

Lagan attributed its change in fortunes to 'thinking in groundbreaking and innovative terms, transforming dynamic concepts into reality and applying these to the real world of commerce' (McGill 2001). Undoubtedly, revenue had increased markedly; however, this could be attributed to a small number of key contracts. Nevertheless, the company proactively publicised its position and, in March 2001, announced that it was planning for a stock market flotation in 2002, which was expected to rise to £100 million. Whether the company actually planned to achieve this is uncertain; however, by 2007, this had still not happened and may reflect (with the exception of 2004) the persistent financial loss that the company has incurred since 1999.

What is perhaps more interesting is the motivation for wanting to pur-sue a stock market flotation. The company was hungry for growth and perceived an Initial Public Offering (IPO) as facilitating this. As CEO Des Speed stated, 'we face many well-funded American competitors. To address that in terms of sales, organisation and product development it is a question of how fast we can grow and how much we can broaden the scope of what we can offer to clients' (McGill 2001).

In the early 2000s, the size of business in the computer software sector was perceived as being a determining factor in business success. Jeffrey Peel, as the vice president (VP) of Global Marketing at Amacis,[5] stated in an interview that:

> It's just a function of size and availability of funds that I can't see any local players [Northern Ireland companies] in the CRM space becoming world leaders unless they are acquired. I have high regard for the CRM community in Northern Ireland and they have grand ambitions but there isn't a huge local market and the support infrastructure in terms of equity to grow huge businesses. It's not going to happen. (McKillion 2002)

Lagan clearly understood the difficulties that existed for a small company to succeed in the international CRM market, and it was keen to pursue different routes, considering both the acquisition of venture capital and a stock market flotation as possibilities. However a strategy that was implemented in the company (and one which had proved successful since 1999) was the formation of partnerships. As David Moody, the chief technical officer, stated: 'While we want to have a global presence, moving into new territory is always a high risk so we have to minimise that and the easiest way is to go through partners – that has to be one of the main ways of developing the business' (McGill 2001).

Developing appropriate business partnerships was a very important strategy for Lagan, and this remains the case in 2007. However, the next contract that Lagan secured in 2001 was perhaps the most significant in the development of the business and one that it won on its own.

A Turning Point: Local Government as Customer

Lagan was introduced to Birmingham City Council by one of the telecoms consultants whom it retained. The consultant suggested that Lagan should talk to the Council, something that it was very reluctant to do, as this was local government and not the customer base that it worked with. Nevertheless, it presented to the Council on the SSL work that the company had undertaken, and, on leaving the meeting, Lagan personnel felt that this had been a complete waste of time. However, shortly afterwards, Birmingham City Council requested that Lagan respond to their call for tenders to implement a CRM system.

---

[5] Lagan Technologies and Amacis were both founded by Tom Montgomery, amongst others.

The purpose of this contract was to assist Birmingham in complying with EU legislation arising from the 2000 Lisbon summit requiring all the local governments to provide public services transactions electronically by 2005. Birmingham, therefore, wished to set up a one-stop entry point interface between the council and the community. The computer-based system would enable citizens to undertake activities such as completing passport applications, motor tax renewals and applications for social welfare benefits online (McGurk 2001). Tony Glew, the head of IT at BCC, stated that 'the system will help us to be more efficient, more directly accountable and more visibly part of the business, residential and voluntary communities which make up the city. The technology gives us the opportunity to put our residents – our customers – at the very centre of the Council's business' (McGurk 2001).

Lagan responded to this and competed with established multinational organisations in the government CRM market. Conscious of the competition, Lagan ensured that their presentation was as comprehensive and informative as possible in demonstrating the advantages of their system, Frontline. Despite the issues about the financial stability of the company, and the need to put in place mechanisms to ensure that the company was financially viable, Lagan was awarded the contract by Birmingham City Council.

The contract – which was for a phasing-in of Frontline over three years under a rental agreement to Birmingham City Council – was reported to be worth more than £5 million and 'one of the most significant e-government contracts in Europe' (McGurk 2001). CEO Des Speed stated that 'the significance of this contract cannot be underestimated. There is now a rush towards meeting targets for getting Europe's e-government transactions online. Birmingham City Council is one of the largest metropolitan authorities in Europe and will be among the first in Britain to adopt the system.'

In a later interview, Speed sought to emphasise publicly the strength of Lagan, stating that it was 'not a flaky dot.com', but instead a company with a 'strong management team which we are continuing to flesh out and we have a track record when it comes to winning business. Our contract with BCC was a watershed for the company in relation to the size of contracts that we will now go after and our credibility in the marketplace' (McDonnell 2001).[6]

---

[6] For an overview of key management appointments announced through the press and the current management team at Lagan, see Table 6.2.

Strengthening the Company: Management Recruitment, New Business Partnerships and Venture Capital Investment

The 'fleshing out of the management team' undoubtedly referred to five new appointments that Lagan had made. These included: Les Stansfield to the board of Lagan as well as acting worldwide VP of sales and marketing; Peter Baker as the worldwide business development director; Stuart Connolly as the solutions director; and Grace Meehan as the European marketing executive. These appointments, announced in June 2001, were closely followed by the further appointment of Yaoshen Wang, a 23-year-old Chinese national who was to be based in Beijing as the marketing executive in the Far East.

The strategy to form partnerships as a means to enter and develop markets was again evident in January 2002. Lagan announced that it had appointed another Northern Ireland company, Consilium Technologies, as a preferred reseller of Frontline. Consilium Technologies, having recently completed a £1.5 million venture capital (VC) funding round, were established as specialist suppliers of software in the government sector and in particular to small- and medium-sized councils. Lagan was clearly aware of the need to develop strong partnerships with companies that were well established in the local government market. As Phil Murray, the VP for sales and marketing for Lagan, remarked: 'We are confident that Consilium's established reputation in the local government arena will give us a strong competitive advantage in our plans to develop new channels and increase market share' (*Belfast News Letter* 2002). Consilium Technologies recognised the potential of Lagan's Frontline product, the proven success of it in Birmingham and the fact that EU legislation would lead to many more councils in the UK seeking to acquire appropriate technology in the very near future.

In early 2002, less than two years from being on the verge of bankruptcy, Lagan was awarded VC funding of approximately £1 million. Again, mirroring the emphasis placed by the company on strengthening the management team, particularly in the area of sales and marketing, the company stated that this funding was to be used to expand sales and marketing activities. Four key sectors were identified, namely government, telecommunications, retail and financial services, with the CEO stating that the investment would 'bring significant value added to our business given its reputation for providing strong management support to its portfolio companies' (McGill and McKillion 2002).

A key focus of marketing activity for the company at this time was in promoting their main (and only) product, Frontline. Whereas the previous marketing attempts had focused on the growth of the company – the management team, new appointments, aspirations to raise finance, increase employment, etc. – attention now turned to the product. This was reflected in the following press articles related to Frontline:

> It enables a more joined-up, more responsive and more personalised service to citizens. The software is transforming the way the public sector does business, complementing traditional channels of service with the efficiency of electronic channels. With Frontline, citizens have real time consistent access to information across their local council. This can be 'assisted service', interacting with a council employee in contact centres or one-stop shops, 'self-service' using, for example Web, iDRV or IVR, and 'message-based service' using e-mail, mail or fax … (*Belfast News Letter* 2002)

> In the public sector it is more about citizen relationship management. It is about providing information and services as opposed to selling and revenue generation. This is a different focus (relative to the private sector) it is about fast access to information by going to a central point. (*Belfast News Letter* 2002)

Another avenue for marketing the activity of the company was that of entering for awards. In March 2001, Lagan was the winner of the Northern Ireland Innovation in Business Awards 2000 in the tradable services section. In April 2001, the company was awarded the Innovation Award of the Year by the Northern Ireland software industry and in May 2001 it was short-listed in the Enterprise Awards 2001. In June 2002, recognising their success with Birmingham City Council and their ongoing efforts to penetrate the local government market, Lagan was nominated in the Government Computer Innovation Awards 2002.

In August 2002, a further partnership was announced with Knowledge Management Software Plc (KMS), which entered into a global original equipment manufacturing (OEM) partnership with Lagan, meaning that the solutions of KMS were to become a major component of the e-CRM solution as offered by Lagan (*AFX.com* 2002).

Announcements of new contracts with UK city councils began to flow from the middle of 2002. In August, a contract with Newcastle City Council was announced followed in January 2003 by a (just under) £2 million contract with Bristol City Council (Daly 2003). This contract with Bristol was claimed to be 'one of 10 major contracts totalling several million pounds inked by Lagan in the last seven months' (Daly 2003). In March 2004, Lagan announced an additional local government contract worth £1.5 million with Blackpool City Council to install their CRM solution (*Sunday Business Post* 2004).

Also in March 2004, Lagan publicised a new business partnership with plaNET Consulting (a division of CSG Systems), a leading provider of telecommunication services in Namibia (*PR Newswire* 2004) to upgrade their version of CSG® ICMS and integrate the Lagan Frontline CRM platform alongside this. Securing contracts in the telecommunications sector and with local government at this time reflected the efforts by Lagan to target both the public (local government) and private (predominantly telecommunications) sectors. In 2007, David Moody, reflecting on this two-track market strategy, stated:

> Any software company will find it difficult to say we are not going to do that, especially in formative years when you haven't understood how you are going to be successful. For us we only learnt that about a year ago. We have operated as a government-focused company for the last 5 years but it is only in the past year that we have put a stake in the ground and said that this is 'only' what we are going to do, and that decision has made a huge difference to us. Even though we operated that way, we were still wasting time looking at this and that and wasting time. (Moody 2007)

Becoming Profitable: Albeit Temporarily!

Sales revenue was markedly increasing as a result of local government contracts, and for the first time since 1999 Lagan was becoming profitable. Des Speed stated in January 2003: 'Being profitable takes the pressure off and we expect to see good, steady growth in profit and revenues in 2003' (Daly 2003). This did occur and by the end of the financial year (March 2004) sales revenue had increased to £4,268,330 with profit before tax of £372,705. As the finance director remarked: 'We have grown revenue by a factor of 10 since 2000 and we are now generating annual revenue worth €6.5 million. Since January 2003, we have been trading profitably' (*Irish Times* 2004).

The rapid growth in sales revenue was again acknowledged publicly through awards. In 2003, Lagan was again listed in the Deloitte Technology Fast 50 Awards, improving their position by thirty-two places from forty-third to twelfth as well as being listed as thirty-eighth in the *Sunday Times* ARM Tech Track 100, based on a 98 per cent sales growth between 2000 and 2002. By the end of 2004, Lagan was to announce that it had raised an undisclosed amount of second-round funding to accelerate the expansion of the company principally into the North

American market (Cresent Capital 2002). VC financing had been led by the London-based DN Capital and supported by the existing investors of Crescent Capital, Invest NI and the Viridian Growth Fund (White 2004). However, while sales revenue continued to increase rapidly (see Figure 6.1 and Table 6.1), profitability again began to decline for the company by March 2005. It once more reported a loss (before tax) of £287,926 on sales of £6,087,263.

Entering the American Market

From the incorporation of the company in 1994 a global sales strategy had been adopted. In serving the UK local government market, Lagan had successfully developed relationships with authorities in the UK to provide them with greater integration between their departments. In the US, integration between state departments was less well-developed than that in the UK, the implication of this being that Lagan was at an advantage in bringing to the US market a product and service that had been tried and tested elsewhere and could offer significant benefits to the US authorities. For Lagan, the US market offered vast opportunities to them to expand their sales, but critical in this decision to target the US market was having an established customer base in the UK.

Lagan, unsure about the best approach to entering the American market, sought advice from another Northern Ireland software company, Meridio, who were already active in that market. Lagan decided to go on a tour of the US, visiting three local authorities on the eastern coast and outlining to them the work that it had undertaken with UK local governments. Following advice given, Lagan decided that it should target the US market directly as opposed to trying to work with US partners.

Within six months of securing VC support to expand the business into the American market, Lagan acquired its first US contracts. One of these contracts was to provide the city of Hampton, Virginia, with improved city services. John Eagle, chief information officer for the City of Hampton, stated:

> We were impressed with Lagan and what they had to offer to a city of our size. In Hampton, we strive to bring our citizens the best services available. Five years ago, we implemented one of the first centralised call centres in the nation. Lagan's Frontlink[7] will allow us to convert our centralised call centre into a full-service contact centre that will streamline our approach to handling

---

[7] The Frontline product was re-branded in the US as Frontlink.

Table 6.1: Financial Data for Lagan Technologies Ltd, 1999–2006 (months: 12; currency: GBP)

End of year date	31/03/1999	31/03/2000	31/03/2001	31/03/2002	31/03/2003	31/03/2004	31/03/2005	31/03/2006
Turnover	844,295	479,463	1,293,990	1,884,249	2,161,885	4,268,330	6,087,263	9,950,344
Profit (loss) before taxation	−30,503	−204,821	−769,148	−1,063,827	−747,037	372,705	−287,926	−1,539,777
Net tangible assets (Liab.)	79,655	396,708	−56,331	464,225	159,710	284,678	2,562,002	1,743,925
Shareholders funds	79,655	396,708	104,074	649,147	435,110	732,815	2,904,541	319,808
Profit margin (%)	−3.61	−42.72	−59.44	−56.46	−34.55	8.73	−4.73	−15.47
Return on share-holders funds (%)	−38.29	−51.63	−739.04	−163.88	−171.69	50.86	−9.91	−481.47
Return on capital employed (%)	−38.29	−51.63	−233.73	−137.42	−146.45	45.43	−9.13	−59.93
Liquidity ratio	1.98	4.93	0.63	1.44	0.93	1.04	1.88	1.25
Gearing ratio (%)	1.88	0.75	247.85	43.09	69.06	71.6	18.29	850.86
Number of employees				42	45	61	82	111

Source: FAME (Financial Analysis Made Easy) database.

105

city services. Our citizens will be able to reach us in a variety of ways – whether by e-mail or phone or even in person – Lagan will provide us with the tools we need to give our citizens quality services. (*Business Wire* 2005)

Once again the key focus of Lagan was to strengthen its sales and marketing team. Lagan announced that it had grown its US sales force and was aggressively looking to showcase its innovative solutions with decision makers across the country (*Business Wire* 2005). The key appointments in 2005 included: Steve Isler as the US eastern region sales director to handle sales outreach in the eastern US (*Tampa Tribune* 2005); Roger Dean Blake as the senior sales engineer and member of the sales team (Grote 2005); Thomas Mazur (previously employed as national sales manager at Motorola Inc.) as the VP of sales in St Charles (*Crain's Chicago Business* 2005); and Rocky Ray to take the responsibility for sales outreach in the western US (*Press Enterprise* 2005).

In just over six months from securing their first US contract with the city of Hampton, Lagan was successful in a $3.2 million bid with Unisys to install a one-call 311 solution to Minneapolis.[8] Unisys were to host the solution at their outsourcing centre near Eagan, Minneapolis, as well as providing training and IT support for the 311 call centres (Butterfield 2006). This deal was soon followed by another US contract worth £308,000 with Fort Wayne, to run a pilot 'One Call to City Hall' programme. This would provide a one-stop call centre for all government departments (Lanka 2006).

Although market entry into the US was a key driver of activity in Lagan in 2005, the company continued to pursue local government contracts in the UK, typically in partnership with other companies. For example, in August 2005, North Hertfordshire District Council signed a £2.2 million deal with public sector IT specialist Anite to overhaul its IT systems and business processes. As part of this contract, Anite implemented Lagan's Frontline Version 5 as the CRM application of the council (*Computer Weekly* 2005). Similarly, in February 2006, Salisbury District Council, in an attempt to improve services – particularly to citizens in rural areas – created a virtual contact centre based on MacFarlane CallPlus contact centre technology and Lagan's Frontline CRM software (*M2 Presswire* 2006a).

The company continued to receive awards over this 2004 to late 2005 period which were mainly based on the sales growth figures. The awards

---

[8] Lagan's share of this contract was believed to be around $1 million (*Business and Finance* 2005).

included being ranked again in the 2004 Deloitte Fast 50 Awards as thirty-sixth (Manley 2004) and, in 2005, as tenth (*Belfast News Letter* 2005), as well as being listed in the Microsoft Tech Track 100 (*Irish News* 2005*a*).

Lagan capitalised on the publicity attached to industry awards and the winning of new contracts. The senior management team promoted the company as a success with John Montgomery (the founding director and the VP of operations) stating that, 'good people, good ideas and a willingness to take risks have been critical in making the company a success' (*Irish News* 2005).

2006 Onwards: A New Era?

Product and Market Diversification

According to Chief Technical Officer David Moody, prior to 2006 Lagan was approached by a customer who expressed a need for adult protective services. More specifically, adult protective services are concerned with the provision of care for the elderly which could include a range of services from domestic assistance to providing a rail on a wall, etc. For service providers, the key priority is to ensure that the services they offer are matched to the citizen's needs. Initially, Lagan felt that this was irrelevant to it; however, the customer then explained how it had configured Lagan's system to serve this market area.

At approximately the same time, CEO Des Speed was looking to identify the possible avenues for diversification for the company. As part of this, he began to look at the market for 'human services'[9] and the potential synergy between the needs of this sector and those that Lagan was already serving.

In moving into the human services market, Lagan acquired a company, Peter Martin Associates Inc. (PMA), which had established human services software products. PMA's HyperWorks and FACTORS software provided 'eligibility screening, referral information management, online benefit applications and collaborative case management' (*ComputerWire* 2006). It was stated that the perceived synergy between Lagan's Frontlink and the PMA products would provide 'off-the-shelf' 311-based human service management offerings for local and state government. While there may have been a technological complementarity in the

---

[9] The term 'human services' is common in the US; however, this is referred to in the UK as 'social services'.

relationship, it is unquestionable that acquiring PMA also provided Lagan with an established customer base and credibility in the human services sector.

Further Venture Capital Investment

With the announcement of Lagan acquiring PMA also came the news of additional VC investment. This represented the fourth round of investment in the company, the first three being at inception in 1994, in 2002 and a third injection of funding in 2004, led by DN Capital. This fourth investment was on a much larger scale than that of the previous investment, reported to be worth £8.3 million (*Belfast News Letter* 2006 and Stinson 2007). Cazenove Private Equity were the investors and the purpose of the investment was to fuel the next phase of growth in the UK and the US. Stuart Chapman, the MD of Cazenove Private Equity, stated the following:

> Lagan is a dynamic company with an excellent proposition for international public sector markets. With its clear strategic vision, market leading solution and strong management team, we believe the company is well-positioned to become a major player in citizen relationship management and shared service delivery worldwide. The take-up of the Lagan solution in the US denotes the strength of its proposition' (*Belfast News Letter* 2006).

As with the previous finance investments, the announcement was closely followed by the appointment of new personnel, this time Jon Brooks, who was coming to Lagan with extensive experience in the business management of application software, having been employed previously at Geac, Software AG and Bull. Since 2000, Brooks had worked with Liberty Management Systems across twenty-five countries and was appointed with account management responsibility for Lagan's UK customers and corporate responsibility for product development, professional services and customer support (*Belfast News Letter* 2006). After a brief period, Brooks was subsequently appointed as the chief operational officer.

The appointment of Brooks mirrored the strategy of Lagan to diversify its product into new market areas. Des Speed, remarking on the appointment of Brooks, commented that 'his knowledge of managing application software will ensure that we continue to meet the requirements of our customers, and also expand the use of our leading CRM technology across more areas of the public sector market, as we continue our ambitious growth both in the UK and internationally' (*Belfast News Letter* 2006.).

Lagan's sales revenue continued upwards during this period (see Figure 6.1 and Table 6.1), with the company being listed again in the Microsoft Tech Track 100 annual league table, having climbed twenty-four places from seventy-third to forty-ninth in 2005, as well as coming nineteenth in the Deloitte Fast 50 Awards. Lagan was listed as having 150 employees and more than 130 government clients in the UK and the US.

Interdependent Partnerships and Deals

Partnership agreements continued to dominate the business profile of Lagan. In October 2006, it was announced that Lagan was partnering with Hyfinity[10] to integrate adapters between back- and front-office applications with the potential to speed up government IT implementation (the system building time) by up to 60 per cent. Lagan would be using Hyfinity's Web application development technology (MVC) to 'build new "integration adapter" modules to connect front-office and back-office applications together seamlessly ... [enabling] these complex integration solutions, involving in-depth, two-way inter-operability, to be brought to market earlier to enable public sector organisations such as local authorities to improve citizen-centric services and efficiency' (<http://webservices.org>).

In December 2006, the partnership between Lagan's Frontline and MacFarlane Telesystems' CallPlus contact centre technology, which had been the basis of their contract with Salisbury (February 2006), was once again successful. This was to lead to a new contract with Tonbridge and Malling Borough Council to improve the quality of service provided to local businesses and citizens (*M2 Presswire* 2006a).

Similarly, in early 2007, two further contracts were awarded which developed from earlier partnerships and pilot activities of implementing a CRM solution. The first of these was with Unisys in Minneapolis, with Unisys serving as systems integrator and hosting the solution at its

---

[10] Hyfinity is an independent software vendor (ISV), with headquarters near Birmingham, UK. Hyfinity is known for its innovation in XML and Web services technology, enabling the rapid visualisation, assembly and construction of enterprise-strength solutions. Hyfinity's technology uses a revolutionary new approach that harnesses the latest developments in XML and Internet technologies to provide a Web services platform that is powerful, agile and extremely lightweight. This enables solutions that take a fraction of time to build, deploy and maintain, compared to traditional approaches, resulting in massive savings for customers. Hyfinity's exciting new technology solutions have gained strong endorsement from customers around the world and leading market analysts.

service centre in Eagan, Minnesota (Bailor 2007). The second contract was with Fort Wayne, which had previously piloted the Lagan Frontlink product and was now moving to full implementation of a CRM 'One Call to City Hall' 311 service (*US States News* 2007).

Creating greater awareness of Lagan and, in particular, of Frontlink in the US, as well as being awarded a number of US contracts, led the company to announce the opening of another office in the US. The new office is based in Bethesda, Maryland, and complements the existing offices in Belfast (Headquarters), Newbury UK, Washington DC and Chicago.[11]

In addition to this, Lagan is now planning to create another 100 jobs at its headquarters in Belfast, focused on software development, implementation and support. In announcing the plans for expansion Des Speed stated that:

> Lagan is now the largest indigenous software company in Northern Ireland and offers challenging and rewarding career opportunities. Our continued growth and success are a tribute to the quality and dedication of Lagan employees who have played a fundamental role in placing the company at the forefront of global technology. The availability of highly skilled workforce in NI makes the region a serious contender in the worldwide software market. (Stinson 2007)

On Reflection

David Moody, the founding director, reflecting on the experience of Lagan to early 2007, identifies a number of important lessons that Lagan has learnt and which he believes are relevant to other companies.

The first lesson relates to the importance of having a *clear market focus*. Up until 2006, Lagan was trying to serve a number of market sectors. The problem with this approach was that this included both the private (mainly in telecommunications) and the public sectors (local government). Applying Lagan's solution in these different markets reflected different priorities of public and private sector organisations and undoubtedly created problems for Lagan in developing their product offerings.

The senior management team of Lagan participated in 'Crossing the Chasm' workshops as organised by the Innovators and Entrepreneurs Association.[12] In this, they critically questioned the mission of the

---

[11] See <http://www.lagan.com>
[12] The Chasm Workshops are designed to provide senior management of high-tech firms

Table 6.2: Managerial Appointments and Current Management Team at Lagan

Name	Current position	Date commenced employment with Lagan	Identified as currently in management team
John Montgomery	Founding director and current VP of operations	1994	✓
David Moody	Founding director and current chief technical officer	1994	✓
John Lillywhite	Appointed chairman of board of directors	1999	
Des Speed	President and chief technical officer. *Considerable experience at senior management level in IT industry*	1999	✓
Stuart Connolly	Professional services director. *Created and developed the solutions delivery capability within the company. Responsible for solutions delivery and customer support*	2000	✓
Les Stansfield	Appointed to board of directors and worldwide and VP of sales and marketing	2000/2001	
Peter Baker	Worldwide business development director	2000/2001	
Yaoshen Wang	Marketing executive in the Far East	2001	
Jamie Andrews	Chief financial officer. *Responsible for finance and administration. Formerly financial controller with BSkyB, New Media Division and KPMG, London and Sydney*	2001	✓
Philip Murray	Senior VP Sales and Marketing. *Responsible for new business sales and marketing UK and Europe. Formerly business unit director in Fujitsu and ICL*	2001	✓
Steve Isler	US Eastern region sales director	2005	
Roger Dean Blake	Senior sales engineer and member of sales team	2005	

Table 6.2 (Continued)

Name	Current position	Date commenced employment with Lagan	Identified as currently in management team
Rocky Ray	Sales outreach in Western US	2005	✓
Tom Mazur	VP of local government sales, North America; Over twenty years' experience with public sector clients	2005	✓
Una Sheehan	Human resources director; Responsible for people development and company resourcing in North America, UK and Ireland	2005	✓
Jon Brooks	Chief operational officer; Responsible for account management, product development, professional services and customer support; considerable application software experience; Formerly with Geac, Software AG, Bull and Liberty Management Systems	2006	✓
Lori Goss	VP of marketing; Responsible for determining strategic position of Lagan's products; considerable experience in marketing technology solutions for the public sector; Worked previously for PeopleSoft, SAP America and Sun MicroSystems	2006	
Claudia Langguth	VP of human services sales, North America; For past fifteen years worked with federal, state and local government agencies in North America to provide solutions that improve government services	2006	✓

Source: Various sources including press and industry articles as referenced throughout text and company website: <http://www.lagan.com>.

company and agreed that their vision was to 'focus relentlessly on providing solutions for government that deliver improved outcomes for them and their customers and best-in-class return on investment.' In other words, the vision was about Lagan providing improved outcomes for its customers, conscious of the fact that 'if your solution does not address the problem, then it is irrelevant.'

In 2007, Lagan is focused exclusively on the public (government) sector. This market sector, it believes, is one in which it has competitive advantage over rival products and one where it can adopt a niche market strategy. A niche strategy is particularly important for Lagan, given that it ultimately has only one product but, by carefully targeting specific market niches and customising the product accordingly, it can expand the range of markets into which it is selling. As David Moody outlines, 'It is the same product, the same focus, the same market but just a different niche' (2007). Building on one software product, Lagan now provides a portfolio of solutions to governments,[13] including:

- CRM, e.g. for local government.
- Customer contact centre and case management solutions for central and regional government.
- Case management for human and social services solutions, such as integrated eligibility and adult protective services.
- Shared service centre solutions, e.g. human resources.
- Single non-emergency number solutions, e.g. 311 in the US and 101 in the UK.

The second key lesson that Lagan has learnt is the importance of *careful planning*, and remaining open-minded to change. For example, Lagan established its UK customer base, and then used the success of this in trying to enter the US market. Lagan also acknowledges that there has been some 'luck' along the way: for example, in being encouraged to present to Birmingham City Council, in developing key business partnerships and in identifying new market niches for diversification, etc.

The importance of forming *strategic partnerships* in helping them to achieve their business goals is the third lesson learnt. From the early days of the company, enabling partnerships have assisted the company in many different ways, from minimising the risk of entering new markets to integrating the Lagan product in the software solution as offered by

with key insights on managing high-tech innovation and marketing. For further information, see <http://www.idea.org.sg/>.

[13] See <http://www.lagan.com> for further details of Lagan's solutions.

other companies. What is not known, however, is the extent to which these relationships have constrained profitability for the business.

The fourth lesson for Lagan has been in ensuring that it has *the right people with the right skills*. Lagan stresses the importance of putting people first and ensuring that the business is equipped with the skills it needs to achieve its business objectives. As Moody states: 'It is about being on a bus, about making sure that the right people are on the bus, that they are sitting in the right seat and that the bus is going in the right direction.' A good management team is critical in achieving this and, as illustrated throughout this case, at each key stage of development, a priority of Lagan's was to recruit the right people, typically with the right experience, skills and business networks. This is reflected in the profile of the management team at Lagan (see Table 6.2) and the breadth of 'appropriate' experience that each manager brought to the company on their appointment.

For Lagan, looking to where the company will be in three years time is important in establishing a vision for the business. In general, companies are risk averse. Yet what this is really about is managing the risk by undertaking a formal process of determining what the size of the market will be, what the human resource implications of this are likely to be, etc., and seeking to develop a solution to these issues.

References

AFX.com (2002), 'Knowledge Management Software in Global OEM Agreement with Lagan Technologies', 5 August.

Bailor, C. (2007), 'When Disaster Doesn't Strike: Lagan Technologies Helps Minneapolis Launch a 311 System to Provide Information on Municipal Issues and Nonemergency Services', *CRM Magazine*, 1 January, 42.

Belfast News Letter (2006), 'Dynamic Firm Secures Growth Funds', 1 June.

Belfast News Letter (2005), 'Meridio's Growth Soars to 1,456pc', 25 November.

Belfast News Letter (2002), 'Partnership Shows Way for E-government; Software Companies Link Up to Serve Councils', 4 January.

Belfast Telegraph (2000), 'Korea Buys NI Expertise', 12 September.

Belfast Telegraph (2000), 'Lagan Tech Rolls Out the Barrel with Major Oz Deal', 21 November.

Business and Finance (2005), 'Selling to Uncle Sam', 30 June.

Business Wire (2005), 'Lagan, a Leader in 311 City Services and CRM Solutions for Local Government, Inks First US Contract with the City of Hampton, Virginia', 27 June.

Butterfield, E. (2006), 'Unisys Rolls Out Minneapolis 311 System', *TechNews*, 10 January.

Computer Weekly (2005), 'Smart Projects New Systems will Improve Efficiency and Hit e-Government Targets; North Hertfordshire Begins £2.2m Project to Transform Processes and Boost Services', 2 August.

ComputerWire (2006), 'Lagan Buys Human Services Software Firm', 31 May.

Crain's Chicago Business (2005), 'On the Move', 31 October.

Crescent Capital (2002), *Lagan Technologies: Case Study*, available at: <http://www.crescentcapital.co.uk/case_study/lagan.asp>.

Daly, G. (2003), 'Lagan Continues Contract Success with Bristol Deal', *Sunday Business Post*, 26 January.

Grote, S. (2005), 'Local Scene', *The Columbus Dispatch*, 23 September, 02E.

Gulf News (1999), ' GCC's First IT Call Centre Planned', 1 June.

Irish News (2005), 'Risk Takers Are Imperative', 22 March.

Irish News (2005a), 'Three Northern Companies Make It into Fast-Growth Table', 24 September, 58.

Irish Times (2004), 'Optimism Makes Reappearance at Tech Gathering Summit 2004 Contrasted Pleasantly with Last Year's Conference during Which the Nasdaq was Languishing at Five-Year Lows', 12 March, 57.

Lanka, B. (2006), '1-Call Access to City Hall Being Tested', *The Journal Gazette*, 8 March.

M2 Presswire (2006), 'MacFarlane Telesystems: Tonbridge and Malling Council Opts for Virtual Approach to Customer Services Excellence', 5 December.

M2 Presswire (2006a), 'MacFarlane Telesystems: Salisbury District Council Improves Quality of Service to Rural Areas with Investment in Virtual Contact Centre', 15 February.

Manley, J. (2004), 'Average Growth of 333 Per Cent among Technology Firms', *Irish News*, 5 November, 35.

McDonnell, F. (2001), 'Lagan Negotiates to Raise Finance for Expansion', *Irish Times*, 17 July.

McGann, R. and Castano, I. (2000), 'Deal Flow', *Daily Deal* (New York), 29 September.

McGill, A. (2001), 'Commercial Review: Radical Software Pushes Company to the Frontline', *Belfast News Letter*, 13 March.

McGill, A. and McKillion, P. (2002), 'Local Hi-tech Firm Expands While Global Telco Cuts Back', *Belfast News Letter*, 12 March.

McGurk, H. (2001), 'Birmingham Online', *Belfast News Letter*, 8 May.

McKillion, P. (2002), 'Proof That Getting Hung up on Bad Service Isn't the End of the Line', *Belfast News Letter*, 28 May.

Moody, D. (2007), 'Growing a Global Software Company in Northern Ireland', presentation to Momentum, the Northern Ireland ICT Federation, 2 February.

PR Newswire (2004), 'Telecom Namibia Expands Use of CSG Systems ICMS Solution to Support Convergent Services', 9 March.

Press Enterprise (2005), 'On the Move', 27 November.

Smyth, J. (2000), 'Lagan Raises Profile with €16m Funding, IBM Deal', *Irish Times*, 24 November.

Stinson, J. (2007), 'Business – Hi-Tech Jobs Boost for City', *Irish News*, June 14.

Sunday Business Post (2004), 'Kainos Signs €2m CRM Deal', 13 June.

Tampa Tribune (2005), 'Business People', 19 September, 9.

US States News (2007), 'City Launches 311 "One Call to City Hall Program"', 21 May.

White, G. (2004), *Daily Deal/The Deal*, 8 November.

CHAPTER 7

ESB International

Chris O'Riordan and Felicity Kelliher[1]

School of Business, Waterford Institute of Technology

Prologue

It certainly seemed like an ordinary Tuesday as Don Moore, the retired managing director of ESB International (ESBI), drove to ESBI offices in Stephen Court, just off St Stephen's Green, in Dublin. Don regularly called in to meet Michael McNicholas, the CEO of ESBI, for lunch and just to chat about the business. Today was different – Michael wished to speak with Don to get his thoughts on a big project for which ESBI had been invited to tender. This was the type of project that ESBI thrived on – it was not only of the large-scale, lucrative type, but also had some element of risk attached. 'When isn't there some risk', Don thought, 'if there is money to be made?' ESBI had been in a similar situation many times before, but each project is different in its own way and needs careful thought. As Don drove towards the office, he reflected on the ESBI he knew very well.

Electricity Supply Board (ESB): Lighting Up a Nation

Before the establishment of ESB (under the Electricity Supply Board Act 1927), Ireland's electricity was supplied by over 300 separate suppliers, including sixteen local authorities and five large companies. Bringing together all these independent businesses was an arduous administrative

[1] The authors wish to acknowledge Mr Don Moore, the former managing director of ESBI, and Mr Michael McNicholas, the CEO of ESBI, for their time, help, guidance and support in the production of this case. Quotations are taken from an interview with Mr Don Moore conducted on 17 April 2007. The information in this case study relates to the position of ESB International up to 2007. This case is intended to be used as a basis for class discussion and is not intended to represent either effective or ineffective management.

task, but one ESB managed to perform well. Most of Ireland's electricity came from imported coal at the time, and the newly established state recognised that this was a risky strategy because of limited national coal sources.

In seeking to produce as much 'home-grown' electricity as possible, a hydro-electric power station was developed at Ardnacrusha as part of the Shannon Scheme[2] in 1923, and ESB were mandated to operate Ardnacrusha power station and to 'control, co-ordinate and improve the distribution and sale of electricity in the country' (O'Riordan 2000) under the 1927 Act. More hydro plants were opened over the period from 1937 to 1949, by which time 75 per cent of the nation's inland waterpower potential was harnessed. ESB then turned to the construction of peat-fired stations, again using indigenous natural resources to fuel the growing energy needs of the economy. By the early 1960s, the potential from peat-fired energy was maximised and the country needed to turn to imported fuel to meet its energy needs. From the 1960s to the late 1990s, ESB developed a portfolio of power plants that used the best available generating technology, starting with oil-fired plants in the 1960s, balancing that with coal in the 1980s (following the oil crises of the late 1970s) and finally using highly efficient gas-fired power plants in the late 1980s and 1990s. Throughout this period, ESB provided a very reliable and effective infrastructure to meet the electricity needs of the Irish economy. The mix of plants also provided a high degree of security of supply, given the diversity of fuel sources used.

Between 1946 and 1979, ESB managed to connect over 420,000 customers in rural Ireland to the national grid through the Rural Electrification Scheme – this was known as the 'Quiet Revolution' because of the major socio-economic impact that it had on the nation. This was so successful that the World Bank, even today, uses this scheme to demonstrate to developing countries what can be achieved in their own nations. The transmission and distribution network was expanded over the intervening years in line with the economic expansion of the country.

Throughout its history, ESB went through regular organisation changes. In 1993, it adopted a business unit structure, essentially delegating significant autonomy to the individual business units, with

---

[2] The Shannon Scheme was the name given to the project, initiated in 1923 as the nation was emerging from the Irish Civil War, that led to the establishment of Ireland's first large-scale power station at Ardnacrusha. In 2006, Ardnacrusha was awarded international recognition for its technical and social impact and is formally rated with projects such as the Golden Gate Bridge and the Eiffel Tower – a great honour for ESB and Ireland.

overall coordination provided by a small corporate centre. While the shape of the organisation changed, reflecting a changing business environment or major restructuring (e.g. the Cost and Competitiveness Review (CCR) 1995 or the Programme to Achieve Competitiveness and Transformation (PACT) 2000), the essential corporate or business unit structure was retained. The current structure in terms of main business lines is set out in Figure 7.1.

Right through to the 1990s, ESB operated as a successful commercial semi-state company. It implemented national energy policy, delivered reliable electricity at prices below the European average and was recognised for its ability to deliver significant infrastructure projects. The advent of deregulation was about to change ESB's role dramatically.

Electricity Supply in Ireland: A Changing Competitive Landscape

From the mid-1990s, the EU policy direction was towards the creation of an internal energy market. EU directives required each member state to introduce competition to its electricity market according to an agreed timeline. The overall model was to strictly regulate the natural monopoly elements of the industry (i.e. the distribution and transmission networks) and to introduce competition to the remaining elements, namely the generation and sale of electricity to customers. In Ireland's case the market was required to be 30 per cent open by 2000 and fully open by 2007. For ESB this meant the end of its monopoly status and the need to redefine its role as an energy provider in Ireland. Essentially, ESB needed to evolve from being the electricity industry in Ireland to become a player in the Irish electricity market. ESB acknowledged this and agreed to play its part in facilitating competition and helping to develop the market structures for Ireland. Indeed, ESB agreed to accelerate the market opening process with full market opening in 2005, two years ahead of the 2007 deadline.

In the period from 2000, ESB implemented significant organisation change, separating regulated activities from unregulated activities, implementing systems and processes to facilitate the opening of the market and reducing significantly its market share in both its generation and its customer supply businesses. It also worked with the government to transfer the operation of the National Grid out of ESB to an independent system operator, EirGrid, which, as the independent market controller or operator, provides assurance to all market participants through its independence. Despite the significant changes, the scale of ESB

Figure 7.1: ESB Corporate Chart 2007

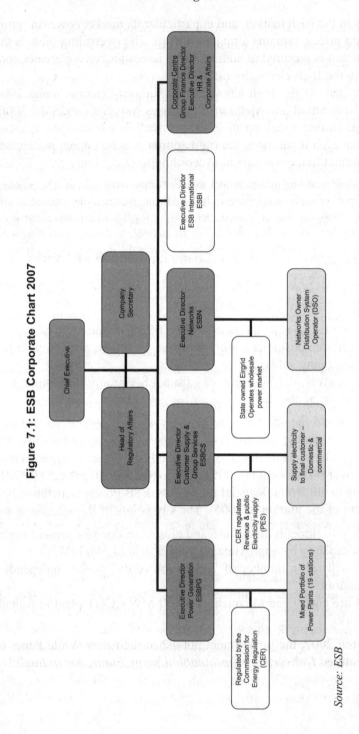

Source: ESB

activities in the Irish market, and in particular its market power in setting generation prices, remains a major concern. The overriding view is that further action is required to address these issues and create greater competition in the Irish electricity market.

Some, such as the Irish Competition Authority (Krawchenko 2006) and the Irish Small and Medium Enterprises Association (ISME 2006), argue that further break-up of ESB is essential, while others question whether an ESB break-up is the right approach to be taking, particularly in this competitive environment. According to Don Moore:

> I do not see it adding to the competitiveness of the Irish market. The problem, in my opinion, with competition in Ireland is that we are a tiny market, in total no bigger than the city of Manchester. It is impossible to create economies of scale and electricity utilities need scale to compete and deliver efficiencies to customers. ... It would be a short-term gain – and I'm not sure that it would even be a gain.

The Commission for Energy Regulation's (CER) preference is for a large-scale structural reform of ESB by:

- Selling off two separate portfolios of ESB generation plant.
- Splitting the customer supply business into three entities, with two of these being sold off.
- The removal of ESB Networks from ESB group, but retaining its ownership by the state.

The CER accepts that this is unlikely to happen and, as a partial solution, has entered into an asset strategy agreement with ESB. The measures, under the agreement, will reduce ESB's share of the Irish market from over 60 per cent in 2005 to approximately 40 per cent by 2010 (according to the group financial statements, ESB Power Generation held 52 per cent of the market in 2006). The key points of the agreement are:

- ESB will, through divestiture and closure, reduce its present generation capacity by approximately 30 per cent (1,500 MW[3]).
- ESB will sell a number of 'generation ready' sites to independent generators.
- ESB are authorised to construct a 400 MW CCGT plant at Aghada in Cork.

In March 2007, the government published their new White Paper on Energy entitled *Delivering a Sustainable Energy Future for Ireland*. The

---

[3] Megawatt

paper states that all the transmission assets held by ESB networks will be transferred to EirGrid by the end of 2008. EirGrid will then be run on an effective 'not-for-profit' basis in an attempt to reduce the electricity prices for businesses and consumers. One of EirGrid's key projects is the establishment of an 'All-Island Market' for electricity by cooperating with its equivalent in the North, System Operator Northern Ireland (SONI). The market went live in November 2007. It is believed that, by sharing the networks, greater efficiency can be achieved and a larger market will attract more entrants, increasing the competition and providing greater market dynamics (see Appendix 7.2 for further details).

In 2007 ESB generated electricity in fifteen single and multi-resource stations (see Table 7.5) and, by the end of 2006, ESB Power Generation had total installed capacity of just over 4,650 MW and supplied 52 per cent of all Irish customers, down 11 per cent on the previous year. The 2005 and 2006 revenues of each of ESB's four key divisions are shown in Table 7.1.

It has been established that the majority of ESB's revenue comes from its core business – electricity generation and supply (Table 7.1). However, with its market share due to fall over the next three years based on the EU directive and CER requirement, and with the global market consolidation on the horizon (see Appendix 7.2 for further details), it is clear that revenue streams from other sources will be essential. According to Don Moore, 'If ESB is to grow in the future, it has to be outside Ireland.' This is where ESBI comes in.

The Birth of ESBI

ESBI was established to facilitate power generation, transmission, distribution, utility consultancy and independent power producer (IPP) investment and management. ESBI is responsible for the non-regulated

Table 7.1: Revenue by Division

Revenue by Business Line	2006 € '000	2005 € '000
Power generation	355,690	222,759
Customer supply	1,837,586	1,816,522
Networks	249,275	273,725
International	687,581	472,830
Other	(42,628)	(29,623)
Group totals	3,087,504	2,756,213

Source: ESB Annual Report 2006

businesses of ESB and provides a wide range of engineering and consultancy services both to third parties and other ESB companies, with offices in Ireland as well as in Hanoi, Brussels and Abu Dhabi.

ESBI's beginnings can be traced back to the 1970s. Up to this time, ESB had a strong and significant engineering resource that had been built up over the previous forty years, and this resource served ESB almost exclusively, supplemented with some small projects for a few specialist clients in Ireland. Following the Arab-Israeli War in 1973, the world experienced a major oil crisis and, according to Moore, 'growth came to a halt over a period of years.' For ESB, this meant that hard decisions were required – the engineering resource was a significant cost but, with expansion curtailed, had little benefit to add in its existing form. One option was to scale it back and, realistically, lose it forever. ESB chose, instead, to find alternative uses for this resource, due primarily to the division's insightful and dedicated leadership at the time. Moore states: 'We were very fortunate at the time that we had very strong and visionary leadership in ESB. ... They were all very strong guys who had come through the rural electrification period and who weren't daunted by anything.' Thus, ESBI was born.

ESBI's technical expertise was derived from the resources in engineering design, planning, construction, investment, commissioning and operation for all types of power plant and electrical networks. In the beginning, international growth was slow and measured, and just began in the Middle East, Saudi Arabia and Bahrain. The flip-side of the oil crisis was that money was plentiful in these oil-rich states, but infrastructure was underdeveloped. In 1981, ESBI was a successful bidder for a sizeable contract in the city of Jubail in Saudi Arabia – a brand new industrial city in the desert, built from scratch and to be powered by gas that was otherwise being flared.[4] Moore recalls:

> This was the single biggest project ever undertaken on the planet at that time, to build a city of 370,000 people from scratch ... We won a [big] contract, against international competition, to design the transmission and distribution system for the city ... The job went very well, it was very challenging, [with] huge publicity and the management and board of ESB sat up and noticed.

A decision now needed to be taken by ESB – would they continue to pursue such business in an active and coordinated way or allow ESBI to continue as a small niche in the bigger company? The management of

---

[4] Flared gas is a by-product of oil refining.

ESBI decided to take the requisite risk and moved the design and construction organisation in ESB into the new division.

ESBI: A New Division

ESBI was set up as a separate division in ESB in 1989 and, in 2000, became a separate, wholly owned subsidiary of the group. This was a novel move or, as Moore describes it, 'a huge step'. Staff with effectively lifetime contracts in the nation's largest semi-state organisation were being asked to move – physically, culturally and conceptually – into a new, more commercially based entity in new offices. This was handled through seconding the relevant staff from ESB into the new firm, whereby they retained their terms and conditions of employment. However, all new staff hired directly by the new entity would be on ESBI terms and conditions. The new firm was different to ESB – the benchmark was to be at the competition, not just internally devised targets. In addition, staff were not simply moved across en masse – they had to be interviewed competitively for jobs with ESBI, and not all who were interviewed were awarded ESBI jobs, even at senior levels, which was a clear initial statement of intent. According to Moore:

> A different working regime was established ... Nobody is watching the clock, there is performance management, it is seen very much as a meritocracy ... People love to be with a winning entity. We discovered that there were no limits as to how hard you could push people to deliver. You think you'd set the bar high, the people who were doing the work would set it even higher themselves ... In a way, ESBI was a home for mavericks as well. The very quality that might make you appear like an awkward customer in ESB, was the very thing ESBI wanted.

Key strategic issues facing the newly created division proved to be planning, scheduling and staff retention.

Planning

Initially, planning was informal, as the division leaders sought to establish themselves in the market. Don Moore states: 'Was there a plan – not really, there wasn't one – what you had were people of vision who were determined to go out and see if these things were possible.' However, as the organisation grew, so too did the need for formalisation. Since its establishment, ESBI has completed numerous projects worldwide, and now have 'very strong internal business plans and very strong monthly reporting', suggesting that planning has tightened considerably since the early days.

Scheduling

Although a separate entity with its own management team, ESBI's obligation remains to its parent and this is fully acknowledged by Moore: '[O]ur mandate was to put our number one client first.' This means that when ESB requires construction or transmission work to be carried out, ESBI must be available. However, these assignments can be intermittent, and timetabling projects can therefore be an issue for ESBI. In the early years, when the resource exceeded the demand, this was not a problem. However, today, ESBI's services and expertise are demanded the world over by multinational and state-owned utilities, making scheduling and completion times critical.

Staff Retention

Retaining all the knowledge built up by its employees is a challenge for ESBI – its technical staff are keenly sought by other companies in the industry and divisions in the company. ESBI consciously seeks to develop people as well as infrastructure and recognises that it has built up a tremendous knowledge resource over the decades. However, as Don notes: 'There is a worrying decline in the number of people and the calibre of people doing engineering worldwide and Ireland is no exception.' This is making the existing resource extremely valuable and potentially difficult to replace.

ESBI Today

ESBI's mission, as per ESB's *Annual Report* 2005, is to:

> Contribute to the growth ambition of ESB with a focus on international investments and provide engineering services to support ESB Group strategic objectives. (29)

To date, ESBI has completed projects in over 115 countries and is recognised as one of the world's most successful utility engineering, contracting and consultancy organisations (<http://www.esbi.ie>). ESBI's technical expertise is derived from resources in engineering design, planning, construction, investment, commissioning and operation for all types of power plant and electrical networks. The company employs

Figure 7.2: ESBI Corporate Chart 2007

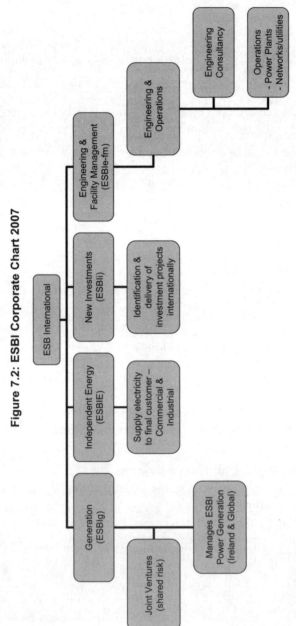

Source: ESBI

approximately 1,200 people who work in partnership with clients, within four main divisions in the organisation (see Figure 7.2).

ESBIg

This division manages ESBI's power generation assets both in Ireland and worldwide. The division holds a portfolio of assets including combined cycle gas turbine plants (CCGTs), windfarms, combined heat and power (CHP) units and renewable generation assets. Some of these assets are held in joint venture (JV) businesses, where ESBIg has a partial holding, thus sharing the risk with other parties. The JVs are led by a general manager and operated by teams from the facility management division. A number of the generation assets held are situated abroad, including the first internationally owned independent power plant in the Spanish market.

ESBIE

This division is a competitive supply business, holding 14.7 per cent of the Republic of Ireland market in 2006 (and 20 per cent of the market in Northern Ireland), with an expectation that this will grow in the future. It was established in January 2000 'to supply electricity to the liberalised electricity markets and build long-term relationships with customers' (<http://www.esbi.ie>). The division does this by tailoring its offering to the customers' needs with a focus on the industrial or commercial market, differentiating it from the competition. Customers include Intel, British Telecom and Tesco Ireland. ESBIE also provides 'value adding' services to customers in the form of green electricity supply, energy monitoring and management services, and electronic billing.

ESBIi

This division 'is responsible for the identification, development and bringing to commercial operation of power related projects in the deregulated markets both at home and overseas' (<http://www.esbi.ie>). Spain and the UK have proven to be the most successful markets for the division to date, with two 800 MW and one 400 MW plants at varying stages of completion. ESBIi is also responsible for the group's renewable energy business. According to the 2007 White Paper on Energy, the government wants one-third of Ireland's electricity to be supplied from renewable sources by 2020.

ESBIe-fm

This is the main engineering and operations wing of ESBI. The engineering division is the centre of engineering services for the ESB group, as well as providing consulting services to foreign governments and private businesses. Consultancy services provided by ESBI Engineering are wide and varied and include power plant engineering, automation and telecommunications, restructuring and privatisation, strategic consultancy, civil and structural engineering, environmental and climate services, and architectural and building services. In total, the division carried out operations in twenty-five countries during 2005. The facility management business provides full operation and maintenance services to ESBI power plants and to international clients and is currently responsible for operating over 5,000 MW of plant worldwide.

Although fully separated from the parent company for seven years, ESBI has had some notable achievements. Over the past eleven years, the company has won contracts all over the globe for a variety of jobs and assignments. The focus has been on consultancy and technical projects, and taking on the role of transmissions operator as these contracts are profitable, numerous and quick paying. Table 7.2 highlights key successes over the years.

Not all the contracts worked out in ESBI's favour. As the size, risk and complexity of projects grew, so too did the dynamics relating to contract negotiation and acceptance (see Table 7.3).

At the time of the Polish bid, ESBI's link to its primary client and owner came to the fore. According to Moore:

> Ultimately, all significant investments or projects require the approval of our main shareholder [the Department of Energy and Natural Resources and the Department of Finance] … Did it do us any lasting harm? No – we built from the experience to work with our shareholder to better understand their needs and our shared expectations so that next time around, we were better prepared on both sides.

As for the Setrans project, Don Moore is notably philosophical: 'We got paid for our time and effort … There was no loss, at the end of the day … You always learn something, even from failure – the next time an opportunity presents itself, you'll be better.'

There are also a number of significant projects in progress that should come to fruition in the near future.

Table 7.2: ESBI Contract Highlights 1994–2007

Year	Location	Value € million	Contract description
1994	Corby, UK		ESBI took a small fractional share as part of the terms surrounding their appointment as the operating and maintenance contractor.
1996	Pakistan	57	ESBI took a 7 per cent share to operate and maintain a power plant for thirteen years.
1997	Malaysia	80	Operate the power supply to an industrial park for nine years.
2001	Nigeria		Provide consultancy services to the National Electric Power Authority.
2002	Georgia	12	Manage the electricity services of the former Russian state of Georgia.
2004	Kosovo	8.8	Oversee the operation of Kosovo's electricity service and to provide training to workers (extended in 2005).
2005	Manjung, Malaysia	9	Operate, manage and maintain a 2,100 MW coal-fired plant – ultimate owner is the national electric company.
2005	Vietnam	4.5	Consultancy contract relating to a 600 MW coal-fired plant, including technical project design, preparation of specifications, tender evaluation and contract negotiation.
2005	Indonesia	5	Advisory services relating to the construction of a 1,200 MW coal-fired plant.
2005	South Africa		A five-year contract with the state electricity supplier for consultancy services in the construction of new power plants.
2005	Amorebieta (Basque Region)	500	Completed CCGT gas toiling plant. Ownership: 50 per cent ESBI/50 per cent Osaka Gas Group; this plant represents the largest ever inward investment in the region and will be managed and maintained by ESBI for an initial twenty-year period.
2005	Northern Ireland	300	Completed 400 MW CCGT plant in Coolkeeragh.
2006	Galway, Western Ireland	72	Completed 60 MW windfarm project at Derrybrien.

Source: ESBI

Table 7.3: ESBI Failed Deals 1994–2007

Year	Contract	Value € million	Reason for failure
2001	Bid for purchase of a network of energy distributors – Poland.	950 (annually)	The Irish government vetoed the deal because of the scale of the spending involved (€1.7 billion) and the perceived risk involved.
2002	Awarded Setrans project – US contract to manage a regional transmission organisation, accounting for 10 per cent of the market.	750	Deal fell through (2003) primarily due to the US Energy Bill – electricity companies were no longer obliged to join regional transmission systems, forcing a suspension of the contract.

Source: ESBI

ESBI sees each tender and project as a stepping stone in its business development and success. For example, in the Corby contract (in 1994), a mandatory share purchase insisted on by the banks worked to ESBI's advantage. According to Moore:

> The banks wanted to put in every add-on, every operation and maintenance system – anything you proposed, they wanted it because it would secure the reliability of the plant. We found this was a very good business and was one that we knew quite well. Suddenly, now it wasn't just about developers, it was about the role that the banks would play in the future and this really opened the next chapter in ESBI's history. We saw a way of leveraging our long experience in the gas turbine [CCGT] market.

Since then, ESBI has become one of the top providers of CCGT plants worldwide. The popularity of CCGT technology is based on its high levels of efficiency and short project completion time (thirty months versus thirty-six to forty-eight months for traditional power stations). Much of ESBI's advantage in this field can be traced back to ESB's decision to use CCGT plants in the 1970s, ahead of much of the competition.

Even in disappointment, there has been potential for ultimate success; because ESBI were in the US for the Setrans project, they are now looking at another Federal Energy Regulatory Commission (FERC) led initiative where they are attempting to place transmission under central management by offering a higher return to existing generation and transmission companies. Moore states:

> Had we not been in the US with Setrans, we would not have seen that. I would say that is a likely future runner for ESBI. Is that proactive or reactive? We're

using our market knowledge to try and position ourselves for something in the future. We can't create the opportunity per se, but if it is there, we want to be one of the first people in and we are already talking with the merchant bankers who are driving this.

Considering ESBI's 'minnow' size in international terms, alliance and joint venture activity has also been a valuable tool in the creation of sustainable competitive advantage for the organisation over the years. According to Moore, 'One of the things we do, because of our size, is to team up with others to win the job'. These partnerships work well for ESBI as, while it can bring their technical expertise, its partner can provide other key elements. For example, in the Southampton project (in 2007, see Table 7.4), Scottish and Southern Energy (SSE) supplied the plant with fuel and will purchase the electricity generated, while 80 per cent of the investment was secured as debt finance from a consortium of five banks, with the two equity partners putting in the balance evenly. Of equal value is the firm's relationship with its parent company (ESB). Moore states: 'Ultimately, being part of an integrated utility has been of enormous help to ESBI and its development … If it is to change in the

Table 7.4: ESBI Projects in Progress 2007

Start Date	Location	Value € million	Contract Description
2006	Cavan		Windfarm development of 19 1.5 MW wind turbines producing up to 28.5 MW of renewable energy – expected completion: 2008.
Early 2007	Southampton England	563	The construction of a new Combined Cycle Gas Turbine plant is a joint (50/50) project between the ESBI and Scottish and Southern Energy plc (SSE). Construction is expected to finish by late 2009 and, at full capacity, this will serve the needs of one million homes.
2008	Northern Spain	500	Construction of an 800 MW CCGT plant in Asturias is expected to start in 2008. The site is owned by ESBI, which is currently working through a consultation process.
2009	Wales	600	The project is in the initial business development stage and construction of an 800 MW gas-fired power station near Port Talbot is expected to commence in the coming years.

Source: ESBI

future, I really hope that someone does the sums – certainly, it wouldn't be helpful to ESBI.'

ESBI: Internationally Competitive, Locally Responsible

ESBI believes strongly in ethical practices and values its integrity highly. It makes this clear at all times so that there is no confusion as to its stance and it has held onto this ethos throughout its existence. Moore says:

> We have a reputation of being a company of the highest integrity. I don't say that lightly, but being a state-owned company helps in that respect as well … That hasn't been a burden, it has been an enormous help to us. There are no incentives to behave incorrectly inside in ESBI. That's been a core value.

A national and international presence brings with it a need for localised social responsibility, a factor that ESBI takes very seriously. Evidence of community inclusion includes:

- The Amorebieta project (see Table 7.2) represents the largest ever inward investment in the Basque region and provided employment for 500 workers during construction.
- ESBI and its staff are keen supporters of the work of the Christina Noble Children's Foundation (<http://www.cncf.org>) in Vietnam, where they have funded the development of a hostel for homeless girls in Ho Chi Minh City.
- In the Coolkeeragh project, an initiative was launched to ensure that local businesses with appropriate expertise were invited to tender for contracts – Stg £30 million worth of business was placed with these firms and a total of 600 people were employed during construction.

Mutual respect between ESBI and individual stakeholders is evident in ESBI's interaction with customers, alliance partners and financiers. Moore affirms that 'Most Irish people working abroad make a very favourable impression in the most difficult of circumstances.' This reputation facilitates country, partner and financier/World Bank business relations and, in ESBI's experience, according to Moore, partners 'want us to lead' in these arrangements. This amounts to a 'key competency of Irish companies … that's why Irish companies are doing so well out of globalisation.'

The Future Looks Bright?

ESBI has built up a significant international business over 30 years, and has completed medium- and large-scale projects in 115 countries over that time. The company has built a reputation for advanced market knowledge, technical expertise and a professional approach, and pride themselves on a reputation for getting the job done. As Don Moore remarks:

> In all of my twenty-five years in ESBI, I can't remember a single instance where we failed to deliver a project. We might have had difficulties, but we always delivered. If we had to spend, we spent. It's a business of long term relationships, it's all about repeat business.

With this experience comes an ability to understand the client's needs and to work closely with the client to help them identify what their real needs are before engaging in a project.

In reflecting on whether, given the chance to go back to the beginning and do it all again, anything should be done differently, Don Moore feels that results probably could not be any better, considering the origin and nature of the company:

> We came from an inward looking, ESB-focused, conservative company. It's hard to change that because that was what we were. That was our fifty-year history; very successful in a particular type of way. Could we have been bolder at certain times? I'm not sure. Remember who we are and what our core business responsibilities are as a state-owned utility. I have to say that we have always had tremendous support from the top management and the board of ESB. Every month, we would be over trying to get approval for a bid or a contract. All bids and contracts go through a tough challenge process. I can hardly remember a situation when we were turned down. Our story is not a conventional business one – you couldn't have planned it. I'm very firmly convinced that, without some of these visionary leaders that we had at the beginning, it would not have gotten off the ground. Many utilities tried to do what we do – there aren't many still standing. Some of them were big at one stage, but most of them have around ten to fifteen people, who are basically agents of their country's bilateral aid. We are one of the last of the utility-based international companies.

The future for ESBI looks to be promising and lucrative. This is an organisation, says Moore, 'always on the lookout for something new', and, in recent years, the company has been more aggressive in targeting high-profile and more long-term projects than in the 1990s. Now the company has the capacity to invest in power plants and wait the requisite time to recoup its investment. In addition, ESBI has used the partnership model to great success with Osaka Gas and SSE and hopes to continue to create such mutually beneficial alliances. Turnover in ESBI grew by over 45 per cent between 2005 and 2006 and by over 50 per cent between

2004 and 2005. It is critical that continued growth is achieved as it is the group's stated intention to make up for the loss in revenues and profits that the opening up of the market will cause for ESB through increased performance in the international division. However, competition in the global market is intensifying (see Appendix 7.2), and there is also the fear that – as happened with the Polish deal – the government may try to rein in ESBI if it feels that it is venturing into projects that carry too much risk from a social or an economic perspective. The ownership situation surrounding ESB and its divisions is likely to resurface in the coming years also – the cases for the splitting up of the group and even its privatisation have their supporters but, equally, have their detractors.

The Meeting

Now, as Don arrived at ESBI offices, he thought about the many challenges that ESBI now faced. He was very proud of what the company had achieved and knew that Michael was the man to bring it forward with his own ideas and plans. Don liked the sound of the project and could see that it had great potential – something he knew Michael believed as well. Now, how to convince others to buy into the idea? That was the challenge.

Appendix 7.1: ESB Power Plants, Ireland (2007)

Poolbeg can operate on both oil and gas[5] and Marina (in Cork) and North Wall (in Dublin) were re-powered with combined cycle gas turbines (CCGT), to take advantage of the Kinsale gas field. Finally, Moneypoint station is of considerable strategic importance as it is coal-fuelled, providing Ireland with an alternative to oil, gas and water.

Appendix 7.2: The Global Electricity Market

According to Datamonitor, the global electricity market in 2005 generated total revenues of over $995 billion, an increase of 9.7 per cent on the previous year.

The compound annual growth rate (CAGR) over the period 2001–2005 was 9 per cent, and forecasts for the market over the period 2005–2010 show the CAGR falling to 7.5 per cent, resulting in predicted 2010 revenues of $1,431 billion (see Table 7.6). As market consumption rates are

---

[5] Most gas now comes over the interconnector from the European sources.

Table 7.5: ESB Power Plants in Ireland

Station	Capacity (in MW)	Fuel type	Year Commissioned
Aghada	525	Gas	1981
Ardnacrusha	86	Hydro	1927
Clady	4	Hydro	Not specified
Erne	65	Hydro	Not specified
Great Island	240	Oil	1967
Lee	27	Hydro	Not specified
Liffey	38	Hydro	Not specified
Lough Ree Power	100	Peat	2004
Marina	115	Gas	1953
Moneypoint	915	Coal	1985
North Wall	266	Oil and gas	1947
Poolbeg	1020	Oil and gas	1971
Tarbert	620	Oil	1969
Turlough Hill	292	Hydro	1968
West Offaly Power	150	Peat	2005

Source: ESB website <http://www.esb.ie>

expected to hit 15,479 billion kWh[6] in 2010, this would suggest that prices will rise faster than output, possibly because of the increased cost of fuel sources as oil, gas and fossil fuel resources approach total depletion. In Europe (which accounts for 30 per cent of the global market), the story is similar, though with considerably lower growth rates (Table 7.6). While the UK electricity market is one of the fastest growing in Europe, this growth is on the back of declining volumes, with a negative compound annual rate of change between 2001 and 2005 of 0.4 per cent. The UK market is the fourth largest in Europe, with a 10.8 per cent share, being just over half the size of the German market (Italy and France are second and third, respectively). The main growth, in European terms, has been in the east where industrial, commercial and domestic demand is growing at a rapid rate coming from a low initial base. This would indicate that lucrative opportunities still exist in the less developed markets. By 2007, 100 per cent of the EU market is supposed to be fully liberalised. However, this is unlikely with a number of states yet to make the necessary changes.

The Irish electricity market has, over the last ten years, grown at an average annual rate of 5 per cent, which is significantly above that of the

---

[6] Kilowatt hour.

Table 7.6: Global Market Consumption Rates and Compound Annual Growth Rate (CAGR)

	2001–2005	2001–2004	2005 (billion)	2004–2009	2005–2010	2010 (billion)
Global Electricity Market						
CAGR (Datamonitor 2006)	9%	8.6%		8.3%	7.5%	
Revenue			$995			$1,431
Market consumption rates (kWh)			12,830			15,479
European Electricity Market						
CAGR (Datamonitor 2005)		2.7%		2.8%		
UK CAGR (Datamonitor 2006a)	10.2%	10.2%		7.2%	6.2%	

Source: Datamonitor

EU25. This is on the back of a sustained period of growth as Ireland's economy expanded at a rapid rate – average real growth in GDP was 7 per cent per annum between 1991 and 2001. Economic growth also had a positive impact on the construction market, with building firms experiencing considerable demand for new houses in a period of rising prices. While growth has slowed down to more reasonable levels in recent years, the infrastructure is playing catch-up. Although current ESB capacity is able to accommodate peak national demand, there is awareness that, with forecast power demand predicted to reach 37.8 kWh by 2020 (CAGR of over 3 per cent), further investment from the existing suppliers and incoming players is certainly needed.

Key Competitive Players in Europe and Ireland

The main player in the market is Électricité de France (EDF), whose main source is nuclear power. EDF, while dominating the French market, also has substantial interests in both the UK and Germany and in 2004 the company showed an increase in net income of 56 per cent. Centrica plc (32 per cent) and E.ON UK (29 per cent) dominate the UK electricity market, and both companies are also major gas suppliers.

In Ireland, ESB's main competition is provided by Viridian and Airtricity:

- Viridian, though a key player in an Irish context, controls less than 1.4 per cent of the UK market. In 2002, it began operations in its

Huntstown Power Plant in north County Dublin, and was granted contracts to become the preferred suppliers to over 500 SuperValu and Centra stores in Ireland in 2004. In 2005, Viridian was awarded a contract to supply the majority of all power required by the Department of Finance, including Garda Headquarters and Áras an Uachtaráin (the President of Ireland's residence).

• Airtricity was established in 1999 as a private company, supplying green electricity in Ireland, the UK and the US. By 2005–2006, Airtricity had 177 MW of wind power in operation, with a further 6,000 MW (including 600 MW in Ireland) under development. One of the company's most ambitious projects, which it hopes will be funded by national governments, is the proposed development of an offshore 'Supergrid' to harness the wind-power resource in the seas of northern, western and southern Europe. The initial plan is to develop a 10 GW[7] Foundation Project, between the UK, Germany and the Netherlands. This project is expected to cost €2 billion and could deliver enough power for over eight million homes.

References

Datamonitor (2006), *Global Electricity: Industry Profile*, August.

Datamonitor (2006a), *Electricity in the United Kingdom: Industry Profile*, August.

Datamonitor (2005), *Electricity in Europe: Industry Profile*, August.

ESB (2006), *Annual Report*, available at: <http://www.esb.ie/main/about_esb/annual_report_2006.jsp>.

ESB (2005), *Annual Report*, available at: <http://www.esb.ie/main/about_esb/annual_report_2005.jsp>.

ESB website <http://www.esb.ie>.

ESBI website <http://www.esbi.ie>.

Irish Small and Medium Enterprises Association (2006), *ISME Critical of Decision Not to Break up ESB*, Press Release, 2 October 2006, available at: <http://www.isme.ie>.

Krawchenko, A. (2006), 'ESB Divestiture: too Little, too Late', *Energy Business Review*, available at: <http://www.energy-business-review.com>.

O'Riordan, C. (2000), *Development of Ireland's Power System: 1927–1997*, EirGrid: Dublin.

---

[7] Gigawatt.

CHAPTER 8

An Post: Addressing Ireland's Mail Market

Kevin Pyke, Theo Lynn, Malcolm Brady and Paul Davis[1]
Dublin City University Business School, Dublin City University

Introduction

After five months of uncertainty and speculation, An Post, the state mail delivery service in Ireland, announced a new chief executive on 22 June 2006. The new CEO, Donal Connell, faced several challenges, including implementing an agreed recovery plan, getting the Fortis joint venture in place by the first quarter of 2007 and boosting revenue growth. While the company posted a €30 million pre-tax loss in 2002 under the outgoing chief executive, it turned around and produced a pre-tax profit of €41 million in 2005. But the real picture lay beneath these figures. An Post faced increased strains: letter mail items per capita in Ireland fell from 203 in 2001 to 183 in 2005. The operating margins were at 2.1 per cent and the quality of service for next-day delivery, a key performance indicator, was 21 per cent below target for 2005 (Quality of Service Monitor 2005). In addition, with full liberalisation of the EU postal market due on 1 January 2009, 58 per cent of mail volume was opened to competition on 1 January 2006 (see Table 8.1 for a timeline for the liberalisation process).

Leadership challenges were nothing new to An Post. The previous incumbent, Donal Curtin, took over as the chief executive in July 2003 from John Hynes. Immediately, he set about the task of returning financial stability as 'An Post had made losses from 2001 to 2003' (see Table 8.2 for key financial results for An Post for the six years 2001–2006 and Table 8.3 for key statistics). The recovery plan, put in place in 2001, identified

---

[1] The authors acknowledge An Post for its support while researching and compiling this case study. The information in this case study relates to the posotion of An Post up to 2007. This case is intended to be used as a basis for class discussion and is not intended to represent either effectivc or ineffective management.

Table 8.1: Regulatory Timeline and Impact of Market Liberalisation

Date	Regulatory Change	Percentage of market open to competition
February 1999	Items over 350 grams and charged at five times the basic letter stamp rate	29
1 January 2003	Items over 100 grams and charged at three times the basic letter stamp rate	37
1 January 2004	All outgoing international mail open to competition	44
1 January 2006	Items over 50 grams and charged at 2.5 times the basic letter stamp rate	58
1 January 2009	Full liberalisation	100

Source: An Post Annual Reports (2001 and 2005)

the need to shed 1,140 jobs to address the losses in the post office net-works and to stem losses in Special Distribution Services (SDS), the parcel division of An Post (*An Post Annual Report* 2001). By August 2003, a new management and business structure was announced, resulting in a plan to close SDS which in 2003 lost €12 million on revenues of €70 million (*An Post Annual Report* 2004).[2] Plans were put in place to re-integrate the parcel business, the post offices division and letter post into a single company. This 'strategic recovery plan' was approved by the board of An Post in September 2003 and then by the Minister for Communications in October 2003. Intense industrial relations activity took place during 2004 and 2005; this included strike action and recourse for binding arbitration under the auspices of the labour court, but resulted in productivity agreements with each of the four trade unions. In May 2005, following application by An Post, the industry regulator ComReg[3]

---

[2] Calculated on revenues from Annual Reports 2001–2002, as a separate figure is not reported for parcel revenue in the *An Post Annual Report* 2003.

[3] ComReg, the communications regulatory authority in Ireland, has responsibility for ensuring that the needs of consumers of the postal service are met; for licensing a universal service provider (which in this case is An Post); for authorising other postal operators; for approving applications for price increases which are examined to ensure that all pricing is transparent, non-discriminatory, geared to cost and affordable; for setting and monitoring quality of service targets; and for ensuring access to the postal service for all citizens of the state.

Table 8.2: An Post Performance 2001–2006

	2001	2002	2003	2004	2005	2006
Turnover (million €)	624.9	683.7	709.2	750.2	752.9	818.8
ComReg next-day measure	N/A	N/A	N/A	71%	73%	74%
Payroll costs	Averaged at 69% of revenue					
Payroll costs, change	Increased by 13.4%	Increased by 11%	Pay frozen (however, all arrears of national pay agreements were made in 2006 – expected to amount to 18.9% pay increase to May 2007)			
Key areas of loss (million €)	Retail network (1.3) USO (6.6)	Retail network (1.2) USO (16.5)	Retail network (1.2) USO (38.5)	USO (parcels) (4.4)	Not yet reported	

Source: An Post Annual Reports 2001–2006

Table 8.3: Key Statistics for An Post

An Post	2006	2005	2004
Turnover (million €)	818.8	753	750
Operating profit (million €)	14.7	16	1.7
– Mails (%)	72	72	71
– Post offices (%)	17.6	18	18
– Other (%)	8.6	9	11
Tariff index (2000 = 100)		96.4	98.5
Items delivered (million)		756.9	757.2
Items per capita		183	187
No. of deliver points (million)	1.99	1.88	1.76
No. of company post offices	84	88	90
No. of sub-post offices	1,277	1,321	1,365
No. of motor vehicles	2,991	2,905	2,908
No. of posting letter boxes		4,500	4,500
Pay (as % of costs)	70	70	67
An Post employees (full-time equivalents)	10,012	11,296	11,440
Contractors/agents	1,300	1,321	1,365

Source: An Post Annual Reports (2005 and 2006)

sanctioned price increases for flats (large envelopes) and packets, but not for standard letters. By 2005, when Donal Curtin was reporting his last annual report review, An Post had made a profit of €41 million and had cash reserves of €185 million (*An Post Annual Report* 2005). However, other performance indicators were not so good. An Post's pay costs averaged 69 per cent of sales for the period 2001–2005, compared to the pay costs in Sweden's Posten AB of 50 per cent for 2005 (see Table 8.4 for a comparison of performance measures across European postal organisations). An Post's mail volumes increased by just 0.3 per cent for the year 2005, and the quality of service for next-day delivery of mail was 71 per cent in 2004 and 73 per cent in 2005. An Post had a profit margin of 2.1 per cent for 2005, while Royal Mail and Austria Post had achieved 6 per cent, Sweden's Posten AB 5 per cent, TNT 9 per cent and Deutsche Post WorldNet (DPWN) 8 per cent (WIK-Consult 2006).

Table 8.4: Performance Measures for European Postal Operators

	Population 2005 (in million)	Population Density per km² 2005	% Revenues from Letter Mail 2005	Mail items per capita 2005	% Revenues from parcels 2005	Basic Tariff 2004	Pay as % costs	Next-day delivery standard % 2005
Small Operators								
Ireland	4.1	60	72	183	In letters	48c	69	72
Finland	5.3	17	60	521	26	65c	55	96
Portugal	10.5	114	82	190	3	45c	58	96
Medium Operators								
Austria	8.2	99	76	554	13	55c	61	94
Denmark	5.4	125	57	269	10	60c	68	94
Sweden	9	22	53	334	28	60c	50	96
Large Operators								
France	60.5	98	58	321	6 (excludes DPD)	53c	62	79
The Netherlands	16.3	481	32	326	Not stated	39c	38	97
UK	59.7	247	70	356	Not stated	44c	66	91
Germany	82.7	231	28	264	57	55c	35	95

Source: EuroStats 2007; Universal Postal Union Statistics; WIK Consult Final Report 'Main Developments in the Postal Sector 2004–2006' for the EU Commission, 2006.

Recent History of An Post

While its origins go back to the foundation of the state, An Post became a commercial-state company on 1 January 1984. It has responsibility under the 1983 Postal and Telecommunications Act to provide postal, communication, retail and money transmission services. These services are provided through its company-owned retail and mail delivery network and through its contracted or agency retail sub-office network.

During the period 2000–2002, An Post pursued a strategy that integrated three key objectives: to pursue operational efficiency, to service the needs of key customers and to explore strategic alliances. An Post developed automated mail processing capacity which improved operational efficiency by minimising the downstream sorting. An Post allowed for discounted pricing to large customers under certain conditions. In common with the Greek and Danish post offices, An Post explored options for a strategic alliance (*An Post Annual Report* 2001). However, company performance deteriorated during this period, requiring the initiation of the strategic recovery plan.

As part of its key customer orientation objective, An Post acquired Kompass Ireland Publishers in 2002 in order to add B2B (business to business) marketing databases to the already acquired databases of the B2C (business to consumer) company Precisions Marketing Information. It also acquired JMC Van Trans and Wheels Couriers, giving them access to new markets. Wheels specialised in the same-day delivery of parcels and documents in the greater Dublin area, whereas JMC operated a nationwide overnight logistics service. During 2002, An Post acquired the UK-based Air Business, a provider of services for the publishing, direct marketing and print industries, including international and domestic mailing and data processing. More importantly, it also sourced final delivery options through a range of alternative delivery channels. The summary of developments in An Post, since it received its commercial mandate, is set out in Table 8.5.

The European Union Postal Industry

The global postal market was worth approximately $263 billion (approximately €274 billion) in 2003, with revenues growing in each of the past twenty years. The EU postal market was worth €90 billion in 2005. Ireland is considered a small operator within the EU, along with Czech Republic, Finland, Greece, Hungary, Luxembourg, Poland, Portugal and Slovenia. These small operators account for just 8 per cent of the letter

Table 8.5: Developments in An Post since its Commercial Mandate

4 January 1984	First day of operation of An Post Ltd – a commercially mandated state company.
1987–1993	Focus on cost reductions through company/union productivity agreements to reduce retail branch system size and introduce roadside deliver letterboxes.
	Creation of separate business unit – SDS to focus on recapturing the parcel and courier market.
1993–2002	Implementation of counter automation programme, and of mails processing automation.
	Transfer of mails distribution from rail to road and concentration of mails processing into four mails centres in Dublin, Athlone, Portlaoise, Cork.
	Cessation of second deliveries.
	Exploration of strategic alliance with other European postal operators.
	Acquisition of same day courier, overnight courier and logistics companies.
	Creation of separate business units – letter post and post offices.
	Purchase of e-commercell (UK and Spain), Kompass (Irl), Air Business (UK).
	Joint ventures formed with FexCo; Western Union.
	Formation of PMI (database and marketing) from former joint operation with Equifax. Kompass (Irl) was later purchased and assimilated into PMI to form DataIreland.
	Increased sales and marketing activity: formation of key account management; utilisation of CRM; setup of customer services centre.
2003–2006	Pay freeze in place.
	Conversion programme for retail company offices to owner/contractor office.
	Cessation of separate business units letter post, post offices and closure of SDS (parcel/courier business) and re-integration into mails operation.
	First price increases for letter mail items in over twelve years.
	Sale of e-commercell (UK and Spain).
	Joint operation with AIB.
	Joint venture with Fortis announced.
	Productivity agreements concluded with each of the four unions to reduce workforce by 1,200.

mail market in the EU, compared to that of Deutsche Post (24 per cent), La Poste (20 per cent), Royal Mail (19 per cent), TNT (formerly TNT TPG – Dutch Post Office) (7 per cent) and Poste Italiana (7 per cent). The medium-sized operators, namely Austria, Belgium, Denmark, Sweden and Spain, between them account for 14 per cent of the market. Tables 8.6 and 8.7, respectively, give data on the postal service usage worldwide and market shares for the European package and express services.

Table 8.6: Worldwide Postal Services Usage

	Letter Mail (%)	Parcels and Logistics (%)	Financial Services (%)	Other Products (%)
Africa	60	10	19	11
Latin America and Caribbean	62	20	3	15
Asia and Pacific	31	13	42	14
Europe and CIS	44	6	26	24
Arab Countries	45	4	30	21
Industrialised Countries (includes Ireland)	60	25	12	3

Source: Universal Postal Union Statistics 2003, <http://www.upu.int>.

Table 8.7: Market Share in the European Parcel and Express Market (2004)

Parcel/Express Operator	TNT estimates (%)	DPWN estimates (%)
DHL	23	20
TNT	11	11
UPS	6	8
Fedex	2	2
La Poste (DPD)	58	12
Royal Mail (GLS)	58	8
Others	58	39

Source: WIK-Consult (2006), 'Main Developments in the Postal Sector 2004–2006' for the EU Commission.

Regulation and Liberalisation

Under the EU Services Directives of 1997 and 2000, An Post has been designated as a universal provider for mail services in Ireland. This designation obliges An Post to deliver mail items of up to 20 kilogrammes to all address points, five days a week, to a standard of 94 per cent next-day delivery for non-deferred items. An additional implication of these directives is that, since 1 January 2006, the only part of the postal industry that remains a monopoly, called the 'reserved area', is that part that deals with mail items weighing less than 50 grams.

The regulation has two roles: to introduce competition into the market and to ensure equal access for all citizens to postal services through the universal service obligation. To help postal operators manage their universal service obligation, the EU Services Directive created a 'reserved area' to fund this aspect of the business. The EU is gradually allowing competition to enter the market with full liberalisation of the market to take place by 1 January 2009. However, the intention is that competition will root out bad practices, and the incumbents will have time to put in place the reach, trust and brand awareness that will allow them to compete favourably and transform themselves into lean, profitable companies.

Two main responses to the issues of universal access and liberalisation have emerged from the European postal operators: forming alliances and shoring up defences. Those that have embraced the liberalisation agenda have made acquisitions or formed joint ventures or strategic alliances. The Dutch post office (TPG) purchased TNT instantly, giving them a strong and well-recognised brand. Deutsche Post has the world's biggest logistics and mail service (DPWN) as a result of a series of acquisitions, including DHL. The Royal Mail Group purchased GLS, an international logistics operator.

Other operators have taken a more defensive position, cautioning against further liberalisation and urging the continuation of the 'reserved area', to ensure the ongoing provision of the Universal Service Obligation (USO). The EU Internal Market and Services Commissioner has suggested that the Irish government impose a levy on new entrants to compensate An Post for losses arising from its legal obligation to deliver domestic mail to poorly populated areas which cannot, under regulation, be subsidised by other profitable sections of the business, or which cannot be charged a different postage rate based on location by ministerial direction (Connolly 2006).

As a result of these responses, partially or fully privatised postal operators now handle 29 per cent of EU letter mail (WIK-Consult 2006). In 2004, the German government lowered its stake to 42 per cent in Deutsche Post and the Dutch government reduced their share of the former TPG-TNT (now called TNT) to 10 per cent. In 2005, the Danish government sold 22 per cent of Danish Post to a British investment group and the Belgian government sold just below 50 per cent of their postal service to the same British investment group and the Danish post office.

But postal workers have reacted to this new situation. On 6 June 2007, the main post offices across Europe shut for one hour as up to 10,000 workers protested at the liberalisation of the marketplace. Irish unions are warning that the opening up of mail markets to full competition could destroy the Irish postal services and lead to extensive job losses (Black 2007). Further industrial unrest in Ireland and across the EU is likely.

Market Moves

As these various strategies have unfolded, liberalisation operators have found themselves at times in competition, and at other times in cooperation, with each other.

UK

The UK market has been fully liberalised since 2006. BT, one of Royal Mail's top ten customers, have recently signed a contract worth £90 million with TNT, covering 170 million second-class mail items. Interestingly, TNT will still inject the mail into Royal Mail for 'last mile' delivery and will pay Royal Mail 13p per item for this 'downstream access' service. UK Mail, a domestic competitor, also won a contract worth £12 million to deliver mail for the UK government Department of Work and Pensions.[4] Royal Mail earns about 12 per cent of its revenues from its foreign operations and cooperates with TNT and Singapore Post for global mail contracts through a joint venture called Spring.

The Netherlands

In the domestic market, TNT has been losing mail volumes to competitors, such as Nederland Royal Mail. TNT is expanding its operation in Germany through EP Europost, a joint venture between Hermes and TNT which links 120 of Hermes's 160 regional mail delivery partners together under a single franchise structure. Hermes was set up to deliver mail-order items for a leading mail-order company in Germany in the mid-1970s. TNT's recent strategy has been to exit their freight and logistics business to concentrate on the UK and the German letter mail market. TNT earns 60 per cent of its revenues from foreign markets.

---

[4] Based on information from <http://www.guardian.co.uk >.

Germany

Deutsche Post WorldNet (DPWN) is active in the Dutch market through its MailMerge and Selekt Mail operations. Competitors are finding it difficult to win large customers from DPWN as these customers have built up long-term relations with Deutsche Post. DPWN strategy is to develop a 'one-stop' shop for business customers as it continues expanding across Europe, e.g. by buying logistics company Excel in 2005. DPWN earns approximately 48 per cent of its total revenues from foreign operations.

Nordic Countries

Since Sweden's Posten AB was privatised in 1993, prices for business customers have fallen by 30 per cent. However, it has lost 8 per cent of the market to Citymail, a company owned by Norway Post (*The Economist* 2007). Yet Citymail and Sweden Posten AB have a jointly owned corporation to maintain a national address database. Norway has also announced its intention to set up a Citymail subsidiary operation in Denmark. Sweden and Norway had earned around 11 per cent from foreign operations, while 50 per cent of Finland Post's revenue growth for 2003 came from foreign operations, mainly printing, e-invoicing, information management and direct mail services. Finland Post's strategy is to develop its business towards integrated information and materials flow management, enabling versatile messaging and logistics solutions.

Ireland

Competition is also experienced in Ireland. DX Ireland, which already handles 40,000 pieces of mail a night for solicitors, banks and financial institutions, and won a three-year contract worth €1 million to provide business mail services to the Registry of Deeds Offices (*Business & Finance* 2006). An outcome of market liberalisation is that a large number of major and minor players exist in Ireland in the parcels, courier, express and international markets. Tables 8.8 and 8.9, respectively, list authorised operators and present key financial data of the parent companies of certain operators.

For An Post, 87 per cent of volume is business mail, in line with the EU average of 88 per cent, and up to 67 per cent of EU business mail is B2C (WIK-Consult 2006). This figure is expected to increase as the customer-to-customer (C2C) segment declines and as addressed direct mail increases. Like most other postal operators in Europe, An Post is heavily

Table 8.8: Authorised* Postal Operators in Ireland

Central Logistics Ltd
Connect Couriers
Cyclone Couriers
Delta Express
DHL Express (owned by DPWN)
Document Express Postal Services (DEPS)
DX Ireland
Fastrack
FedEx Express
First Direct Logistics/Medical/Quickstream/Brief/Cobra/Rapid Despatch/FDS
    Worldwide Couriers
General Logistics Systems in Ireland
Hurricane Couriers
INDN City Express
Interlink Ireland/Interlink Express (owned by La Poste)
Irish Swift Post
Lettershop Services
Nightline
Olympus Couriers Ltd
Pony Express
Relay Express
River International Forwarding Ltd
Roadrunner Couriers LTD
Securispeed Despatch
Spring (joint venture of Royal Mail, Singapore Post and TNT on international
    mails)
Streetlink Couriers
Target Express Ireland
TNT
UPS
Wheel Couriers (An Post owned)
World Courier Ireland Ltd

* *'Authorised' means approved by ComReg to provide services as specifically notified to the regulator. All postal operators with a turnover in excess of €500,000 must be authorised to operate in Ireland.*

dependent on a small number of key customers for mail revenue.[5] Just under 80 per cent of mail is now paid by customer-owned franking meter or by Ceadunas (paid under licence), for which An Post offers variable dis-

---

[5] CEO presentation to An Post Group of Unions Conference on 'The Future of the Irish Postal Service', 1 March 2007.

Table 8.9: Key Financial Data for Certain National Postal Operators Authorised to Compete in Ireland

Mail Group	2005	2004	Services from Ireland
Royal Mail Group			
– Revenues	£9,056 million	£8,956 million	Offers international mail through Spring Delivers logistics through GLS
– Operating profit	6.5%	5.8%	
TNT			
– Revenues	€10,105 million	€9,106 million	Offers national and international express; international mail
– Operating Profit	9%	9%	
Deutsche Post			
– Revenues	€44,168 million	€43,168 million	See DHL (Ireland)
– Operating Profit	8%	7%	(in Appendix)

Source: Annual Reports.

counts based on volume levels, pre-sorting and deferred delivery options. To offer these types of discounts, An Post sought an interim price increase in 2006, claiming that it has had to absorb wage cost increases of 18.9 per cent agreed under national pay agreements between August 2003 and May 2007, and also increases in energy and fuel costs. The effective date of any interim price increase would be 1 March 2007, forty-two months since An Post last increased prices for letter mail in the 'reserved area'.[6]

Future Prospects

Not all commentators subscribe to the need for price increases with some suggesting that further price increases will have a negative impact on the already declining growth rate of letter mails (An Post Group of Unions 2006). They argue that with continued growth expected in gross domestic product (GDP), in population and in e-commerce over the coming years, An Post should pursue a no-price-increase policy, making its products cheaper in the long run and promoting growth. The experience of other postal operators may support this view. For example, the Swiss generate 749 mail items per person per year, the USA averages 670 and Norway averages 574. Ireland generated only 183 per person in 2005,

---

[6] An Post Application to ComReg for Interim Price Increase, 6 December 2006.

suggesting that letter per capita in Ireland has scope for growth (An Post Group of Unions 2006). Others argue that volume growth driven by low prices, e.g. via direct mail, will merely increase costs and create network capacity issues for An Post, and therefore such growth should be avoided.[7]

An Post also referred, in its price application, to the declining mail volumes due to e-substitution. Other postal operators' activities suggest an alternative view. In the run-up to Christmas 2005, Royal Mail delivered 70 million items that had been ordered online over the Internet. In the USA, the online DVD order business alone added 100 million pieces per year to the mail stream (*Postal Technology International*, 14 June 2006). The Web auction company eBay is said to have generated an additional $1 billion (approximately €1.3 billion) in priority postage for the United States Postal Service (USPS) in just two years. In response to demand from eBay sellers, the USPS launched a new flat-rate mailing box, the 'shoe-box', which comes with both the eBay and USPS logos. According to the European E-Commerce and Mail Order Trade Association (EMOTA), representing 2,000 companies from twenty-one countries, the presence of eBay has developed consumer and retailer confidence and trust in e-commerce, particularly in countries that have not been strong in mail-order. They also state that the development of online sales is directly linked to Internet penetration, broadband access and the performance of postal operators in particular (see <http://www.emota. org>). They suggest that the market for online sales is developing synergies with traditional mail, as many consumers like to browse, mark and refer to hard-copy catalogues before ordering online. They also report that the year 2005 saw a 10 per cent increase in online sales, with 29 per cent of retailers carrying out cross-border transactions through e-commerce.

Due to this evident growth from e-commerce, big brands such as TNT, DHL (DPWN), UPS, GLS (Royal Mail) and DPD (La Poste) are becoming interested in the small- to medium-sized mailers. DHL intends to double its access points from 15,000 to 30,000 by 2008, and UPS is using a franchising model to expand its access and distribution. In response to Hermes's capture of market share in the C2C segment (up to 22 per cent in 2005) and in the B2C segment in Germany (up to 35 per cent in 2005), DHL has targeted customers and small businesses with a 10 per cent price cut (WIK-Consult 2006).

---

[7] An Post response to report commissioned by the An Post Group of Unions.

Other approaches to serving and retaining this market can also be observed. Regional operators have banded together to build regional logistics. For example, Norway and Denmark set up Pan-Nordic Logistics (PNL) to service the Nordic countries. An Post operates a number of bilateral commercial agreements with competitors of postal operators in some European countries in order to assure high quality of delivery in parcels and express markets, e.g. with Express Parcels in Northern Ireland and with ANC in the UK.

Due to strong rivalry among incumbents in the industry, companies keep to themselves figures on market share and on revenues by market segment. However, the European Commission estimates that 'the total revenues earned in EU parcels and express markets at €33 billion in 2000 and €36 billion in 2001' (An Post Group of Unions 2006). According to the Universal Postal Union, which is the international cooperative for all the national postal authorities, 28 industrialised country members hold 28 per cent of the domestic and 18 per cent of the international parcels market.[8]

Delivering the Future

During his announcement confirming liberalisation of the EU postal market for 1 January 2009, EU Commissioner McCreevy stated that countries that had fully opened their postal markets to competition were reaping benefits:

> All have shown, not only that market opening is feasible but those who opened up and started early gained the most. There is no reward for sitting on the fence.

Not one for sitting on the fence, Donal Connell, the new chief executive,[9] on taking up his position immediately sought approval from the board of An Post to pay its employees €20 million in frozen wage increases due from 2003 under national pay agreements. Commenting on this development, the Communications Workers Union said that 'while many serious challenges face our members in An Post, no one can deny

---

[8] See UPU Postal Market Review 2004 and UPU Postal Network Figures, available at: <http://www.upu.int>.

[9] Under the leadership of the new chief executive, stakeholder relationships improved and, with a strong focus on agreed change activity, An Post increased turnover by 6.6 per cent, grew operating margins to 3.3 per cent and significantly improved next-day delivery standards during 2007.

that this decision is a very good start by the new CEO' (Flynn 2006). Notwithstanding this 'very good start', the real issue is what An Post must do to 'get off the fence' and meet 'the many serious challenges' ahead. Should An Post concentrate on defending the domestic market? Should An Post look to grow this market? Should An Post look for an ally in these uncertain times?

Appendix 8.1: Postal Operators

- DHL (Ireland) is now a single entity comprising the former Securicor, Omega Express, Danzas Eurocargo and DHL International businesses, now wholly owned by DPWN.
- DPD has 22,000 employees and 500 depots across Europe. It is owned by La Poste, through a subsidiary, GeoPost, which owns the Interlink brand.
- GLS employs 11,000 people and operates in 34 states across Europe. GLS contributed 12 per cent to Royal Mail Group revenues and over 30 per cent to group profits for the year 2005–2006 (*Royal Mail Annual Report* 2005–2006).
- Spring is the brand name for a global joint venture in cross-border mail between TNT, Royal Mail Group and Singapore Post.

References

An Post, *Annual Reports* 2001–2005, available at: <http://www.anpost. ie/>.

An Post Group of Unions (2006), *An Post: A New Vision*, May.

Black, Fergus (2007), 'Protest at EU Plan to Open up Mail Markets', *Irish Independent*, 7 June.

Business and Finance (2006), 'Stamps of Approval RSVP', 16 November.

Connolly, Niamh (2006), 'An Post Will Get Cash to Open Up the Market', *Sunday Business Post*, 22 October.

Flynn, Gerald (2006), 'Postal Chief Seeks €20m in Unpaid Wages', *Irish Independent*, 30 August.

Quality of Service Monitor (2005), available at: <http://www. comreg.ie>.

The Economist (2007), 'Europe's Postal Services', 382(8512), 77.

WIK-Consult (2006), *Main Developments in the Postal Sector 2004–2005*, final report for the EU Commission, available at: <http:// ec.europa.eu>.

CHAPTER 9

Vivas Health

Breda McCarthy[1]

Department of Management and Marketing, University College Cork

Introduction

Vivas Health is the fastest growing health insurer in Europe. Founded in 2004, it quickly gained 6 per cent of the market, confounding analysts who predicted that the duopoly of VHI (Voluntary Health Insurance) and BUPA (now Quinn Healthcare) would be in no way challenged by the latest entrant. Product differentiation, aligned with price follower tactics, was the key element in its market entry strategy. A new branding strategy, 'More Power to Your Health', was launched in 2006, which helped the company differentiate itself from its competitors. The company has managed to create 'new market space' in a well-guarded market (Kim and Mauborgne 1999; Bryce and Dyer 2007). Its vision centres on the notion of 'wellness' as opposed to 'illness'. The company adopts a broad definition of health, seeing it as a complementary mix of physical, emotional and spiritual well-being. With this in mind, Vivas aims to launch new products and services to meet the needs of its growing subscriber base.

Characteristics of the Irish Health Care and Private Health Insurance Sectors

As health systems can be structured in different ways, different kinds of private health insurance (PHI) networks emerge.

[1] The author is grateful for the contribution of individuals and organisations to this case study. This case is based on interviews conducted with Marketing Director Deirdre Ashe and CEO Oliver Tattan of Vivas Health, and interviews with VHI and BUPA, managers of private hospitals and the Irish Hospital Consultants Association. The information in this case study relates to the position of Vivas Health in 2007; Vivas Health has since become part of the Hibernian Group. This case study is intended as a basis for class discussion. It is not intended to illustrate either effective or ineffective management.

The Irish health system is a mixture of a universal public health system and a fee-based private system. PHI arrangements in Ireland are complementary (covering services excluded by the state) and supplementary (for faster access to non-crucial services and better amenities). The key features (OECD 2004*a*) of the Irish PHI system are as follows:

- Community-rated premiums: the absence of discrimination in premium calculations on the basis of age, gender, health status, claims history or other factors.
- Open enrolment: insurers are compelled to accept all applicants for PHI.
- Minimum benefit: insurers cannot provide health insurance below a minimum level.
- Lifetime coverage: refers to guaranteed renewal; as individuals get older, their health may deteriorate, but insurers cannot deny individuals the right to renew coverage from one year to the next.

The proportion of the Irish population covered by PHI, at 52 per cent, is amongst the highest in the EU. This statistic is quite striking given the full entitlement to public hospital care and reflects a lack of confidence in the public health system. A range of government policies exist to ensure affordability of PHI, such as tax relief and subsidies on public pay-beds for private patients (Health Insurance Authority 2005*a*). People buy health insurance because it frequently improves the individual's choice of health providers, treatments and timing of care (OECD 2004*a*). The high level of governmental support for PHI has been justified in terms of taking pressure off the capacity-constrained, public hospital system. However, there is controversy about whether support for the private sector undermines the equity and efficiency of the Irish health care system (Wiley 2005). This aspect of the debate is replicated in Australia, a similar market. In the context of Australian health care, Deeble (2003) notes that nearly all emergencies and most of the oldest, poorest and sickest patients will be cared for publicly. Critics of the for-profit sector note that private hospitals have an incentive to seek out the most profitable cases (Segal 2004) such as day surgery within elective care (generally refers to surgeries and treatments that can be planned, for example, hip replacements and scans). In Ireland, acute and emergency care (i.e. heart bypass surgery, appendix removal, childbirth, etc.) for adults and children is, in the main, covered by the public health system. Private hospitals provide acute care as well as elective care. There is no private insurance for long-term care.

Key Players in the Market

VHI, a state-owned company, was the sole provider of insurance prior to 1997. After the Irish market was opened up to competition, BUPA entered the market in 1997 (subsequently taken over by Quinn Healthcare) and Vivas Health entered the market in 2004. Private health care is seen as a growth area, private hospitals have profited from long waiting lists in the public sector, and the sector has attracted the attention of banks, medical entrepreneurs and venture capitalists. Tax breaks were introduced in 2001 to meet a shortfall in public bed capacity. According to the Prospectus Report (2003), a large increase in hospital capacity is planned for the period 2000–2010. In 2007, a controversial 'co-location' policy was announced by the Fianna Fáil government, which refers to the building of private hospitals on the grounds of public hospitals.

The opening up of the market intensified competition and stimulated the design of new products. New entrants sought to differentiate their products by offering coverage for out-patient services and non-core medical treatments, e.g. medical screening, dental and optical services, home nursing, domestic assistance, dieticians, physiotherapy and podiatry, private A&E care and alternative therapies such as acupuncture and reflexology. Certain services reflect contemporary clinical practice, and disease prevention measures prevent future hospitalisation and can be delivered safely 'outside the hospital gate'. All insurers struggle to compete on the basis of offering the lowest premium, nationwide coverage and the best customer service. New entrants have to cover operating costs and meet shareholder expectations (i.e. the need to maintain prudential reserves, invest, reward entrepreneurial risk-taking and remunerate capital appropriately). According to the OECD (2004: 208), the overheads are as follows:

> Marketing, policy management and underwriting represent the largest fraction of administrative expenses but insurers also incur the cost of billing, product innovation, agents' commission and distribution. Where insurers enter into contracts with health care providers, multiple contractual negotiations add to insurers' administrative burdens.

Thus, new entrants incur additional costs. Insurers are expected to compete on the basis of providing the best coverage at the lowest cost. A price-following strategy is evident, with the market leader setting the premium and market followers charging a similar, albeit marginally lower, price. Small companies, who lack bargaining power with suppliers, generally have to negotiate higher rates to secure agreements with suppliers; thus

Table 9.1: Private Health Insurers in Ireland – Key Characteristics

Company	Market Share	Major Products	Market Segmentation	Differentiation
Vivas Health	6% with more than 70,000 members	The 'me plan' for the first time buyer; the 'i plan' for individuals; and the 'we plan' for couples/families.	All segments, families and children, young singles, and retired.	Branding; Product innovation, being the first to offer laser eye and teeth whitening treatment; Treatment for new and emerging procedures abroad which are not available in Ireland; Supporter of the Marie Keating Foundation.
Quinn Healthcare	24% with more than 320,000 members	Family Care Personal Care Essential Essential Plus Health Manager Starter Health Manager Health Manager Gold	All segments, families and children, young singles, and retired.	Discounts on motor and household insurance; 'Recommend a friend' to receive a €100 reward; Sponsor of the Great Bupa Ireland Run, Dublin; UK Cover.
VHI	70% with over 1.5 million members	Plan A to E and Options Life Stages	All segments, families and children, young singles, retired.	Primary care through VHI; SwiftCare Clinic; First to offer dental insurance; Health shop; Sponsor of the Cúl Camps – GAA summer camps for children.

there is limited scope for lower provider prices due to competition (Health Insurance Authority 2003). The market leader continues to exert strong bargaining power over providers with regard to reimbursement levels, and the other insurers follow the prices set by the market leader (OECD 2004a). For a small number of hospitals in Ireland, there is some scope for leverage: a provider who offers acute care benefits or who is located in a region with a shortage of providers has a relatively strong bargaining position. The market leader's share of the market has fallen as a result of new arrivals, but it remains a dominant player with a large share of the market. Table 9.1 outlines products, customer numbers and aspects of the market segmentation strategies of the three players in the marketplace.

Regarding Table 9.1, there are two things to note: (1) due to the complexity of the product sold, it is not easy to compare one particular service with another, and the subscribers are advised to check the services available in the participating hospitals in their location along with the level of coverage and type of hospital accommodation that they require. Products are geared towards a person's stage in life. Therefore, as a person's needs change over time, they need to review their policies; (2) all companies must provide a minimum level of coverage with respect to day care/in-patient treatment, hospital out-patient treatment, maternity benefits, convalescence, psychiatric treatment, and substance abuse. The minimum accommodation level is semi-private in a public hospital.

Government Regulation

Government regulation has a strong impact on the insurance sector. A risk equalisation scheme (RES) was implemented in 2006 by the Irish government – almost ten years after the market was opened to competition. Recently, the issue of risk equalisation has been hotly debated in the media, attracting vocal critics as well as proponents. The Health Insurance Authority (2005, 2005a) has published several reports on the issue. Proponents argue that RES is essential in a community-rated health system (where everyone pays the same for an insurance package, irrespective of their age) and a logical response to the strong incentives of new entrants to select healthier individuals, leaving the incumbent with the burden of claims. According to the OECD (2004), risk equalisation is designed to help spread the cost of caring for less healthy populations. It involves transfer payments from one insurer to another and is designed to 'neutralise differences in insurers' costs due to variations in the health status of its members' (Worz and Foubister 2005: 27). Opponents argue that it limits competition, impedes innovation, rewards inefficiency and does not serve the customer in the long run. BUPA Ireland challenged this ruling in court (BUPA vs. the Health Insurance Authority, November 2005), lost its case and withdrew from the market. It was taken over by the Quinn Insurance Group, and Quinn Healthcare is now the third player in the market. VHI is faced with threats such as new solvency requirements, EU regulation and shifts in government policy. For instance, the Barrington Report (an investigation into PHI in Ireland from a business point of view) recommended that the required level of capital solvency for VHI Healthcare should be in the order of 30 per cent of gross written premium. The report also recommended that risk equalisation payments be discounted by 20 per cent (Department of Health and Children 2007).

Insurer–Provider Relationship: Its Impact on the Achievement of Health Care Goals and Profit Margins

The insurer is part of a health care network consisting of general practitioners (GPs),[2] health care workers who are state-trained, consultants, private hospital amenities and ambulatory services. Price competition is a feature of the insurance sector and many cost drivers lie outside the control of the insurer.

The insurer–provider relationship is a contractual one. A health insurer is a classic intermediary: it negotiates with providers on behalf of its members and pays for medical services. The original purpose of insurance is to pool risk for catastrophic events. With an appropriately structured pool, the cost of participating in the pool (i.e. the insurance premium) is an acceptable price for protection against the risk of a high-cost, but a low-probability event. PHI contracts contain highly technical information and cover every conceivable medical treatment. They include:

- Technical charges (e.g. charges for theatre, disposables, diagnostic tests such as X-rays, drugs, prostheses, etc.).
- Accommodation (e.g. daily rates for private beds; pay beds in public hospitals).
- Salaries (e.g. consultants).

---

[2] In many health care systems, a patient can only be admitted to hospitals with a referral from the GP. These referrers have an influence on consumers' choice of health care providers. The Irish health care system is paternalistic in nature and patients rely on their GPs for referrals.

Relationship with Consultants

Consultants have strong bargaining power and insurers have little influence over fees. They are obliged to pay the professional fee directly to the hospital consultants. The relationship between insurers and consultants is an 'arm's length' one and consultants jealously guard their clinical independence. From the insurer's perspective, clinicians have little incentive to minimise the costs. Clinicians are not always aware of, or responsible for, the economic consequences of their medical decisions (Doyle 2006). However, Doyle (2006) found that if hospital managers enter into dialogue with clinicians and involve them in new management accounting practices then that helps change attitudes. Despite the cultural differences between insurers, consultants and hospital managers, they share common goals – the provision of quality health care at affordable cost.

Consultants' contracts are standardised and, prior to 2006, fees were the object of collective negotiation between the insurer and the Irish Hospital Consultants Association (IHCA).[3] The lack of price competition in this sector was the subject of an investigation by the Competition Authority. The idea of 'pay for performance' has been mooted by the Competition Authority. Pay-for-performance initiatives are designed to link fees to outcomes and encourage providers to comply with currently accepted medical standards (Nichols and O'Malley 2006). According to the IHCA, this new reimbursement model would not work in practice. Firstly, there are a limited number of consultants and it is not uncommon to have only one specialist in a region. Secondly, the clinical work is carried out by a team of consultants, and the complex and customised nature of health care makes it difficult to estimate performance and negotiate fees in a definitive manner. Finally, patients are not in a position, or are at a serious disadvantage, in the matter of 'shopping around' for a particular specialist charging a particular fee.

Traditionally, the public hospital consultants in Ireland have been the dominant providers for private patients (White Paper on PHI 1999). Wherever public consultants engage in private practice, they are not employed by the hospital but are self-employed and have admitting rights within that hospital (Doyle 2006). In 2007, the consultants'

---

[3] Previously, the insurers normally negotiated a standard salary contract with the Irish Hospital Consultants Association, a representative body, but the Competition Authority deemed that practice to be anti-competitive in 2006; therefore, insurers now write to each consultant in an attempt to get agreement on fees.

contract was changed and public-only contracts were advertised. Reform was prompted by concern about a 'two-tier' health system in which consultants' contracts facilitate private practice and where patients who are privately insured can jump the queue (Worz and Foubister 2005).

Health Care Costs

In many health care systems, hospital costs are driven by demographic change (ageing of the population), rates of utilisation, increases in bed capacity, labour costs, pharmaceuticals, regulatory compliance, clinical equipment and information technology. There is some evidence from the literature that health care costs are relatively higher in the private sector as a result of over-servicing (Hindle and McAuley 2004). The not-for-profit organisations tend to be 'conservative, risk averse and not as commercial as shareholder-owned for-profit entities ... an implicit conflict of interest between service to members and acting more aggressively to contain rising healthcare costs' (Bowie and Adams 2004). Cost structures vary across hospitals depending on clinical research, teaching status and provision of specialised services (Robinson 2003). Although the government policy aims to refocus on primary care and strengthen the role of the GPs, the Irish health care system is heavily biased towards hospitalisation (OECD 1990).

Numerous cost control mechanisms exist (Jacobs and Goddard 2002), both on the demand side and on the supply side. In Ireland, attempts at controlling hospital expenditures began in earnest in the 1990s. Insurers introduced the concept of 'procedural pricing' or 'fixed price' packages. This is a standardised pricing model. Fixed price packages are all-inclusive packages, where all the costs incurred in treating a patient, doing 'tests' or dealing with a particular medical case is assessed, such as need for an X-ray, blood test, theatre fee, disposables, post-operative dressings and prostheses. Thus, the cost of a medical procedure, such as a cataract operation, hip replacement or tonsil removal, was calculated and a schedule of fees was developed. Utilisation of health services is crudely measured by nights spent in the hospital. In response to the rising costs, insurers introduced hospital 'length-of-stay' guidelines by drawing on claims data and international experience. This new reimbursement methodology influenced some hospitals to develop improved activity costing systems (Doyle 2006). These new reimbursement models signalled a move away from passive funding to the more active involvement of the insurer in health care. Certain surgical procedures that once required hospitalisation are now performed on a day-care basis and this has lowered the cost. In Ireland, during the period 1996–2005, there was a 166 per cent increase in day care and a 5 per cent reduction in the average length of in-patient stay (Sheridan 2006). Another cost-control mechanism that exists in some health care regimes is 'co-payments' by which the insured has to pay a part of the fee for each visit to a hospital or consultant, which transfers financial responsibilities to the insured (Simonet 2004). Irish insurers are wary of introducing co-payments for fear of a consumer backlash and being placed at a competitive disadvantage.

In health care, new opportunities for treatment arise through techno-logical advances and through medical research. For instance, micro-surgery has benefits over open surgery in terms of reduced mortality, length of stay, duration of recuperation and return to work. New drug treatments have benefits over overly invasive surgery. Innovation is driven by the provider. For instance, Blackrock Clinic was the first hos-pital to use the cardiac CT scanner in Ireland, and the Galway Clinic was the first hospital to offer a private A&E service. Given the cost implica-tions, these providers negotiate with insurers before investment in new drugs, new technology or new services is made. Insurers have a Medical Advisory Council, which comprises leading medical physicians and consultants to advise them about the new developments in health care. While innovation has the potential to benefit patients, there are few con-cerns over ineffective health technology and overuse. Providers are struggling to fund medical innovation and insurers are struggling to keep premium rates at low levels for their members. Insurers argue that they have to contend with price elasticity of demand for health insurance (it is argued that healthy people would have little incentive to buy health insurance if there was a sharp rise in premiums). This conundrum – elevating quality of care and containing health care costs – is present in all health regimes.

Quality Initiatives

The impact of quality initiatives on the way health care is purchased and provided has been the subject of recent academic research (Bowie and Adams 2004; Porter and Teisberg 2004, 2006). There is growing interest in quality management programmes that capture certain aspects of good or poor service provision, as measured by infection rates, returns to the-atre, rates of clinical errors, waiting times for surgery and patient satisfaction rates. According to Bowie and Adams, quality management benefits both providers and insurers:

> ... quality improvement can help contain costs if one expects the maxim that quality can cost less if one factors in the savings from not having to fix things when they go wrong ... the transition from passive funding to more active involvement in outcomes is a long process of educating clinicians as to the value an insurer can add to the pursuit of better quality in healthcare, without the threat of loss of their clinical independence. (2004: 25)

Although insurers buy medical services on behalf of their membership, the Irish consumers do not receive good information on performance indicators (i.e. waiting times, price of treatments, treatment options available), and this restricts their ability to exercise real choice. Consumer perceptions of quality are limited to personal experience and anecdotal evidence (Porter 2006). Porter's assertion is that 'consumers today have little choice about providers and treatments and are in no position to make informed decisions given the limited information available to them' (2004: 4). It is predicted that quality certification and compliance with international standards will become a requirement for insurance coverage in Ireland in the future. Irish hospitals will, inevitably, have to invest more in information technology (IT), since private insurers will pay for 'evidence-based medicine'. According to the *British Medical Journal*, evidence-based medicine refers to the use of current best evidence (from systematic research or clinical trials) in making decisions about the care of individual patients. It is designed to help doctors maximise the quality of care and life expectancy for patients, it invalidates previously accepted diagnostic tests or treatments and replaces them with new ones and in some cases it raises, rather than lowers, the cost of care. It is predicted that reimbursement models will be more strongly linked to the quality improvement choices made by Irish providers in the future.

In the US, managed care[4] was introduced to reduce the costs of treatment (one example is the management of chronic disease to slow its progression). Employers or groups such as Medicare are more powerful agents than individuals in negotiating coverage conditions with competing insurers. As noted by Simonet (2004), managed care is a system that may achieve cost control, but only in return for high sacrifices (erosion

---

[4] Managed care describes a situation where the market is constrained by rules or regulation, either enforced by governments or, in the case of the US, by employers wanting to contain costs.

of decisional power of physicians, exclusion of patients at risk and little or no freedom of choice of provider). Berry *et al.* (2006), in a study of the US health regime, noted that physicians, employers and insurers need to restructure their working relationships, which tend to be adversarial and distant. Traditionally, the clinician regarded 'production' as an internal matter, and any involvement of insurers in clinical activity was strongly resisted, with arguments ranging from the cost-driven focus of insurers, lack of data on outcomes, the complex and customised nature of health care to the suppression of clinical freedom (Porter 2004). In Ireland, insurers have no desire to adopt managed care principles in the face of strong medical power.

Controlling the Cost of Health Care

In many health regimes, rationing has been used to control health care costs on the supply side. In some circumstances, an increase in hospital beds is associated with increased utilisation of health care and increased health expenditure. The supplier-induced demand theory, formulated by Evans (1974), suggests that providers and clinicians are able to favour demand for care in order to secure an income, although a strong ethical tradition in health care limits this practice. In Ireland, over-capacity or a large expansion in hospital capacity is of concern to insurers. The market leader attributes low premiums in Ireland to control over-capacity along with community rating and insurable risk (i.e. insurance coverage is for major illness and not minor illness).

In other health regimes, network structures exist that channel consumers towards a restricted number of economical providers (Robinson 2003), such as the US. According to Robinson, as the economy falters and inflation raises, 'the market may experience a renewed willingness to purchase narrow-network products if they come at a premium much lower than those for insurance products within a broader network'(2003: 137). In the UK, private insurers offer coverage for the use of approved preferred hospitals, but only partial coverage for the use of other hospitals (Health Policy Consensus Group 2003). In a case study of the Swiss insurance system, it was noted that having to pay 'all willing providers' prevents insurers from selecting from approved lists of cost-effective, safe, or consumer-friendly doctors or hospitals (Health Policy Consensus Group 2003). In Ireland, the market leader enters into contracts with all hospitals. The general public is not generally supportive of network exclusion. Insurers are eager to avoid the opprobrium that results from denying patients' freedom of choice; network exclusion would mean patients would have to travel for care, giving rise to geographical barriers to health access. A major weakness of this system is that it limits selective contracting. Under selective contracting, insurers negotiate agreements with certain doctors, hospitals and health care providers to supply a range of services to insurers at reduced cost. It facilitates cost containment by giving insurers direct purchasing power in relation to providers. The literature shows that insurers face challenges in implementing this type of risk management policy, such as the difficulty in categorising hospitals by price and efficacy, and fear of low-cost providers being labelled low quality (Robinson 2003). In relation to Ireland, the OECD states that:

> They [the insurers] have not leveraged the potential of more selective contracting to strengthen their ability to negotiate on the volume and quality of care, nor on quality standards, clinical practices, and special programs for high risk individuals. (2004*a*: 208)

There is evidence of a change in strategy in recent years. In relation to diagnostic tests, such as MRI tests,[5] some insurers are seeking to hold down prices by excluding some facilities from the network and by channelling consumers towards more economic facilities. Centres are nominated using the following criteria: cost, demographics and quality of service. The market for diagnostic tests is characterised by over-supply, and it can be classified as a commodity health service, with the result that the insurer is liable to switch providers on the basis of price.

To summarise, health care goals include the delivery of care at optimal prices, the funding of medical innovation, performance measurement and patient safety. The insurer is part of a health care system and the insurer–provider relationship has an impact on the achievement of key health care goals and on profit margins (or losses) of parties to the contract.

Entry Barriers: Raising Finance and Changing Consumer Behaviour

The PHI sector is characterised by high barriers to entry, including financial (start-up costs, the need to maintain adequate reserves, solvency requirements) and marketing barriers. A survey published by the Health

---

[5] Magnetic response imaging (MRI) scanning has become an increasingly important tool in early and accurate detection and diagnosis of brain, spine, disc and bone diseases, diseases affecting bone marrow, and muscle and sports injuries.

Insurance Authority in 2003 showed that consumer behaviour was highly conservative, with only a fraction of customers switching between insurers, despite the fact that such a move could save them money. Brand loyalty was seen as a major entry barrier. VHI Healthcare was seen as one of Ireland's most recognised and trusted household brands; people accepted the motto that 'VHI cares' and trusted that their insurer would pay claims when the need arose.

In 2004, after founding a strong management team, the CEO of Vivas Oliver Tattan approached Dermot Desmond, a key player in the private venture capital market. Tattan was successful in persuading Desmond to support his venture. Desmond invested in the company and sold his share several years later in 2008. A key question facing Vivas Health from the beginning was whether a market characterised by inertia would be interested in its brand proposition.

Brand Proposition and Market Segmentation

Building brand name awareness among stakeholders was the first marketing task, all the more important given that Vivas decided to sell its plans through intermediaries, mostly life insurance agencies and bank branches of AIB. Financial advisers were paid by commission to offer advice and sell the most relevant and best value health insurance plan to their clients. Stakeholders included the government, health care providers, hospital administrators, corporate business, human resource directors and the consumer. As a new, unknown company, Vivas had to provide answers to questions of who they were and how they were different.

According to the marketing director, Vivas Health is a 'challenger brand': in a market dominated by one player, it is positioned as an Irish entrepreneurial company that represents innovation, choice and value for money. Vivas Health prides itself on being the first to provide:

- Access to private A&E in the Galway Clinic.
- Home help after major operations and the birth of a baby.
- Prescriptions.
- GP referred MRI scans.
- Overseas coverage for procedures not available in Ireland.
- Coverage for laser eye surgery.
- Coverage for tooth whitening treatments.
- Coverage for primary care (GP, dentist) and alternative medicine such as reflexology, massage therapy and homeopathy.

Vivas Health's strategy is to offer customised plans as opposed to what the CEO calls the 'one size fits all' mentality of other insurers. Vivas Health is the first Irish insurer to offer health insurance plans tailored to suit the specific needs of the consumer. For instance, following research, a plan was developed to suit teachers and nurses. The latter plan includes benefits such as counselling, stress management and protection of a person's back – a common concern in the nursing profession.

Analysis of competitors' plans revealed that health coverage automatically included maternity benefits – even if the subscriber was a single man. Thus, Vivas Health developed the 'me plan', giving the customer the flexibility to opt out of coverage they feel is unnecessary. All plans have tiered pricing, ranging from a basic no-frills plan, which strips down the insurance plan to the core minimum benefits required by law (level 1), to a premium-priced plan (level 5), aimed at older consumers who want comprehensive coverage.

Vivas Health's goal is to create a fresh and exciting brand proposition that captures the imagination of the consumer. The name Vivas caught the marketing director's attention because of its connotations of living life to the full. Considerable thought has gone into the design of logo, the website and promotional materials, which differentiate the brand. People buy health insurance because it represents protection against the costs of major illness; thus the brand logo symbolises nurturing, peace of mind, support at a time when one needs it the most. Vibrant colours, red and green, are used and visual material is interwoven with text on the website to convey a feeling of energy and activity. Brand values relate to wellness, dynamism, fulfilment, reflected in the slogan 'more power to your health'. According to the marketing manager, advertising is 'anti-category'.

In the insurance market, the ideal customer is one who is unlikely to claim against their insurance. Yet, Vivas Health actively encourages their customers to make a claim. Younger customers in particular want to pay for what they are most likely to use, such as laser eye surgery. According to the marketing director, offering extra benefits to the customers – developing added-value insurance plans – has helped the company create a 'bonded customer'. Churn rate is not a problem for the company. Creating an emotional bond with the consumer can be difficult in a product category that is viewed with disinterest by many consumers. Research conducted by the Health Insurance Authority in 2003 found that many consumers never read the information sent to them by their insurer. However, Vivas Health appeals to a distinct type of customer.

Focus group research shows that their customers are very loyal, and once they are satisfied with their initial encounter with the company, they spread positive word-of-mouth advertising.

Market Segmentation

According to the marketing director, the company attracts the 'early adopters, individuals who are well informed, savvy, empowered ... they are people who tend to be early adopters in a number of categories such as telephone, mortgage, health.'

The market was segmented according to the following factors:

- Demographics (age, gender, occupation, income, family life cycle stage).
- Behavioural (benefits sought, attitudes towards health, predisposition to switch).
- Psychographics (lifestyle, personality).

Age and gender are important segmentation variables; for instance, younger customers are less likely to claim for catastrophic illness. Anecdotal evidence suggests that females are more health conscious than males. Male consumers do not need cover for maternity benefits. The names of the plans were carefully chosen to suggest benefits: for instance, the 'me plan' was designed for a lifestyle without the responsibilities of parenthood; and the 'we plan' is aimed at families and parents-to-be and includes benefits such as three days post-natal home help, child counselling and speech therapy.

Pre-disposition to switch is an important segmentation variable. Most of Vivas Health's customers come direct to the company from either VHI or BUPA, with 70 per cent of the subscribers coming from VHI and 30 per cent of them from BUPA. According to the marketing director, consumer behaviour has evolved considerably, which surprised her, given that the Health Insurance Authority survey in 2003 found that only 6 per cent of the consumers surveyed had switched. The switching behaviour can be attributed to the new entrant, the rise of the price-sensitive customer and growing consumer awareness of how easy it is to transfer insurance.[6] Sales promotion has helped the company attract switchers. Analysis of competitors' plans showed that students over the age of

---

[6] The HIA survey 2003 highlighted the need to educate consumers and make them aware that they can transfer between insurers without being subject to additional waiting periods.

eighteen years were charged an adult rate, and Vivas decided to increase the age to twenty-three years, thus families moving from VHI to Vivas Health could make significant savings. Analysis of market trends revealed that students live at home and stay in higher education for longer periods, and many do not enter full-time employment until they are twenty-one years of age. Focus group research revealed that having eighteen years as a cut-off point was contentious. Special promotional offers, such as 50 per cent discount for children and for students up to the age of twenty-three years, sent a strong message to the market that the brand represented value for money.

Founder

Oliver Tattan's decision to enter the PHI market was based very much on a solid business plan. His experience in the industry convinced him that the market for private health care and health insurance was in its infancy in Ireland, and that there was room in the Irish market for a third player. He would appear to have many of the characteristics associated with successful entrepreneurs, being resourceful, an innovative problem solver, hard working, confident and a risk-taker.

Tattan brings a wealth of experience to Vivas Health. He was the co-founder and the CEO of Daon, recognised as the global leader in population biometrics. He served as chief executive of the Irish Trade Board between 1996 and 1998, during which time Ireland's export growth rate rose more than doubled. He has also served as a non-executive director of Forfás, Ireland's industrial policy agency. He previously worked in Germany and Brazil for leading multinationals.

He is a former CEO of VHI Healthcare and contributed significantly to the strategic refocusing of the organisation. Describing himself as a 'gamekeeper turned poacher', his decision to enter the market has upset the well-entrenched traditions of the Irish, not-for-profit, VHI system. Detractors claim that the company engaged in 'cherry picking' – in other words, it targeted the young, healthy members of the population and profited from the absence of an RES when it entered the market in 2004. However, Tattan argues that his company has been quite responsive in meeting the needs and expectations of consumers.

This company has won awards for its quality of customer service. The entry of new insurers to the market has been welcomed by providers of private health care, since it gives consumers more choice. The element of competition serves the provider well by giving them some bargaining power. A health care provider who has many insurance partners has the opportunity to extract higher charges or coverage for more services. Tattan aims to establish strong working relationships with providers and will negotiate on the basis of cost and volume of treatments, quality standards and clinical practices.

Dealing with Competitors

The company strategy is to grow aggressively in the future, and strategic and marketing plans need to be reviewed in the light of a changing marketplace.

A key marketing task is the attraction and retention of customers in a more competitive marketplace. Both VHI and Quinn Healthcare (formerly BUPA Ireland) are innovating to keep rivals at bay. VHI's Life Stages Plan, launched shortly after Vivas Health entered the market, illustrates the trend towards tailoring products for consumers. This plan is designed for individuals who do not envisage a need for coverage in high-tech hospitals where cardiac procedures are performed, but who want coverage for day-to-day expenses, including maternity care, visits to dentists, doctors and alternative practitioners. Vivas Health considers that its innovative approach towards business will keep it one step ahead of the competition.

Although innovation is a feature of the insurance sector, it can be difficult to decide which areas to invest in and which to ignore. Should more cosmetic surgeries and treatments, dental care, GP coverage and outpatient coverage be offered? Should greater protection be provided from out-of-pocket expenditure associated with major illness? Should a 'whole-life' or 'preventative' approach to health be encouraged? Irish insurers are looking with interest at developments in other markets. In South Africa, health reward plans have been developed, which reward subscribers for leading healthy lifestyles, for instance, undergoing regular screening, smoking cessation and joining a gym. However, the Irish health insurance market is a highly regulated one and insurers are precluded from adopting price discrimination tactics. As a small company, Vivas Health has a limited marketing budget and, like every insurer, it has to balance tensions between attracting customers and attracting a high frequency of claims.

Customer satisfaction lies at the heart of marketing. Research suggests that subscribers are not knowledgeable about health insurance and that consumer expectations are often unrealistic. The Health Insurance

Authority (HIA) survey in 2003 revealed that people did not know what plan they were on, the benefits of the plan or for what they were paying. Many insurance plans require the subscriber to contribute a certain amount towards their medical expenses, known as the excess. However, many consumers only educate themselves about the coverage they have taken out when they need to make a claim. The issue of under-insured consumers is of growing concern. The latest study by the HIA (2005*a*) found that 10 per cent of claimants were dissatisfied with the way in which their claim was handled, with the main reason cited relating to expectations not being met and treatments not being covered. Thus, bringing clarity to insurance plans, fulfilling promises and offering a high level of customer care are seen as the keys to long-term business prosperity.

The marketing department undertakes focus group research on a regular basis. Focus group research is seen as a good medium for exploring the reaction of different segments to the company's marketing strategies. It gives the company the opportunity to explore people's motivations for taking out health insurance, test their reactions to new insurance benefits and advertising concepts and help them deal with adverse comments.

Upcoming Management Meeting

Vivas Health has its own direct sales force, responsible for dealing with corporate business. Research suggests that this segment treats health insurance plans as commodities, and cost savings are the motivating factor for many switchers. Employers play an important role in sponsoring health coverage as a work-related benefit, and employees who buy into a group scheme normally obtain a discount of 10 per cent. BUPA Ireland benefited from the growth of multinationals in Ireland when it entered the market in 1997. A key issue for the management team is the development of a marketing strategy that will result in greater market penetration of the corporate sector.

After reviewing the financial performance of the company, Oliver Tattan has to decide on future strategy. Targeting the consumer market entails brand-building and he has reservations about continuing to spend substantial amounts of money on advertising. Oliver believes that the corporate market will generate a higher volume of business and will ultimately be more profitable. He believes that, with his experience and his contacts in the high-technology sector, he could take on the task of building relationships with the corporate sector. He feels confident and enthusiastic about the future. He decided to call a management meeting to select the most effective strategy for expanding into the corporate market.

References

Berry, L., Mirobito, A., Williams, S. and Davidoff, F. (2006), 'A Physicians Agenda for Partnering with Employers and Insurers: Fresh Ideas', *Mayo Clinic Proceedings*, 81(12), 1592–1607.

Bowie, R. and Adams, G. (2004), 'Financial and Management Practice in a Voluntary Medical Insurance Company in the Developed World', background paper for *Conference on Private Health Insurance in Developing Countries*, Wharton Business School, 15–16 March 2005.

Bryce, D. and Dyer, J. (2007), 'Strategies to Crack Well-Guarded Markets', *Harvard Business Review*, May, 2–9.

Deeble, J. (2003), *The Private Health Insurance Rebate*, report to the State and Territory Health Ministers, Canberra: NCEPH, ANU.

Department of Health and Children (2007), *Report of the Market Review Group: A Business Appraisal of Private Health Insurance in Ireland*, Dublin.

Department of Health and Children (2003), *Audit of Structures and Functions on the Health System* (prospectus report), Dublin.

Doyle, G. (2006), 'Innovations in Accounting in Health Care: A Public/Private Comparison', paper presented at the *Irish Academy of Management Conference*, UCC, September 2006.

Evans, R.G. (1974), 'Supplier-Induced Demand: Some Empirical Evidence and Implications' in M. Perlman (ed.), *The Economics of Health and Medical Care*, London: Palgrave Macmillan, 162–72.

Government of Ireland (1999), *The White Paper on Private Health Insurance*, Dublin.

Health Insurance Authority (HIA) (2005), *The Private Health Insurance Market in Ireland*, study undertaken by Insight Statistical Consulting.

Health Insurance Authority (HIA) (2005a), *Report of the HIA to the Tánaiste and Minister for Health and Children on the Commencement of Risk Equalisation Payments*, December 2005.

Health Insurance Authority (HIA) (2003), *Assessment of Risk Equalisation and Competition in the Irish Health Insurance Market: Final Report*, York Health Economics Consortium.

Health Insurance Authority (HIA) (2003*a*), *The Private Health Insurance Market in Ireland*, study undertaken by Amárach Consulting.

Health Policy Consensus Group (2003), *Step by Step Reform*, study undertaken by Civitas, UK.

Hindle, D. and McAuley, I. (2004), 'The Effects of Increased Private Health Insurance: A Review of the Evidence', *Australian Health Review*, 28(1), 119–38.

Jacobs, R. and Goddard, M. (2002), 'Trade-offs in Social Health Insurance Systems', *International Journal of Social Economics*, 29(11), 861–75.

Kim, W. and Mauborgne, R. (1999), 'Creating New Market Space', *Harvard Business Review*, January–February, 83–93.

Nichols, L. and O'Malley, A. (2006), 'Hospital Payment Systems: Will Payers Like the Future Better Than the Past?', *Health Affairs*, 25(1), 81–93.

Organisation for Economic Cooperation and Development (OECD) (2004), *Private Health Insurance in Ireland: A Case Study*, Health Working Paper No. 10, Paris: OECD.

Organisation for Economic Cooperation and Development (OECD) (2004*a*), *Private Health Insurance in OECD Countries*, Paris: OECD.

Organisation for Economic Cooperation and Development (OECD) (1990), *Health Care Systems in Transition*, Paris: OECD.

Porter, M., and Teisberg, E. (2006), *Redefining Health Care: Creating Value-Based Competition on Results*, Harvard: Harvard Business School Press.

Porter, M. and Teisberg, E. (2004), 'Redefining Competition in Health Care', *Harvard Business Review*, June, 2–15.

Robinson, J. (2003), 'Hospital Tiers in Health Insurance: Balancing Consumer Choice with Financial Incentives', *Health Affairs*, January–June, 135–45.

Segal, L. (2004), 'Why It Is Time to Review the Role of Private Health Insurance in Australia', *Australian Health Review*, 27(1), 3–15.

Sheridan, V. (2006), 'The Future of Private Health Care in Ireland – The Insurer's View', presentation given by Vincent Sheridan, CEO, VHI Healthcare, at the *National Private Healthcare Conference*, 5 April 2006, Dublin.

Simonet, D. (2004), 'Managed Care: US Experience and European Initiatives', *Journal of Generic Medicines*, 1(4) 322–35.

Wiley, M. (2005), 'The Irish Health System: Developments in Strategy, Structure, Funding and Delivery Since 1980', *Health Economics*, 14(1), 169–95.

Worz, M. and Foubister, T. (2005), *Mapping Health Services Access – National and Cross-Border Issues* (*Health ACCESS – Phase 1*), summary report, Berlin University of Technology, and London School of Economics and Political Science.

CHAPTER 10

Bulmers Original Cider: A Case in Strategic Repositioning

Paul Ryan, Mike Moroney and Will Geoghegan[1]
J.E. Cairnes School of Business and Economics,
National University of Ireland, Galway

Introduction

It was 2002, and the apples were maturing in the orchards that supplied the raw material for Bulmers, the brand that had become synonymous with cider in Ireland. For Brendan McGuinness, the managing director of Bulmers for more than a quarter of a century, the harvest time always prompted reflection on past developments and future challenges. Looking back, he could derive considerable satisfaction from the repositioning of the company's original vintage cider from a cheap, down-market drink with a poor image, to being one of the premium and most popular alcoholic beverages of Ireland. The transformation in the company itself had been no less impressive.

However, Brendan McGuinness was not one to dwell long on past successes. The drinks industry in Ireland, as elsewhere, was dynamic, and the nature and scale of change presented many challenges to Bulmers, externally in its markets and internally within the company. There were two issues that particularly occupied the thoughts of Brendan McGuinness and his management team. Firstly, the successful repositioning of the company's core product brought its own challenge, that of continued domestic market growth for original vintage cider.

[1] The authors wish to acknowledge Bulmers and in particular the interviewees for their time, help, guidance and support while researching and compiling this case study. Information in the case study is based on interviews carried out from 2001–2. This case study is intended solely as a basis for class discussion. It is not intended to illustrate either effective or ineffective management.

Furthermore, for the first time, the company confronted the issue of significant expansion into overseas markets. Secondly, changing market tastes had indicated the need for a new version of the original vintage cider, with lower calories and a lighter taste.

It was clear to Brendan McGuinness that the implications of these challenges were potentially as significant as the previous repositioning of the company's core product. It was important to embrace the changes that would result from these challenges. However, from experience, Brendan McGuinness also knew that the appropriate lessons of the past needed to be carried into new areas of business.

Company Background and History

Bulmers Co. is the leading manufacturer of cider in Ireland. Its activities began in 1935, when a Clonmel native, William Magner, decided to produce the drink commercially in Dowds Lane, Clonmel. In 1937, he joined forces with the established English cider maker H.P. Bulmer and Co. In 1949, Magner retired from the firm and the name Bulmers came to the fore. In 1964, it changed its name to Showerings (Ireland) Ltd and moved its operations to Annerville, which is located about three miles from the centre of Clonmel town. It is currently one of the main employers of the regional town of Clonmel with 470 people in its ranks. In 1999, it further showed its commitment to future growth with a €24.4 million extension, including a €12.7 million bottling line, a new 75-unit tank farm with a storage capacity of 16.5 million litres, fully automated processing facilities and a new 75,000 sq. ft warehouse. It announced further plans in 2001 for another plant increase in the magnitude of €25.4 million.

In 2001, the company changed its name back to Bulmers to reflect the importance of the brand to the company and to further heighten its profile among the general public and licensed trade. However, Bulmers cider is not the only brand produced in the Clonmel plant. It also manufactures Strongbow Cider, Linden Village Cider, Samsons Cider, Ritz Crisp Dry Perry, Cidona, Britvic Orange Juices (orange, pineapple, grapefruit, tomato, tomato cocktail) and Britvic Orange 55.

Repositioning Bulmers

The image of cider in the late eighties was deplorable. It was thought of as cheap and strong in alcohol, and was associated with binge drinking and unruly behaviour. It served as a convenient scapegoat for the alcohol abuse problems of the time. This poor image also existed amongst the licensed trade and many publicans refused to stock the drink because of this perceived image problem. Added to this, it had low margins and showed little promise of future growth.

Bulmers decided to start off its marketing campaign in 1988 with a strategy of drawing parallels with the beer industry. They initially tried to position the product as a beer, using rather tacky advertising such as ZZ Top type imagery aimed at the binge drinker, reinforced with rather coarse poster slogans. This approach did not do anything for the brand or the correction of the image problems that it was suffering from. As Managing Director Brendan McGuinness recalled:

> Clearly, the first attempt to reposition cider as beer failed and it was out of that we said let's get back to basics and the basics were telling us that it was all about tradition, naturalness and heritage. Those are our properties.

From this early failure, Brendan McGuinness and his management team learned a very valuable lesson: cider was not beer and that trying to fool the consumer through a smokescreen of advertising portraying it as such was not going to work. Through an extensive marketing research effort, they were able to identify several key attributes of the product. These would serve as the creative platform that they built upon. Cider has several qualities that beer does not possess. It is natural and made from apples. As Colin Gordon (the marketing director from 1989 to 1994) stated:

> Apples growing and then being crushed, wow, brilliant! It is not as if it's a funny thing that takes place with chemistry in the background. Apples grow, apples get crushed, and it gets bottled ... there you go more or less. Well yes, that is it essentially. Leave aside all the consumers and all the research that we did, even just watching the whole process gave you that kind of confidence that, you know, this is something that you could get a lot of movement out of.

Cider is also seen as being a very traditional product that has been around for a long time (having been introduced to Britain by the druids and further perfected by the Romans and the Norman invaders). This also led Bulmers to believe in a sense of heritage that beer did not have. Beer could be seen as relatively modern and artificial compared to wine and cider. However, none of these points of differentiation had been inculcated in the mindset of the consumers. Brendan McGuinness noted this fact:

> We did a lot of research at the time that showed that cider in general had enough properties that beer did not have. It was seen as natural and was made with apples. It was seen as being a very traditional product that had been around for a long time. [It was] traditional in the terms you know wine was

traditional, whereas beer was new. It was seen as having heritage as a category and it was out of that that we said, 'Well, what are our points of difference to beer? Let's focus on tradition, natural and heritage as our creative platform.'

Key research carried out by Bulmers' marketing department showed that people were put off by the product's negative image and its adverse effects. Bulmers at this time had colloquial labels such as 'lunatic juice' or 'rocket fuel', and this was in part due to the high alcohol content of the drink. Nevertheless, the marketing department discovered that the public would not like to see the drink removed from the marketplace. Essentially, people had a certain regard for the product but abhorred the image and baggage that came with it. This research also allowed management of Bulmers to identify the faults in its previous strategy of positioning the product head to head with beer and highlighted the fact that it was too big a challenge to try to convert all the major drinkers to cider drinkers. The fact was acknowledged that this would never happen, so the company now looked at their own consumers. They established three varieties of Bulmers drinker: the first being the regular core drinker, the second being the regular repertoire drinker and the third being the occasional repertoire drinker. The regular core drinker drank cider the majority of the time due to its taste and alcohol strength. The regular repertoire drinker was identified as the kind of consumer who went out to play a football match on a Wednesday night and started off on Bulmers before moving on to Guinness after two or three pints, simply using Bulmers for the refreshment value. The final category that they identified was that of the occasional repertoire drinker who only drank Bulmers when he was in the countryside or when the sun shone on a Sunday afternoon.

Colum Carey (the managing director of The Research Centre, a research company engaged by Bulmers) summarised the approach to the classification of cider drinkers thus:

> Instead of saying 'all or nothing', you started to say, 'Just let me hang out with you sometimes.' Rather than have a gang that insists that you either hang around with them all the time or you are not part of the gang, this was, 'No, you can hang around with us on Tuesday or whenever, you can play football with this group, your old college mates are that group, the friends you grew up with on the street are that group, your wife's friends are that group. You don't need to bring them all together into the party and you don't have to choose between them.'

Now that Bulmers had identified their drinkers and separated them into categories, the problem now faced was how were they going to expand this circle and bring in more consumers? Management decided that, rather than trying to make everyone a regular core drinker, they would first attempt to move people from the occasional repertoire bracket to regular repertoire, and then from regular repertoire to regular core drinker. The idea was, as Colin Gordon (the marketing director) said, 'to move the centre out all the time, try to make the centre the bigger part all the time'.

Bulmers could also look to learn from the success of Guinness regarding product positioning using such attributes as tradition and culture. Bulmers then identified a gap at the start of the nineties when Guinness went off in a new direction, forsaking its image of tradition, naturalness and culture. At this time, Guinness pursued a variety of strategies aimed at positioning their product as 'cool and hip' rather than emphasising the ingredients and heritage of the product. Brendan McGuinness cited the fact that, 'We almost moved into all of that ground that Guinness used to occupy and, let's be honest, that was helpful.'

Image Makeover

Simultaneously, the poor image of cider was a critical issue that Bulmers management needed to address. Colum Carey recalls that, 'The image was the tail on the kite that was pulling the kite down, so you had to cut that free so that it could soar.' The first element addressed was the image of cider as having very high strength. This was compounded by the sort of adverse coverage that cider was receiving in the media in this regard. Newspaper headlines such as 'Cider crazed youths', 'Residents at war on cider parties and vandals', 'Cider thugs started library blaze' and 'Cider party turned nasty, court told' were commonplace. Needless to say this did little for the Bulmers image in the mindset of the general public.

Brendan McGuinness identified the problem thus:

I think a lot of the poor image had probably come from the history of cider being very cheap. Historically, it was always very high strength. We were getting very bad headlines in the media. Clearly when we investigated a lot of those cases it was apparent that just alcohol was involved. It was underage drinking. Today it would be Alco-pops getting the brunt of it, but cider was the convenient scapegoat of the day. Where was it all coming from? It really started life as a very marginal category. It started life at very high alcohol level and it was very cheap. It was sold primarily in flagons and it was for thirst-quenching purposes. Also, the strength was never really controlled in the early days. You could get cider at 4 per cent alcohol one day and another day you could be getting it at 8.5 per cent and that is how it sort of got its reputation of 'Johnny jump up' and 'drives you crazy' and stuff like that. So there is a whole history of it being a cottage industry, which wasn't very well controlled.

The only way to resolve that was to go through what we call a total repositioning exercise and that involved a whole range of initiatives. Obviously, we had problems with consumer attitudes to cider, we had huge problems with perceived trade attitudes to cider. [Shops] wouldn't stock it or were reluctant to stock it because of the type of consumers it attracted. We also had a problem with the media in that any form of alcohol abuse by the young was attributed to cider so we addressed these three areas. To do that, clearly advertising was an issue and public relations was an issue. We had to look at the product, we had to look at the pricing and packaging. So I would summarise it by saying that every single element of the marketing mix needed a remake.

It is difficult to capture in a short period the extent of the remake the brand went through and the consistency with which we followed all that. In terms of the product itself, it was a 5.5 per cent or 6 per cent alcohol product, high alcohol, so, on a phased basis, we reduced the alcohol level down to the current 4.5 per cent to bring it in line with beer.

In 1998, the Cider Industry Council (CIC) was set up with a substantial initial fund of €125,000. Its aims (as stated on the website) were:

- To encourage an appreciation of cider amongst responsible and mature drinkers.
- To encourage the use of cider in cooking as an accompaniment to food.
- To help combat underage drinking.

Although claiming to represent the major companies engaged in the production, distribution and marketing of cider in Ireland, Bulmers provided CIC with 95 per cent of its funding. Bulmers moved to get all the other industry players involved in an effort to camouflage the fact that they were the principal drivers behind the scheme. The CIC played a very important role for all of the industry members in changing the media and consumer attitudes to the product. Colin Gordon reflected on the motives for the creation of the CIC:

We were always scared that a misreported accident attributed to cider would have a seriously detrimental impact on the whole business. Trade could have delisted us and whatever ... so everything we did was fundamentally around how to continually improve the image, where we could bring truth into the public domain, truth around underage drinking, truth in terms of what the causes of underage drinking were, as well as what the products were that were actually involved in the underage drinking scene at the time. Truth also in terms of how any so-called 'park parties' and so on were reported, because regularly they were cited as 'cider parties'.

Figure 10.1 illustrates how effective the establishment of the CIC proved over time in reducing the negative associations with cider in the minds of the general populace.

Figure 10.1: Negative Media Stories about Cider

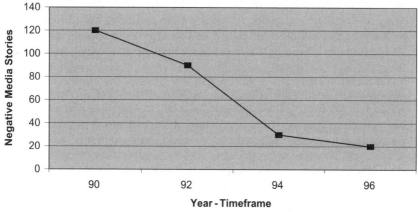

Source: Cider Industry Council

Further Marketing Initiatives

Other efforts to reposition Bulmers in the mind of the consumer were used. The first of these measures was to repackage the product to bring it more clearly in line with premium product industry norms. First of all, this involved introducing the product in draught, long-neck bottle and can forms. Another major step in this strategy was to discontinue with the two-litre plastic flagon, which had become renowned for underage drinking and its relative inexpensiveness. The major success of this repackaging was the introduction of the glass pint bottle traditionally served with a glass of ice, which has become synonymous with Bulmers in Ireland. Brendan McGuinness highlighted the emergence of this strategy:

> I think we recognised how some people were beginning to use it and developed that as opposed to starting out from the very outset saying we wanted to create this concept. We noticed that people were beginning to use the pint bottle over ice as a refreshment proposition. We recognised that and started

building on it. We upgraded the packaging and put nice foil packaging on it, took it out of the 'Sunday morning hangover cure' area and into the 'occasional refreshment' area and it is now supported separately with advertising. To me that is a good example of recognising a trend that was beginning to emerge and grabbing it and taking ownership of it and developing it and bringing it to a position where the pint bottle is about one-third of our business.

Bulmers also decided to stop the in-pub promotion policy, which was deemed by the management to show Bulmers in a bad light. The assumption was made that, by giving out free Bulmers in pubs and bars, Bulmers were increasing the negative image through encouraging drunkenness. This was stopped completely and the money was utilised elsewhere in the marketing budget. One of the measures taken in attempting to upgrade Bulmers' image was the sponsorship of golf events. Colin Gordon recalled:

> I was very conscious that you went into trade and regularly the bar owner would tell you that, 'I'm not going to have that in here because I've heard a bad story,' or, 'I've had a bad experience.' A lot of it was driven by the promotions that were run. The promotions on cider tended to be a volume- driven activity rather than an image-building activity and therefore, for a lot of publicans, as indeed consumers, their only real experience of cider was people drinking it and getting too much of it, which was negative. We withdrew all promotions to the trade, every single thing and we put all the money into image correction.

Another issue addressed was the relatively low price of Bulmers in relation to the other major beers. The price was increased to reflect its new premium product positioning. However, this was not done overnight. The late 1980s and early 1990s was a time of very high inflation in Ireland. This allowed Bulmers to employ a phased increase in the price of their product over an eight-year period. Initially, it was brought up to the level of stout prices. Next it was increased to the price of ale and then to the same level as lager. In 1994 and 1996, the Irish government introduced two selective duty increases, which meant that cider prices went up but beer was not subject to this. This allowed Bulmers to pass on these duties to the consumer and again increase the price of the brand. This resulted in a position where, from 1996, Bulmers sold at a premium to lager.

Advertising Consistency

One aspect of the Bulmers strategy that has proved unflagging during the years has been the commitment to consistency of message. This has been achieved through several mediums, all portraying the same messages – those of naturalness, tradition and heritage. Bulmers have kept the theme of time in all of their advertisements. It initially began as 'Nothing added but time' (Scrumpy Jack, the English cider company, humorously responded to this with their own campaign slogan of 'Nothing added but apples'). This proved to be very successful for Bulmers. The next campaign focused on 'All in its own good time'. This in turn was superseded by 'Time dedicated to you'.

Colin Gordon reflected on the inception of the idea and the snowballing consequences:

> Once you had the copy line, it actually became unstoppable what you could put in against it. So, 'Nothing added but time' allowed you to be natural. What is natural? Well standing in the middle of a river fishing on your own is as natural as you can think of. You have time; you have all day to fish. You can pick on the tradition, the craft, heritage, all to do with time. You could pick on the absence of things because of the 'nothing added' part of the byline. It really became a way of having one central ad and then having loads of different themes to address different consumers in different ways to try and tweak peoples' emotional responses to the image, giving Bulmers absolutely something unique within the alcohol business.

John Keogh (Bulmers marketing director 1994–2001), however, noted how the exercise in stability could be a struggle over time:

> The people who worked on the brand changed over time, the creatives changed, the marketing people changed, the account handlers changed in the agency, the administrators in the Cider Industry Council, everyone. I remember worrying every time there was change, particularly on the creative side, that the new team would want to do something new. You know, 'Ah, for Christ's sake. You've been doing that for the last … you can't keep doing that, you've got to do something new, you got to challenge the customers.'

John Keogh thus commented on the process of educating the new management team on the consistent nature of the Bulmers marketing plan:

> You do need to get somebody into the mindset of the brand, not the mindset of 'I'm the new broom, I'm going to do something distinctly different to what was done before and I'm gonna take this brand on to the next level'. You'd want them to know a Bulmers concept, to know instantly whether it was right or wrong.

The dedication (as in 'Time dedicated to you') aspect of the campaign highlighted that single-minded devotion to success is needed to be first in a particular field. Bulmers drew a parallel between itself and the person that is determined to succeed, using many symbols and legends from different skills and professions. For example, Jules Léotard, the world's first flying trapeze artist, is depicted in one of their advertisements. Another advertisement focused on the 'ski jump', featuring Sondre Nordheim, the first person to 'fly' through the air.

The second creative platform added was that of 'craft'. The advertising reflected the brand's mood and style, but successfully added another aspect to the brand's character, focusing on the time and craft necessary to produce the product. The aim of this constant brand building and learning was to allow the Bulmers brand to evolve while, at the same time, retaining the initial focus and qualities that were identified at the outset of the campaign.

The set of initiatives involved in the repositioning strategy proved to be immensely successful in the enhancement of the image attached to Bulmers cider. They significantly changed the image of a product that looked to be in decline. The result was a huge increase in sales of cider (see Figure 10.2), of which Bulmers, as the dominant market leader, was the chief beneficiary.

Future Challenges

By 2002, the repositioning of Bulmers in the domestic market was largely complete. The fruits of the company's success were clearly evident. Bulmers' share of the Irish beer market stood at more than 10 per cent from a meagre 2 per cent in 1988. Moreover, the consumption of cider in 2002 was an impressive 55 million litres (equivalent to 15 litres per head per annum) and was worth more than €200 million annually. Of this total, Bulmers accounted for the vast proportion. It commanded 89 per cent of the 'on-trade' market, which in turn accounted for some 75 per cent of total cider sales.

Such success brought its own issues. It was evident to management that continuing to grow in Ireland at the pace of the recent past would pose challenges. Further gains in the domestic beer market would be hard-won but, nonetheless, achievable. The hegemony of Guinness was again an issue, in terms both of long-established consumer preferences and the marketing and distribution muscle of the St James' Gate giant. Beer consumption in Ireland was in decline. At the same time, sparked by media reports focusing on late night street violence involving young people, elements of public opinion were pushing for greater regulation of alcohol advertising and pub opening hours.

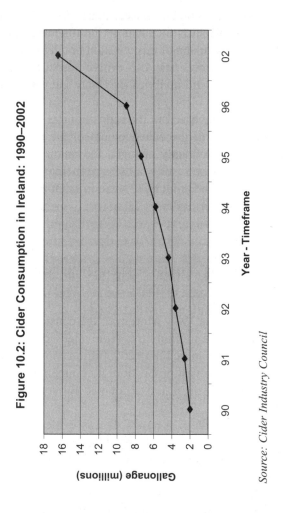

Figure 10.2: Cider Consumption in Ireland: 1990–2002

Source: Cider Industry Council

Against this background, Brendan McGuinness and his team had begun to pursue the expansion of Bulmers original vintage cider into overseas markets. A successful product roll-out had already taken place in the USA and the UK. Initial results from both markets were very encouraging. This provided a high incentive to enter the Spanish and German markets.

Apart from the general issues of market share and continued domestic and international growth, shifts in consumer preferences were also exercising the thoughts of the management of Bulmers. Market research had highlighted a desire among certain consumers, many female, for a different version of Bulmers Original Vintage Cider that was lighter in taste and lower in calories. This clearly pointed to an opportunity to develop a new market segment, one that traditionally had not been heavy consumers of the product. A decision was made to launch Bulmers Light, involving the use of pub endorsements as a marketing tool.

While this opportunity was potentially an exciting one, the company was aware that it was not without risk. As with any modified version of an established core product, Bulmers Light would need to quickly establish its own identity and market position. Warm summer weather during the introduction period was critical for early consumer acceptance. The record of recent Irish summers was not auspicious in this regard. In addition, it was uncertain what effect, if any, the introduction of Bulmers Light would have on the core Original Vintage Cider product, which had been so successfully repositioned by the company.

CHAPTER 11

Cloon Keen Atelier: A Passion for Scent

Ann M. Torres[1]

J.E. Cairnes School of Business and Economics,
National University Ireland, Galway

Introduction

Margaret Mangan, the co-founder of Cloon Keen Atelier,[2] always had a passion for scent. She believes scent forms the heart of her products whether candles, soaps, creams or lotions. Although these types of products are commonly found in other shops, Cloon Keen's products are *not* ordinary. Cloon Keen develops high-quality products where fragrance, design and functionality are blended carefully to create a mood of authenticity and pleasure.

The challenge for Cloon Keen, a small operator, is to develop a strategy that reinforces its chosen market position as it develops new products and expands into other markets. However, Cloon Keen is facing robust competition; some of these rivals have a powerful competitive base because they are long established, highly regarded and well resourced.

Background

Margaret Mangan and Julian Checkley experimented with candle making during Christmas of 2001. It was at a time when Julian, a special effects

[1] The author wishes to acknowledge Cloon Keen Atelier for its support while researching and compiling this case study. Information in the case study is based on interviews with Margaret Mangan carried out in February 2007. This case study is intended solely as a basis for class discussion. It is not intended to illustrate either effective or ineffective management.

[2] Atelier is a workshop or studio for an artist, artisan or designer. Cloon Keen is an anglicised version of cluain caoin, which is Irish for beautiful meadow or beautiful lawn. Cloon Keen is the name of Margaret's family home and the name of a townland in Co. Galway where Margaret's father spent his summers as a child.

model maker, was between film projects, and Margaret, a financial controller with an advertising agency, was looking for a new direction. Margaret read an article in *The Toronto Star* (<http://www.thestar.com>) about the art of candle making and was intrigued; candles were described as a comfort product and an affordable luxury (Korchock 1998). More importantly, Margaret believed hand-crafted candles could provide her with a platform for entering other product markets and developing a lifestyle brand. To test their idea, Margaret and Julian took a stand at the Windsor Christmas Market; to their delight everything sold. In June 2002, Margaret and Julian established Cloon Keen Candles in Galway, Ireland, and began making their hand-poured candles.

Place

In the early days of their start-up, Margaret spent a number of weeks travelling around Ireland to find shops that are a good fit for Cloon Keen candles, primarily high-end gift and craft shops, such as Blarney Woollen Mills (<http://www.blarney.ie>) and Kilkenny Design (<http://www.kilkennydesign.com>), as well as upmarket interior and furniture shops with a modern flair, such as Instore (<http://www.instore.ie>), and Meadows and Byrne (<http://www.meadowsandbyrne.com>). Margaret's sales drive was successful, as she secured orders from over sixty retailers across the country. Margaret attributes this auspicious beginning to offering retail buyers something new for the increasingly sophisticated Irish consumer who seeks out superior modern design, but who still appreciates handmade, quality Irish products. To their credit, Cloon Keen has retained 90 per cent of their original retailers. They also sell through a limited number of exclusive gift shops in England, Spain and Germany.[3] Despite Cloon Keen's achievement with select retailers, the firm is shifting its focus away from wholesaling to developing its own retail initiatives, which are ultimately more profitable. Cloon Keen does not have a dedicated website, but it is possible to buy Cloon Keen candles from several online retailers.[4]

In August 2005, Cloon Keen opened its retail premises, Cloon Keen Atelier, at No. 3 Kirwin's Lane, located in the heart of Galway City. In

---

[3] Cloon Keen sells to ten retailers in the UK, a chain of fifteen shops in Spain and two retailers in Germany.

[4] Several online retailers who sell Cloon Keen candles are: Buy Gifts Here (<http://www.buygiftshere.com>), iWoman (<http://www.iwoman.ie>), Sophie Perks Ward (<http://www.perksward.co.uk>) and Tess Designs (<http://www.tessdesigns.co.uk>).

designing the shop interior, Julian took particular care in developing an atmosphere to reflect the look and feel of the Cloon Keen brand. The shop has a warm, modern look that is clean and uncluttered, but not quite minimalist. Julian, who refurbished the shop himself, created a unique space 'fusing modern design and functionality together with traditional features, such as wooden beams and exposed stonework. [Margaret and Julian wanted to generate an ambience] to attract consumers who enjoy the conveniences of modern life, but still appreciate the objects, fragrances and sensations that filled the homes of yesteryear' (Mangan and Checkley 2006: 1).

An opening in Ceardlann Spiddal Craft Village (<http://www. ceardlann.com>) in July 2006 was an opportunity for Cloon Keen to move their production operations from Rossaveal to Spiddal, Co. Galway. Ceardlann, conveniently located fifteen kilometres from Galway City, is also a scenic tourist destination where visitors can see Cloon Keen's master chandlers pour candles and can then purchase the finished product from the adjoining shop. Although the studio shop reflects aspects found in the Kirwan's Lane venue, the Ceardlann retail venue was tailored to showcase the craft studio and its environs. The effect is sufficiently similar to recognise Cloon Keen's *look*, but suitably different to intrigue customers with variety. Margaret and Julian endeavour to open three to five Cloon Keen Atelier shops over the next seven years; they aspire to apply this design concept, so as to avoid 'cookie-cutter sameness' among their venues.

Product

Cloon Keen's anchor products are their hand-finished candles. The firm employs the expertise of three perfumers to create fragrances exclusively for their range of thirty-five scented candles; they do not use generic scents. The quality of fragrance is especially important. Cloon Keen avails of authentic aromas, which do not smell harsh, bitter or like a chemical. Superior quality wax and cotton wicks are used to ensure optimum absorption and diffusion of fragrance. The craft for producing premium candles requires a highly scientific approach. For example, each scent requires a different wick to ensure the candle burns effectively; spicy scents require a thicker cotton wick than sweet scents. Additionally, softer wax is more effective in scented candles, as harder wax poorly disperses fragrance. Cloon Keen assembles 300 to 400 units per week, which increases to 1,500 to 2,000 units per week during the busiest period between September and December. Table 11.1 outlines Cloon Keen's sales turnover for candles since its establishment.

Table 11.1: Cloon Keen Atelier's Sales Turnover for Candles

Year	Wholesale Unit Sales	Cloon Keen's Retail Unit Sales
2002	9,230	–
2003	22,189	–
2004	20,049	–
2005	22,313	–
2006	22,846	5,000

Source: Cloon Keen

Cloon Keen produces two lines of premium-scented candles; these candles provide the maximum concentration of fragrance, with burning times of fifty to sixty-five hours. The gourmet collection, priced at €13.95 per unit, is packaged in tins and is a more playful, funky product. It comes in scents such as Basil and Lime Pesto, Crazy as a Coconut, Just Baked Apple Pie, Fresh Linen and Swedish Sauna.[5] Irish consumers generally prefer the softer floral scents in the gourmet range, such as Wild Irish Lavender, Galway Honeysuckle and Bluebells of Barna Woods; these floral scents are among Cloon Keen's best sellers.

The spa collection of luxury candles, priced at €14.95 per unit, came into production in 2005. This line offers more sophisticated, subtle scents, such as Blackcurrant, Exotic Woods and Fig Tree.[6] Moreover, its sumptuous packaging reflects its more sensuous, indulgent qualities. Customers often buy candles from the spa collection to give as gifts.

Currently, the majority of Cloon Keen's sales are achieved through wholesaling their candles to other retail outlets. However, Margaret and Julian established Cloon Keen with the intention that premium-scented

---

[5] The full complement of scents in Cloon Keen's gourmet range are: Aegean Jasmine, Al Fresco, Basil and Lime Pesto, Bluebells of Barna Woods, Christmas Morning, Christmas Pomander, Christmas Pudding, Christmas Tree, Cinnamon Devil, Country Garden Rose, Crazy as a Coconut, Fresh Linen, Galway Honeysuckle, Irish Soda Bread, Grapefruit and Citronella, Hot Mulled Wine, Juicy Melons, Just Baked Apple Pie, Oooh Baby!, Poached Pear, Powder, Saucy Cranberry, Surf's Up!, Swedish Sauna, Wild Irish Lavender and Yummy Vanilla.

[6] The full complement of scents in the spa range is: Blackcurrant, Exotic Woods, Fig Tree, Hyacinth, Lavender Rosemary, Lemon, Lilia de Mer, Lily of the Valley, Rose Tea and White Flowers.

candles would serve as their entrée into providing complementary lifestyle products through their Cloon Keen Atelier shops. Hence, their next product venture is a line of Cloon Keen branded soaps, creams and lotions in four scents: Cassis Leaf, Lavender, Linden Blossom and Wicklow Honey. The prototypes have been in development over the past two years and should be in production by the end of 2007. Considerable care has been taken in developing Cloon Keen's skin care products. Margaret has been extending her expertise by studying an advanced cosmetic science course through the Society of Cosmetic Scientists (<http://www.cosmeticlearning.com>) to ensure that the skin care products are made to the highest standards and with the highest quality ingredients. Other body, bath, hair and skin care products (e.g. hand soap, shower gel, body scrub, bath foam/salts/oil, shampoo and hair conditioner) will be added to their Cloon Keen line as a natural progression. In time, they aspire to creating a signature perfume, which will serve as the brand's hallmark.

Of Cloon Keen's current product mix, 75 per cent is 'devoted to their established range of candles and commissioned handmade accessories, [while] 25 per cent is devoted to high-end body and bath products [that demonstrate] a similar passion for detail, quality and authenticity' (Mangan and Checkley 2006: 1). Some of Cloon Keen's select suppliers are:

Comptoir Sud Pacifique (<http://www.comptoir-sud-pacifique.com>)
La Compagnie de Provence Marseille (<http://www.lcdpmarseille.com>)
Côté Bastide (<http://www.cotebastide.com>)
Cowshed Products (<http://www.cowshedproducts.com/uk>)
Tadé Pays du Levant (<http://www.tade.fr>)
Parfums DelRae (<http://www.parfumsdelrae.com>)

Over time, Margaret and Julian may eliminate these suppliers in favour of showcasing solely Cloon Keen branded skin-care and fragrance products.

Price

Cloon Keen's pricing strategy reflects its positioning as quality producer. However, its prices are more reasonable than products at the most exclusive price points. Margaret and Julian follow a policy of offering exceptionally high quality for the price they charge and regularly monitor rivals' price levels to ensure their products remain competitive. As the brand gains momentum and customers recognise the value its products offer, Cloon Keen would be well positioned to accrue higher profit margins. Nevertheless, Cloon Keen's average sales per square foot is €430 (Mangan and Checkley 2006) and compares favourably with established competitors in the home interiors market, such as Yankee Candle, which earns average sales of €450 per square foot (Yankee Candle 2007). With the implementation of an integrated promotional campaign and the launch of its personal care products, Cloon Keen expects average sales per square foot to increase to €650 (Mangan and Checkley 2006) during the next couple of years. Such a figure would enable Cloon Keen to compete more effectively with personal care competitors, such as The Body Shop, which has an average sales per square foot of €998 (Euromonitor 2006*a*).

Brand

Margaret and Julian believe Cloon Keen's brand values have greatly facilitated in generating word-of-mouth to build a loyal customer base. Cloon Keen's brand is based on offering accessible pricing for superior products, and a unique store experience through its upscale store design, attentive customer service and product presentation. Cloon Keen strives for authenticity in its branding approach. As a speciality retailer, Margaret and Julian are positioning Cloon Keen as a worthy alternative to the high-priced designer brands offered in department stores. The combination of smell, touch and sight in Cloon Keen's retail ambiance is meant to inspire and heighten the customer's experience. Brief descriptions highlighting product benefits and ingredients are presented to provide an information-rich environment in which to educate customers. Attractive merchandise displays, well-designed and aesthetically pleasing product packaging are important in enhancing Cloon Keen's brand image. Cloon Keen generally minimises layers in packaging while striving to maintain a distinctive visual image. Margaret and Julian work hard to convey Cloon Keen's luxurious aspects. The brand colours are black and white, but care is taken to ensure that the brand does not look cheap by carefully selecting the media on which the brand appears.

Promotion

Margaret and Julian avail of traditional media, such as press features in quality news and fashion magazines, such as the *Irish Times Magazine* (<http://www.irishtimes.com>), *Image* (<http://www.image.ie>), *Irish Tatler* (<http://www.harmonia.ie>) and *The Gloss* (<http://www.thegloss.ie>).

Cloon Keen sponsored the launch of the new *Irish Times* building and the *Irish Tatler* magazine in October 2006 by providing candles for the event. Margaret and Julian have found that this type of select sponsorship is fruitful in generating awareness and opportunities for feature articles in the press. Margaret and Julian believe merchandising within the shops, along with the product packaging, have been Cloon Keen's strongest forms of promotion. Other promotional efforts such as the matchbooks given with the purchase and the loyalty cards (i.e. one free candle after ten candles have been purchased) keep the Cloon Keen brand foremost in consumers' minds.

To promote Cloon Keen Atelier, Magaret and Julian are more interested in using electronic (i.e. digital) media, which also generates the opportunity for audience involvement. Interactivity in media is novel to people over thirty years of age but, to younger people, it is expected (Lockhorn 2006). More importantly, for a small- and medium-sized enterprise (SME) such as Cloon Keen, interactivity can facilitate brand objectives and be a powerful tool for eliciting an immediate response from customers (Lockhorn 2006). Internet access has increased significantly among Irish consumers. As of 2006, 50 per cent of the Irish consumers have Internet access in their homes[7] and 44 per cent use the Internet at least once a week (Burns 2006). Cloon Keen aims to build a website, which would not only serve as an online retail environment, but also as a platform for Margaret to initiate her lifestyle blog. The purpose behind a blog is to 'create a community of rapid, informed responses on developments' (McKeon 2007: 20) about Cloon Keen's ethos, brand and products. Blogs may also be a source for stimulating viral marketing (i.e. buzz marketing or electronic word-of-mouth) where customers talk positively amongst themselves about a firm's brand and recommend it to others.

Customer Profile

Even with its limited promotional efforts, Cloon Keen has garnered a loyal customer base, as 80 per cent are repeat customers. Cloon Keen's

---

[7] Note that only 13 per cent of consumers have Internet access through a broadband connection. Men have a slightly higher weekly Internet use at 45 per cent, compared to women at 42 per cent. Younger age groups of sixteen to twenty-five years demonstrate the highest weekly Internet use at 59 per cent, followed by twenty-five to fifty-four years at 48 per cent, and dramatically falling to 17 per cent for those between the ages of fifty-five and seventy-four years (Burns 2006).

marketing efforts primarily target working women aged twenty-five to fifty years, who have traditionally purchased premium scented candles and skin-care products in department stores such as Brown Thomas (<http://www.brownthomas.com>), Debenhams (<http://www.debenhams. com>) and Clerys (<http://www.clerys.ie>). They use these quality products on a daily basis as affordable luxuries. Cloon Keen's loyal customers are well travelled, have reasonably high levels of disposable income and are open to trying new products. Margaret and Julian believe these women are increasingly seeking better pricing without sacrificing high quality and service. Cloon Keen's strategy has also been successful in attracting a broad cross-section of other consumers beyond its primary target, such as metrosexual males,[8] who are attracted to the quality toiletries from among Cloon Keen suppliers, as well as young teenage girls (i.e. young Generation Y[9]), who are attracted to Cloon Keen's gourmet range of scented candles.

Consumer Trends in Personal Care Products

Although Cloon Keen's anchor products are candles, the firm's future developments are in the area of personal care products. Margaret and Julian's vision is for Cloon Keen to become a specialist retailer of personal care products. Prominent market trends influencing consumers' decisions with respect to personal care products are:

- A plethora of new products that avail of food-themed scents and food-based ingredients.
- An increasing consumer demand for natural and organic products created in an ethical manner.
- A new aesthetic approach to bestow eco-conscious products with a more fashionable and chic presentation.
- The elimination of potentially harmful substances in favour of safer, more natural alternatives.

Although traditional floral and spice notes will never go out of style, food-themed and food ingredient products are popular sellers. 'Some products have almost true-to-plate scents that would be hard to discern

---

[8] A metrosexual is defined as an urban male with a strong aesthetic sense, who spends a great deal of time and money on his appearance and lifestyle.

[9] Generation Y, or the Millennial Generation, describes the cohort of people born in the 1980s and the 1990s, immediately after Generation X. However, there is no consensus as to the precise birth years that constitute Generation Y.

from the real thing in a blind sniff test, [where] consumers are hit with those familiar notes that engage the senses' (Summerfield 2005: B10). The popularity of food-scented products is encouraged 'in part that to an overstressed, emotionally frazzled society, food connotes comfort and safety' (La Ferla 2001: 1). These scents are a salve; they make consumers feel cared for and energised. Moreover, food-based scents and ingredients in beauty products are perceived as being healthier and coincide with the burgeoning consumer demand for organic, eco-conscious style (Musselman 2007).

'Passions about the environment are skyrocketing. Simplicity is yearned for and is increasingly a necessity [in products]' (Zimbalist 2007: 35). The growing trend among consumers is an attitude that is more conscientious than conspicuous (Euromonitor 2007). There is a substantial shift in the way consumers buy products; consumption is more reflective and concerned (Euromonitor 2007). Prestigious personal care manufacturers and designers are responding to this trend by supporting environmental organisations and reducing their ecological footprint through planting trees, reducing energy consumption, eliminating unnecessary packaging, as well increasing efforts to recycle and minimise waste (Lennon 2007).

Conscious sensualists are 'women who want to do the right thing for their health and the environment, but not at the cost of living well' (La Ferla 2001: 1). An additional force catering for these conscious sensualists is a new aesthetic approach to product presentation. Although natural, organic and eco-conscious products are in vogue, consumers also want to experience something exceedingly fine. 'If a consumer is really going to use the product, [the consumer] has to feel good about it, but if … the product [is] too costly, or ugly, a consumer might applaud its intentions, but won't buy' (La Ferla 2001: 1). Thus, conscious sensualists want products that are also stylish, edgy and fashionable.

Many working in the industry recognise natural, organic and eco-conscious products are a current trend, but they believe it is an enduring one, and note it is evident in other areas of consumer purchases such as food, fashion, furnishings and transport (Euromonitor 2007). Organic Monitor (<http://www.organicmonitor.com>) estimates European sales of natural and organic personal care products to have increased by more than 20 per cent annually and have exceeded €1 billion in 2006 (Musselman 2007). Increasingly, not only eco-conscious manufacturers but also many other manufacturers throughout the industry are eschewing synthetic chemicals[10] in favour of more natural, plant-based alternatives. This trend for reflective manufacturing accompanies legislation for greater transparency in the substances used in personal care products.

Although few health problems have been linked with personal care products, 'momentum has been building for greater oversight of the chemicals in everyday products, with the European Union and California taking the lead in imposing new rules for monitoring what is in the perfumes, creams, nail polish and hair sprays that are sold' (Singer 2007: 1). Manufacturers are intensifying self-monitoring, but emphasise the ingredients under regulation are not a health risk when applied topically, especially given the small amounts used in personal care products.[11]

Personal Care Market in Ireland

Favourable economic conditions and health consciousness are driving increased consumer spending on discretionary items, particularly in those markets related to beauty, health and wellness; these markets are expected to remain dynamic through to 2015 (Hoffman 2006). Although the Irish grooming market is small, it is advancing rapidly. Irish exporters report personal care items (i.e. toiletries) grew 14 per cent in 2004 (Euromonitor 2005). This highly fragmented market, which includes skin care products, hair care products, colour cosmetics and fragrances, achieved annual sales nationwide in excess of €1.6 billion in 2006 (Euromonitor 2006b). In Ireland, the personal care sector is forecast to grow a further 25 per cent by 2010, reaching a value of over €2 billion (Euromonitor 2006b).

Personal care products or toiletries are a highly intimate purchase; consumers prefer to buy their own products than receive them as gifts. Indeed, toiletries are identified as the least popular Christmas gift to receive (Euromonitor 2006b). In buying their toiletries, Irish consumers demonstrate a strong preference for expensive brands. Evidence of Irish

---

[10] Examples of synthetic chemicals in personal care products are the use of parabens as preservatives as well as foaming agents such as sodium laureth sulphate and sodium lauryl sulphate.

[11] No rigorous large-scale clinical trials have been conducted to indicate that cosmetics trigger major diseases in humans. But some small case reports published in medical journals suggest a few substances used in cosmetics may affect hormone function in humans (Singer 2007).

consumers' desire for luxury products is demonstrated by the 62 per cent increase in premium fragrances since 1998 (Euromonitor 2006*b*). Yet, consumers view personal care products as more than merely vanity products.

Historically, a leading distribution channel for personal care products has been pharmacies, which accounted for 54.5 per cent of sales in 2005 (Datamonitor 2006). While specialist retailers and department stores account for only 18 per cent of personal care product sales (Datamonitor 2006), retailers of personal care products are numerous and individually command a very small portion of the market. For example, Boots the chemist, with 13.7 per cent of the Irish personal care market, had the highest market share among retailers in 2005, while specialist retailers such as The Body Shop and L'Occitane held only 0.7 and 0.4 per cent of the Irish market, respectively (Euromonitor 2006*b*). Overall, supermarkets accounted for 27.5 per cent of sales in 2005 and are becoming more important channels through which to access personal care products (Datamonitor 2006). Supermarket groups that operate as mixed retailers, such as Tesco (<http://www.tesco.ie>) and Dunnes (<http://www.dunnes stores.ie>), are steadily increasing their presence within this market by offering a greater range of branded products as well as introducing their own lines of sophisticated private label brands (Euromonitor 2003, 2007). The supermarkets' heightened interest in this market is unsurprising, as health and beauty retailing is among the most dynamic of Ireland's retail categories.

Skin Care Market in Ireland

As noted, the personal care market encompasses a diverse product range and, through the proliferation of brand extensions and new product developments, this market continues to expand. Cloon Keen's entry into the personal care product market is through its line of Cloon Keen branded scented soaps, creams and lotions. Hence, Cloon Keen is operating within the skin care sector of the personal care market, which incorporates facial, body and hand care products. The Irish skin care sector was valued at €74 million in 2005 and is expected to grow to €94 million by 2010 (see Table 11.2).

Facial care is the largest sub-sector within the Irish skin care market and its growth is driven by technological innovations. These innovations are not mainstream developments and are dominated by well-resourced manufacturers, such as L'Oreal (<http://www.lorealparis.com>) and Nivea (<http://www.nivea.ie>), as well as premium beauty houses, such as Estée

Table 11.2: Irish Retail Sales of Skin Care Product by Sub-sector – Value in €million, 2005–2010

Sector	2005	2006	2007	2008	2009	2010
Facial care	54.9	57.2	59.1	61.0	62.3	63.2
Body care	16.4	18.6	21.1	23.5	28.8	27.7
Hand care	2.8	2.9	3.0	3.0	3.1	3.1
Total skin care	74.1	78.7	83.2	87.5	91.2	94.0

Source: Euromonitor (2006*c*), *Skin Care – Ireland*, London: Euromonitor International, May.

Lauder (<http://www.esteelauder.com>) and Clarins (<http://www.clarins. com>) (Euromonitor 2006*c*). Product innovations increase the level of segmentation within the market. In the longer term, highly specific products may be replaced by more cost-effective, multipurpose products, which are progressively popular in the body care sub-sector.

The body care sub-sector is anticipated to experience the fastest growth within the Irish skin care market. According to Euromonitor, 'Sweet-smelling, enriched premium [body care] products proved to be irresistible to a better educated Irish consumer base that is willing to trade up across pricing gaps to take advantage of these offerings' (2006*c*: 2). Products that have performed well within the Irish body care sector are those that offer value-added benefits, such as intense moisturising, through the addition of natural ingredients such as ginko and shea butter; the addition of vitamins and minerals to promote and maintain healthy skin; and those that offer some cosmetic benefits, such as providing self-tanning with regular use, or toning and firming agents to reduce the appearance of cellulite (Euromonitor 2006*c*). Hence, a multipurpose body lotion with value-added benefits allows busy women to simplify their skin routine and save time. These value-added innovations are highly appealing to Irish consumers who are willing to pay premium prices for desirable attributes.

Competitors

Cloon Keen operates in two overlapping markets: candles and home fragrances and the personal care market. The candles and home fragrances market is where Cloon Keen originated, but Margaret and Julian are aiming to position Cloon Keen in the skin care sector of the personal care market. The personal care market is highly competitive. Cloon Keen has numerous rivals that manufacture functionally similar products, sold through a variety of channels, including pharmacies, department stores, supermarkets and catalogues. Moreover, many of these rivals have substantially greater resources, higher name recognition and sell through broader distribution channels.

Cloon Keen also competes directly against speciality retailers of personal care products, including international chains such as The Body Shop and L'Occitane, as well as local speciality retailers, such as the Burren Perfumery. The number of speciality retail outlets selling personal care products has increased significantly in the recent years, and the lack of significant barriers to entry may result in new competition, including possible imitators of Cloon Keen Atelier. Some of the firms that compete most closely with Cloon Keen are listed in Table 11.3; all of these firms operate in *both* the candles and home fragrances market and the skin care sector of the personal care market. However, the firms are categorised according to the market in which each firm has a *stronger* presence. A fuller description of these competitors is outlined in Appendix 11.1.

Table 11.3: A Selection of Cloon Keen's Competitors

	Candles and Home Fragrances Market	Skin Care Sector of the Personal Care Market
International competitors	Sia Yankee Candle	The Body Shop Jo Malone L'Occitane en Provence
Irish competitors	Fragrance Boutique	Burren Perfumery

The Challenge Ahead for Cloon Keen

The challenge for Cloon Keen Atelier is to find the optimum market position that provides a strategic advantage. Given the kinds of competitors identified, what are the strategic alternatives open to Margaret and Julian in developing their business? One pressing consideration for Margaret and Julian is whether to open additional retail outlets and whether to develop an online presence to pursue electronic sales. How could Cloon Keen leverage its competencies into competitive advantages to position itself successfully in the sectors it pursues? For instance, Cloon Keen is known for its premium-scented candles, but Margaret and Julian are seeking to expand into the personal care market by creating their own line of skin care products and complementary accessories, such as body brushes, soap dishes and dispensers. In outlining a specific strategic direction for Cloon Keen, consider the impact on the firm's marketing mix (i.e. product, price, place and promotion) as well as the consumers they target. Of particular concern to Margaret and Julian is finding the most effective and cost-efficient methods to promote Cloon Keen Atelier to relevant audiences, which they believe is essential to establishing their lifestyle brand.

Appendix 11.1: Profiles of Selected Competitors

The Yankee Candle Company Inc. (<http://www.yankeecandle.com>)

In 1969, when he was sixteen, Michael J. Kittredge made his first candle as a Christmas gift for his mother (Donovan 2000). 'But a neighbour admired it so much he sold it to her [and] used the profits to buy wax and make more candles' (*Chain Store Age* 1996: 70). By 1973, Kittredge's hobby had become a business, which went public in July 1999 (Donovan 2000). Yankee Candle's headquarters is located in South Deerfield, Massachusetts and has a staff of over 4,000 people. In the US, Yankee Candle is one of the biggest manufacturers and distributors of scented candles (Yankee Candle 2007). Through its global multi-channel network, Yankee Candle manages 420 retail venues, wholesales to 19,900 other retailers and operates direct sales through its catalogues and websites (Yankee Candle 2007). Yankee Candle offers over 2,900 types of candles in more than 200 scents and also sells many other home fragrance products, such as electric fragrance dispensers, scented oils, room sprays, automobile air fresheners and home accessories (Yankee Candle 2007). 'By building on its strong brand name, Yankee Candle has successfully extended its expertise and leadership in premium-scented candles into fragranced products for the home and personal care' (*Worldwide Videotex* 2003).

The SIA Group (<http://www.sia-homefashion.com>)

Sonja Ingegerd Andersson and Kjell Melander founded SIA in 1963 in Sweden. The SIA Group, an eminent brand within home decor, represents over €130 million in annual sales, with distribution in thirty countries throughout Europe, as well as in the US and Japan (Heinzen York 2005). Its distribution channel includes 30 exclusive boutiques and over 330 points of sale through its network of partner stores (*Inside Franchising* 2006). SIA creates two home fashion collections each year and offers 'over 3,000 items including accessories for the home, seasonal products, gifts and artificial flowers and plants. SIA has become a leader in European decorative home accessories, personal care and giftware' (Spring Fair Birmingham 2007). Headquartered in Paris, France, the SIA Group employs approximately 450 people and the investment company Industri Kapital is its major shareholder.

Fragrance Boutique Ltd (<http://www.fragrance-boutique.com>)

Fragrance Boutique, established in 1987 by a father-daughter team, Roy and Sarah Donaldson, is located at the Malahide Marina in Co. Dublin, Ireland. Fragrance Boutique is a manufacturer of candle and scented gift-ware collections, including a range of soaps, candleholders, flower settings, body toiletries and natural bath accessories (*Irish Independent* 2000). Fragrance Boutique produces themed collections of decorated candles, potpourri and candle gift sets for the large retailers where 60 per cent of their turnover is attributed to the export market (Shanley 2005). The millennium candle was among the firm's most successful products. The design of the millennium candle, on the basis of a fire-retardant transfer that burns more slowly than the wick, proved to be a hit with retailers and consumers (Devane 2005). The Fragrance Boutique employs over thirty-five people, rising to seventy during the busy pre-Christmas period (*Irish Independent* 2000). The John Hinde Group, a firm know for its postcards, bought Fragrance Boutique in 2003. The Donaldsons continue their involvement in the firm's operations and creative direction (Devane 2005).

The Burren Perfumery (<http://www.burrenperfumery.com>)

The Burren Perfumery, located in Carron in the heart of the Burren, Co. Clare, is Ireland's first perfumery. Established almost forty years ago, Sadie Chowen and Edward Briggs are the perfumery's third owners (Kennedy 2007). The perfumery's products are hand-produced using natural essences, plant extracts and spring water. Given its location, the Burren Perfumery is also a tourist destination where visitors can observe the traditional distillation and blending of perfumes (Drinkwater 2006). Even though tour buses are not accommodated, visitors to the perfumery can number more than 300 a day in high summer (Amos 2003). The Burren Perfumery produces cologne, perfume, shower gels and soaps. Half of the perfumery's business is allocated to wholesaling to gift and craft shops in Ireland, Europe and North America. The other half comes from people visiting the shop and repeat business through mail order and online sales (Sweetman 2002). In addition, the perfumery works with a number of hoteliers to provide aromatic toiletries for the guest bathrooms (Sweetman 2002).

The Body Shop International plc (<http://www.thebodyshop.com>)

In 1976, Anita Roddick established The Body Shop in Brighton, England. The Body Shop is known for its activism in social and environmental causes. This firm is generally credited with pioneering the use of natural ingredients in cosmetics and personal care products. The Body Shop frequently 'received more attention for its ethical stances, such as encouraging recycling, avoiding ingredients tested on animals, and forging partnerships with developing countries, than for its products' (Euromonitor 2006a: 1). Another feature of The Body Shop's strategy was to rely on window displays, catalogues and point-of-purchase product descriptions to attract and inform customers. In 1999, The Body Shop left manufacturing in favour of focusing on retailing (*International Directory* 2002).

The Body Shop operates a broad, multi-channel network; there are more than 2,100 stores, two-thirds of which are franchised, across 55 countries (Anderson 2007). Additionally, the firm sells products online as well as through an in-home sales programme – The Body Shop at Home – in the UK, US, Australia and, in 2008, Germany (Datamonitor 2006a). The Body Shop has been differentiating itself by pursuing a *masstige* position, whereby it 'combines excellent [customer] service with a comprehensive range of naturally-inspired personal care products offering high performance benefits and competitive pricing' (Datamonitor 2006a: 22). The Body Shop believes product innovation successfully drives this strategy. Currently, the firm sells over 800 products, including skin care and sun protection products, hair care products, colour cosmetics, perfumes, home fragrances, men's grooming products and accessories (Datamonitor 2006a). In March 2006, The Body Shop was purchased for £625 million and became a subsidiary of the L'Oréal Group (Datamonitor 2006a). L'Oréal's skills in nurturing global brands should facilitate The Body Shop in communicating its unique position through higher profile methods to reach more consumers (Datamonitor 2006b). However, consumers loyal to The Body Shop's ethical and natural branding may find it hard to believe multinationals can trade ethically and that their products are as natural as those of smaller businesses (Datamonitor 2006b).

Jo Malone Ltd (<http://www.jomalone.co.uk>)

The firm Jo Malone was established in London in 1983 by Jo Malone and her husband Gary. They founded the luxury skin care line with a single product, a nutmeg and ginger bath oil (*Soap, Perfumery & Cosmetics* 1999). Jo Malone is known as a perfectionist perfumer, whose loyal customers appreciate her long-lasting fragrances. Today, the firm has well over 200 skin care, personal and home fragrance products. The company's flagship store is in Sloane Street, London, but it has outlets in prestigious department stores in the US, Canada and Italy as well as selling online and through catalogues (*Soap, Perfumery & Cosmetics* 1999). Indeed, Jo Malone's select distribution strategy has meant it has achieved high penetration through its online business because the products are so limited in the marketplace (*Fair Disclosure Wire* 2007).

In October 1999, Estée Lauder acquired Jo Malone and since its acquisition has transformed Jo Malone into a top global brand by heavily investing in its product range rather than promoting a personality (Datamonitor 2006*d*). In every exclusive department store where Jo Malone is sold, it ranks among the top five brands (*Fair Disclosure Wire* 2007). In addition to its innovation in products, Jo Malone is innovative in its positioning strategy and is aggressively pursing the gender-neutral fragrance market. Industry observers recognise consumers are increasingly buying perfume that is neither conventionally masculine nor feminine (La Ferla 2006). Through its neutral packaging (i.e. chunky glass bottles with a white label with black lettering) and neutral sounding names (e.g. Lime Basil Mandarin or Pomegranate Noir), Jo Malone avoids being stereotyped. Moreover, the firm's marketing is distinct from how unisex scents were marketed the late 1990s. Jo Malone circumvents the issue of gender by allowing customers to decide what is appropriate and by selling their products away from men's and women's fragrance counters (La Ferla 2006). The gender neutral approach has meant Jo Malone has become highly desirable within the corporate gifting market (*Fair Disclosure Wire* 2007).

L'Occitane en Provence (<http://www.loccitane.com>)

In 1976 Olivier Baussan founded L'Occitane, which is headquartered in Manosque in Haute Provence in the southeast of France. L'Occitane manufactures its own prestige line of skin care, hair care, men's grooming, colour cosmetics, as well as personal and home fragrance products, all of which are composed of essential oils and natural ingredients from the Provence area. Although the majority of Baussan's shares were bought by an investment fund, he still is L'Occitane's public ambassador. 'He promotes the company's perfume school for the blind in Provence and L'Occitane's Braille labelling' (Carvajal 2006: 1). In a burgeoning personal care market, L'Occitane has abundant opportunity for expansion. Under the auspices of the investment fund over the last ten years, L'Occitane has grown from 10 to over 750 shops across Europe, the US and Asia (Carvajal 2006).

Within the natural cosmetics sector L'Occitane inhabits a prestigious position, but competitors, such as The Body Shop, are pursuing a more upscale position by remodelling stores and developing premium products for customers who appreciate personal luxuries (Carvajal 2006). However, the *mêlée* is about perceived quality rather than price. Industry observers recognise that competitors at the premium end of the personal care market aim to achieve a distinct market position to minimise duplication (Cohen 2000). Hence, even though customers of these high-end competitors may look similar according to demographics, they are quite distinct according to psychographics. Similar to other prestige personal care firms, L'Occitane's customers are educated, well travelled and wealthy. However, L'Occitane's customers have a psychographic profile where they perceive themselves as worldly connoisseurs who appreciate quality products (Cohen 2000). L'Occitane is successful in attracting the male customer and they account for 30 to 35 per cent of its total customers (Cohen 2000). Its appeal to male customers is attributed to 'the store design, which evokes the French countryside rather than a boudoir, the vintage-style packaging, and the products themselves, which can be used by men or women' (Cohen 2000).

References

Amos, S. (2003), 'Scents of a Place', *Country Living*, June, available at: <http://www.burrenperfumery.com/press/press-CL.shtml>.

Anderson, L. (2007), 'The Body Shop PLC', Hoover's, available from: <http://www.hoovers.com>.

Burns, E. (2006), 'Half of European Union Population Uses the Web Regularly', *ClickZ.com*, 5 November, available at: <http://www.clickz.com/showPage.html?page=3623956>.

Carvajal, D. (2006), 'Whiffs of Combat Waft Over Natural Cosmetics', *New York Times*, 12 August 2006.

Chain Store Age (1996), 'Retail Entrepreneurs of the Year', December, 72(12), 70.

Cohen, N. (2000), 'L'Occitane: An Upscale Flair in Personal Care', *Shopping Centers Today*, available at: <http://www.icsc.org/srch/sct/current/sct0500/07h.html>.

Datamonitor (2006), *Hand and Body Care in Ireland: Industry Profile*, London: Datamonitor Reports, December.

Datamonitor (2006a), *The Body Shop International PLC – Company Profile*, London: Datamonitor Reports, September.

Datamonitor (2006b), *Market Watch Global Round-up Industry Comment – Body Shop: Aiming to Satisfy a Worldwide Appetite for Natural Cosmetics*, London: Datamonitor Reports, August.

Datamonitor (2006c), *Personal Care – Industry Update*, London: Datamonitor Reports, August.

Datamonitor (2006d), *Industry Comment – Market Watch: Personal Care*, London: Datamonitor Reports, March.

Devane, M. (2005), 'Sweet Smell of Family Success', *Sunday Business Post*, 21 August, available at: <http://www.archives.tcm.ie/businesspost/2005/08/21/story7182.asp>.

Donovan, D. (2000), 'Odor of Magnitude', *Forbes*, 7 February, 165(3).

Drinkwater, C. (2006), 'Carol … Meet Clare: Carol Drinkwater Sets Out to Explore the Glories of Co. Clare', *Mail on Sunday* (London), 15 January 2006.

Euromonitor (2007), *Cosmetics and Toiletries – World*, London: Euromonitor International, February.

Euromonitor (2006), *Euromonitor International Spending choices: Discretionary Income Patterns to 2015*, London: Euromonitor International, December.

Euromonitor (2006a), *The Body Shop International Plc Retailing United Kingdom*, London: Euromonitor International, November.

Euromonitor (2006b), *Country Market Insight: Retailing – Ireland*, London: Euromonitor International, September.

Euromonitor (2006c), *Skin Care – Ireland*, London: Euromonitor International, May.

Euromonitor (2005), *Consumer Lifestyles – Ireland*, London: Euromonitor International, September.

Euromonitor (2003), *Boots on the Edge*, London: Euromonitor International, April.

Fair Disclosure Wire (2007), 'The Estée Lauder Companies Inc.'s Analyst and Investor Day', Conference Transcript, 6 March.

Heinzen York, J. (2005), 'SIA selects One Coast for U.S. Distribution', *Home Accents Today*, 1 April, available at: <http://www.homeaccents today.com/article/CA525719.html>.

Inside Franchising (2006), 'SIA Home Fashion Franchise System Profile', available at: <http://www.insidefranchising.com.au/sia_pofile.asp>.

International Directory of Company Histories (2002), *Encyclopaedia of Company Histories About the Body Shop International Plc*, The Gale Group, Inc., available at: <http://www.answers.com/topic/the-body-shop-international-plc>.

Irish Independent (2000), 'Sweet Smell of Success for Award Finalist: The Fragrance Boutique', *Irish Independent*, 18 December, Business Section.

Kennedy, E. (2007), 'Artisans: the Burren Perfumery', *Sunday Business Post Online*, 11 February, available at: <http://www.archives.tcm.ie/businesspost/2007/02/11/story20900.asp>.

Korchock, K. (1998), 'News of Candle's Death Greatly Exaggerated; Candle Maker was Good Bet for Career Change', *The Toronto Star*, 21 December.

La Ferla, R. (2001), 'Beauty Goes Fruity', *New York Times*, 28 January.

La Ferla, R. (2006), 'Scent of a Person', *New York Times*, 23 March.

Lennon, C. (2007), 'Behind the Pretty Pictures', *Time Style and Design*, Spring, 35–7.

Lockhorn, J. (2006), 'Are You Ready for Ubiquitous Interactivity?' *ClickZ.com*, 4 December, available at: <http://www.clickz.com/showPage.html?page=3624090>.

Mangan, M. and Checkley, J. (2006), *Cloon Keen Atelier Business Plan*, July.

McKeon, B. (2007), 'Meet the Blogonistas', *Irish Times Magazine*, 10 March.

Musselman, F. (2007), 'Organics Abound at Beautyworld', *Women's Wear Daily*, 9 February.

Shanley, V. (2005), 'Firing the Ideas to Shape the Designs of Tomorrow in a Kiln of Innovation: RDS Showcase is a Huge Market Stall for Designers but it's a Tough Task to Catch the Eye of the International Buyer', *Sunday Tribune*, 23 January,

Singer, N. (2007), 'Skin Deep: Should You Trust Your Make-up?' *New York Times*, 15 February.

Soap, Perfumery & Cosmetics (1999), 'Lauder Buys Malone', November, 72(11), 3.

Spring Fair Birmingham (2007), 'SIA (UK)', available at: <http://www.springfair.com/page.cfm/action=Exhib/ExhibID=02410>.

Summerfield, R. (2005), 'Sweet Enough to Eat: The Ever-Expanding Menu of Yummy Bath and Body Products', *Sault Star* (*Sault Saint Marie Ontario*), 15 February.

Sweetman, M. (2002), 'For One Couple, Making Perfume in the Isolated Burren is More a Way of Life than a Business', *Irish Times Magazine*, 27 July.

Swengley, N. (1998), 'The Woman with the Perfect Nose', *The Evening Standard*, 17 April.

The Yankee Candle Company Inc. (2007), *The Yankee Candle Company Inc*, United States Securities and Exchange Commission, Form 8K Report, 22 January.

Worldwide Videotex Update (2003), 'Yankee Candle Revamps E-commerce Website', August, 22(8).

Zimbalist, K. (2007), 'Clean sweep: Goodbye to All That Gaudy Stuff', *Time Style and Design*, Spring, 35–7.

CHAPTER 12

U2: Keeping the Rhythm[1]

Thomas C. Lawton
Cranfield School of Management, Cranfield University

Denis G. Harrington
School of Business, Waterford Institute of Technology

James A. Cunningham
*J.E. Cairnes School of Business and Economics,
National University of Ireland, Galway*

'It's stasis that kills you off in the end, not ambition.'

Bono

The Creation

Bono, The Edge, Adam Clayton and Larry Mullen Jr – the name recognition may not be as instant or universal as John, Paul, George and Ringo but, for fans in Cape Town or Cork, Toronto or Tokyo, the music these four make is equally entertaining and uplifting. Ever since breaking onto the international stage in the early 1980s, the quartet has inspired rock music lovers across the world. What is the secret to the band's international reach and enduring appeal? How have they survived and thrived in a notoriously fickle business?

The global music industry is renowned for its tendency towards trends and the 'next big thing'. It is rare that an artist or band maintains a premier position in the business for more than a few short years. Most are little more than one-hit wonders, rising and falling within the space of

---

[1] This case was compiled using published secondary resources. The information in this case study relates to U2's position up to 2007. This case study is intended solely as a basis for class discussion. It is not intended to illustrate either effective or ineffective management.

two to three years. Some endure but lose much of the critical acclaim and commercial appeal they once possessed. A rarefied few last the course, consistently delivering innovative, attention-grabbing music and delighting both fans and critics alike. Over the course of the last thirty years, Irish rock group U2 has stood head and shoulders above most of its contemporaries, creating an almost unassailable position as the world's best rock band.[2] The numbers are impressive even by rock stardom standards: a dozen albums, more than 120 million copies sold worldwide, 14 Grammy Awards and sold-out concerts from London to Los Angeles.

As 'The Band of the Eighties',[3] U2 started with an advert posted on the bulletin board of Mount Temple High School in Dublin in 1976 by fourteen-year-old Larry Mullen Jr.[4] Interested in forming a band, Mullen put out a call to musicians and interviewed them at home. Two of these boys – Dave Evans and Adam Clayton – met in Mullen's kitchen in suburban Dublin. When Paul Hewson joined the trio, he was meant to play guitar but his charismatic character and enthusiasm made him the natural front man. Although the only member who could actually play an instrument, Mullen quickly realised that he was no longer the lead. He later remarked in 1986, 'There were no jobs to get. It was like we were all going nowhere, so we decided to go nowhere together and form a band.' Originally, the band had six members – including Dave Evans' brother Dick and Ivan Mc Cormick – but in 1978 they became the four-piece they are today.

Originally performing cover songs, the band evolved quickly to writing their own music. They had been performing under names such as 'Feedback' and 'Hype' but, at the suggestion of a friend, renamed themselves 'U2'. The name had a direct association with the Cold War spy plane U2 used by the United States and a more indirect play on a notion of inclusivity between the band and their audience. In fact, Paul Hewson later admitted that he did not like the band's name and never thought of it as 'you too'. Paul Hewson was given the nickname 'Bono Vox' at around the same time – a variation of the Latin for 'good voice'. Different opinions exist as to where this name came from. One theory is that he was named after a hearing aid company's advertising sign in

---

[2] Some might argue that this title belongs to The Rolling Stones and they are undeniably in the same category. However, 'The Stones' have had their ups and downs over the past twenty-odd years, whereas U2 have rarely lost their competitive edge since the mid-1980s.
[3] *Rolling Stone* magazine dubbed the group 'The Band of the Eighties', saying that, 'for a growing number of rock-and-roll fans, U2 has become the band that matters most, maybe even the only band that matters.'
[4] See <http://www.en.wikipedia.org/wiki/U2_(band)>.

Dublin City centre (which is still there today). An alternative theory is that Gavin Friday, his friend and a well-known Irish singer, named him such because he always sang so loudly. Bono subsequently re-named Dave Evans 'The Edge', apparently because he was always on the edge of new ideas and trends. These different stories and an absence of one accepted view helped to enhance the legend and mystery that is U2.

The band's first break came in 1978, winning IR£500 in a talent contest on St Patrick's Day in Limerick. A judge at the show, Jackie Hayden – who worked for CBS Records – helped the band to produce its first demo. Live performances led to a modest following and the first single, 'U2-3', was independently released in 1979 with CBS Ireland as a three-song EP. One important fan of the U2 style was Bill Graham, a journalist with the music paper *Hot Press*. Graham was an early champion of the band and also introduced them to their manager, Paul McGuinness (often referred to as the fifth member of U2). The single did not do well outside of Ireland (where it topped the charts), but they toured to promote it and landed a contract with record label Island Records in 1980. Their live performances were a key part of their early success, as their shows were energetic and, with Bono's charisma, people began to notice them. Between 1980 and 1983, they released three albums: *Boy*, *October* and *War*, with reasonable sales. *War* gave them their first number one hit and ensured that the band became a mainstream. From here on, adolescent bluff turned into adult confidence.

The Band of the Eighties

In April 1985, *Rolling Stone* magazine dubbed U2 'The Band of the Eighties'. This accolade followed their show-stealing performance at 1984's Live Aid concert, coupled with the critical and commercial success of their latest album, *The Unforgettable Fire*. Produced by Brian Eno and Daniel Lanois, it marked a departure from the anthems and stadium rock beats of the previous three albums. This haunting and mature album contained songs that explored themes such as nuclear warfare and heroin abuse. It firmly established U2 as a band with their finger on the pulse of modern society and in touch with the concerns of a new generation.

Despite the consequent global success, the group did not rest on their laurels and continued going from strength to strength. *The Unforgettable Fire* was eclipsed by the release of *The Joshua Tree* in 1987. Generally regarded as U2's best-known recording, their fifth album (named after a small town in California's Death Valley; the album cover featuring a photo of one such tree from the area) went platinum in the UK forty-eight hours after being released, winning them both Grammy Awards and the front cover of *Time* magazine. This latter privilege had previously been bestowed on only three other rock bands – The Beatles, The Band and The Who. *The Joshua Tree* was the band's most idealistic, spiritual and melodically consistent album.

Containing three of the band's most successful singles, 'Where the Streets Have No Name', 'I Still Haven't Found What I'm Looking For' and 'With or Without You', this album swept the boards at all the award ceremonies. The accompanying sell-out tour included over 100 shows, and cemented U2's reputation as what *Time* magazine called 'Rock's hottest ticket'. The video for 'Where the Streets Have No Name' high-lighted U2's imagination and ability to use the PR machine. Playing live on a Los Angeles rooftop, they caused traffic chaos below as fans and passers-by stopped to watch, much to the increasing displeasure of the Los Angeles Police Department, who eventually told them to shut it down (but not before they got the necessary footage and played four other songs as well).

Their music was now instinctive but not aggressive, fusing the melancholy of folk music, the angst of blues music, the passion of gospel music and the splendour of operatic arias.[5] Anthems such as 'Sunday Bloody Sunday' (1983) and 'Pride' (1984) blended easily with more soulful tunes like 'A Sort of Homecoming' (1984) and 'Running to Stand Still' (1987). The fact that older songs sound so consistent with newer material, yet don't sound formulaic, is astounding, and is a reaffirmation of the band's efforts to keep the chemistry alive by reinventing itself but remaining fundamentally the same.

Style Change

With the escalating success of their first five albums, it was probably inevitable that there would have to be a let down at some point. This came in the guise of 1988's *Rattle and Hum* album, bringing them back to the early days when U2 was simply a rock band – none of the moody undertones of what had emerged in the previous two albums. A documentary film of the same name accompanied the album and, while both were well received by fans, the critics were disparaging. Bono announced at the end of 1989 that they would need 'to go away and dream it all up again'.

---

[5] This assessment is derived from <http://www.scaruffi.com/vol4/u2.html>.

All bands want to be fashion conscious and cool, and in the 1980s U2 almost single-handedly made earnestness cool. By the end of that decade the band had started to hint about re-inventing themselves. The result was the radical departure of 1991's *Achtung Baby* album, inspired in part by the excitement of Berlin around the time of the fall of the wall. The 1990s saw a transformation in this political rock-and-roll band from guitars and idealism to electronica, starting with the *Achtung Baby* album and going right though to *Pop* and the single 'Lemon'. *Achtung Baby* hit the right chord with fans and critics. *Rolling Stone* magazine said that U2 had 'proven the same penchant for epic musical and verbal gestures that leads many artists to self-parody which can, in more inspired hands, fuel the unforgettable fire that defines great rock and roll'. The subsequent tour, ZooTV, was a huge extravaganza, which seemed more about the show than the songs. The show was built around a stage backed up with hundreds of TV screens, flashing satellite TV images and subliminal messages to an enthralled audience. Characters formed an important part of the performance, such as 'The Fly' and 'MacPhisto'. Not everyone 'got it' and some interpreted ZooTV as U2's egos being vastly inflated and out of control. In reality, the band was parodying the rock-and-roll lifestyle through extreme exaggeration.

The late 1980s to early 1990s was the most turbulent time for U2. Adam Clayton was the only member of the band not to become a fervent Christian in the early 1980s. As the band grew ever more successful, he more than any of the others bought into the rock-and-roll lifestyle with his playboy lifestyle, peroxide blonde hair, cigarettes, shades and engagement to supermodel Naomi Campbell. He was responsible for songs such as 'Zoo Station', 'Until the End of the World' and 'Lemon'. He was arrested in Dublin in possession of cannabis with the intent to supply but got around this conviction with a large donation (IR£25,000) to the Dublin Women's Aid Refuge Centre to avoid serious repercussions on the band's touring schedule. But, due to a romantic break-up and spiralling alcoholism, Adam went on to miss a gig, forcing U2 to go on stage with a replacement. This necessitated his confronting his problems and rehabilitating.

Achtung Baby was followed by *Zooropa* in 1993 and was a further change for the band since it embraced a more electronic, techno style. *Zooropa* was less commercially successful than other albums and is illustrative of U2's experimentation period. During their subsequent 'break' period, Clayton and Mullen recorded the soundtrack and theme song for the 1996 movie *Mission: Impossible*, and the whole band, under the name

'Passengers', released an Eno-produced album called *Original Soundtracks No. 1* in 1995. The album was experimental and did not attract considerable attention, though it is notable for collaboration with Luciano Pavarotti on 'Miss Sarajevo'. After this, U2 decided to take a break from each other before re-uniting for their ninth album, *Pop*, in 1997.

Pop was as far away from classic U2 as was possible. It was a difficult album to record because of time pressure. Yet another world tour followed again with extravagance, computer generation and a giant rotating lemon and huge olive on a 100-foot cocktail stick. This ultimately was not what the band was about and left many of their core fans numb, though *Rolling Stone* magazine said U2 had 'defied the odds and made some of the greatest music of their lives'. 'PopMart' signified the last of this type of concert for U2 as it was back to basics from then on. The tour itself was the second highest grossing tour in 1997 with revenues of $80 million. Unfortunately, it had cost $100 million to produce. Change was inevitable and essential. The group would have to go back to basics. This they would successfully do, but it took them several years to pull it off.

Conquering the 21st Century

Every release from U2 represents an evolution of their sound. *All That You Can't Leave Behind*, released in 2000, returned to what the band was about originally and is, in effect, the spiritual follow-up to *The Joshua Tree*. Returning to their guitar driven sound, they sold more than ten million copies. One song, 'The Ground Beneath Her Feet', was a bonus track on the European and Australian versions of the album and featured lyrics written by Salman Rushdie, the controversial author of *The Satanic Verses*. The tour accompanying the album (the 'Elevation' tour) was a scaled-down affair compared to their more recent forays and their eighty American shows grossed revenues of $110 million – the second highest total ever, behind The Rolling Stones 'Voodoo Lounge' tour in 1994. After the tour ended, U2 performed at the half-time show during Super Bowl XXXVI. Some months earlier, the band's emotional and fully live rendition of 'Where the Streets Have No Name', paying tribute to the victims of the 9/11 bombings, helped to renew U2's place amongst music's greats (Tyrangiel 2002). The album subsequently won four Grammy Awards.

Their 2005 album *How to Dismantle an Atomic Bomb* falls squarely into the category of a band in mid-transformation. After *All That You Can't Leave Behind*, one quickly gets the impression that *How to*

Dismantle an Atomic Bomb is very much The Edge's album musically, given its guitar dominance. Bono has himself commented that the title has to do with his complex relationship with his father and not with any obvious association with nuclear disarmament. On first play, it is not what a U2 fan would expect but continued play causes it to grow on most people. Its debut track, 'Vertigo', has seen much overexposure thanks to Apple's iPod marketing campaign. The band did not receive any royalties for this, but it ensured early interest in the album among a younger generation (Ali 2005). Indeed, U2 appears to have embraced the iPod culture, licensing a special version of the player with their design and allowing the iTunes website to sell *The Complete U2*, a digital box set featuring all of the band's albums, singles, B-sides and some previously unreleased material.

Somewhat reminiscent of earlier albums such as *The Unforgettable Fire* and *The Joshua Tree*, *How to Dismantle an Atomic Bomb* playfully examines where U2 have been and where they are going. Their usual signature topics – war, peace, life, death, God and love – are all touched upon in this album and it contains a number of songs that might last the distance and become classics, including the haunting ballad 'Sometimes You Can't Make it on Your Own'. In its first week, the album sold 840,000 copies in the USA (a record for the band) and topped the charts in 32 countries. The 'Vertigo' tour, which followed the album, was a huge success. In Ireland, their concerts (150,000 tickets) sold out within 50 minutes. The tour generated $260 million in revenue and drew more than three million people to ninety concerts, all of which were sell-outs. The European leg of the tour ended in August 2005 in Portugal where President Jorge Sampaio presented the band with the Order of Liberty – the country's most prestigious honour – because of their work to combat poverty in Africa and worldwide. This award had never before been presented to a foreign music group.

New Dimensions, New Directions

While other big acts felt threatened by the new 'music download culture' or, in the case of Metallica, sued online music file-sharing pioneer Napster, U2 was busy working on a new business model. Even as early as 2000, U2 had opened an extensive website, with an index to every song and album, lyrics, tour news that is refreshed nightly and subscriber features that allowed access to tickets, exclusive content and streaming downloads of every song and video the band has ever made. In

November 2005, U2 struck up a deal with Apple to offer an iPod music player special edition model tied to the group. Apple also introduced the iPod Photo, which stored digital photographs along with music. The group also partnered with Apple to promote the iPod, performing its single 'Vertigo' on an iPod TV commercial, and releasing 'Vertigo' as a single exclusively through Apple's online music download service, iTunes. The collaboration with Apple gave visibility to the band at a time when most radio station playlists did not extend much beyond a narrow selection of pop singers. Equally, the members of U2 are passionate proponents of Apple's iPod – 'it's the most interesting art object since the electric guitar in terms of music' remarked Bono in an interview to *Rolling Stone* magazine. The Edge, in a prepared statement after the partnership had been announced, commented: 'iPod and iTunes look like the future to me and it's good for everybody involved in music' (Mullins 2004). But the band's partnership with Apple Computer is still something of a surprise. In their 25-year history, U2 had never previously licensed their music for commercial use or even accepted tour sponsorship.

Bono is also involved with Elevation Partners, launched by former Silver Lake Partners' co-founder Roger McNamee and former Electronic Arts executive John Riccitiello in 2004. Elevation Partners has made investments in the music and entertainment industries in an attempt to profit from ongoing turmoil in these sectors, including online piracy and competing home entertainment technologies such as DVDs and video games. Elevation's first investment in 2005 brought together video game producers Pandemic Studios and BioWare in a $300 million deal. Then followed an investment in *Forbes* magazine and, more recently, in June 2007 Elevation made its biggest investment to date, taking a 25 per cent stake in Palm for $325 million (*Irish Times* 2007).

Paul McGuinness: The Fifth Member of U2

At the core of U2, long-time manager and confidante Paul McGuinness has been part of the band since the early days and is widely regarded as the band's fifth member. His ability to create and *think the future* and his courage to take bold decisions that allowed the band members to exploit their creative talents over the decades has ensured that U2 maintains a commercial and temporal relevance. McGuinness recognised the importance of being outwardly focused in creative terms to take advantage of business opportunities but, at the same time, he identified the need for the band to keep a firm handle on operations. As he pointed out in an interview with the *New York Times*: 'The band members and I were always aware that it would be pathetic to be good at music but bad at business. They shared my understanding that great rock and roll is a complex equation involving art, commerce, advertising, fashion, sex, politics and all sorts of things' (Olsen 2005).

While he has honed his business and management talents with U2, he has also represented acts like PJ Harvey and Sinead O'Connor. McGuinness has also diversified into other ventures such as his Celtic Heartbeat label, established with Barbara Galavan and former Clannad manager David Kavanagh. From the start he had a clear sense of how the band might develop strategically. As he has pointed out, in 1983, during the early days of MTV, U2 were achieving a reputation as a live band but had not yet had a hit album. He decided to produce a TV programme at the Red Rocks Amphitheatre in Denver, Colorado and use the film to illustrate U2's emerging status in the United States. McGuinness remarked on the importance of using the concert footage 'to try and get on MTV'. They subsequently invested all available resources in the programme. On the day of the show the rain poured down but as the *New York Times* reported, 'luckily the rain and fog concealed the fact that the show was not sold out. There were only about 2,000 people in the audience, but it looked like there were 10,000.'

Whilst other bands have had difficult relationships with their managers, McGuinness's thirty-year tenure as U2's manager is widely regarded as one of the most successful in the music business. Such sustainability and continuity is impressive. McGuinness's ability to think about and deliver on the band's evolution over the long term has been a significant and often overlooked asset possessed by U2.

In 2006, U2 moved some of their business affairs to a Dutch finance house in order to avail of a virtually tax-free status on their royalties. Defending the move, McGuinness argued: 'The reality is that U2's business is 90 per cent conducted around the world. 90 per cent of our tickets and 98 per cent of our records are sold outside of Ireland. It [Ireland] is where we live and where we work and where we employ a lot of people. But we pay taxes all over the world. And like any other business, we're perfectly entitled to minimise the tax we pay.'

The Political and Humanitarian Motivation

Music and image aside, another way that U2 have long stood apart from other bands is through their political awareness and social concern, with songs such as 'Sunday Bloody Sunday' referring to the troubles in Northern Ireland and 'Miss Sarajevo' dealing with events within the Bosnian city during its siege in 1993. Bono in particular has much to say to anybody who will listen, regardless of where they sit on the political spectrum. He rarely sees limits to his reach or his efforts and routinely meets with world leaders, whom he impresses with his charisma, passion and knowledge of detail. His celebrity status has opened doors to the Oval Office and Number 10 Downing Street. His knowledge of issues and his dedication have won over Washington's elite and power brokers elsewhere around the globe. These qualities were commented on in *BusinessWeek*, where an interviewer remarked: 'After listening to Bono share his personal story, I realised that he is a wonderful example of a person who has not only changed his behaviour but also his identity, or definition of who he is – while remaining authentic and not becoming a phony.' Since 1999, Bono has helped persuade US Republicans and Democrats, presidents and law makers, to provide millions to help end the scourge of AIDS, eliminate poverty in Africa and forgive Third World debt. In 2002, President Bush pledged $15 billion towards African poverty and said of Bono:

> Here's what I know about him: first, he's a good musician; secondly, he is willing to lead to achieve what his heart tells him, and that nobody – nobody – should be living in poverty and hopelessness in the world. (Associated Press 2005)

In a similar vein, *Rolling Stone* magazine, in a detailed interview with Bono in November 2005, suggested that the story of Bono and U2 is a story of commitment to one another – after twenty-nine years they remain a remarkably stable unit – and to the greater causes of social justice on which Bono has staked his reputation. The singer, they suggest: 'gives us a vision of how tomorrow can be better than today. He appeals to something greater than ourselves. He tells the story of his life and struggles in terms everyone can understand. He speaks about faith in a way that even a nonbeliever can embrace.' The *New York Times* magazine referred to him as 'a one-man state who fills his treasury with the global currency of fame ... the most politically effective figure in the recent history of popular culture.'

Bono began his crusade in 1997 when he was asked to help out on the Jubilee 2000 campaign for complete cancellation of the debt Third World nations owed to richer countries. Greater involvement convinced Bono that he was 'way out of [his] depth' and a tutorial with the then Harvard

Professor Jeffrey Sachs soon followed. In 2000, Bono lobbied to get $115 million for debt relief in the foreign operations bill. A year later, there was $435 million. More lobbying resulted in the AIDS initiative of $15 billion over five years and double the US assistance for Africa. In 2003, the American Ireland Fund (AIF) presented The Humanitarian Award to Bono for his efforts to encourage debt cancellation and increase aid and trade incentives for Africa's impoverished nations through DATA (Debt, Aids, Trade, Africa).

Playing Tony Blair's guitar, posing for photographs with George Bush and meeting with Nelson Mandela and the Pope, Bono definitely plays all sides and alienates nobody, especially if they are willing to support his many causes. He is well aware that no one else has this type of access to media and money (Tyrangiel 2002). The band itself are experienced enough to know that donating millions to poverty-stricken Africa or speaking at United Nations assemblies against Third World debt has more impact than proclaiming good intentions on an album (Ali 2005).

The Secret of the Band's Longevity

To most people, the music of The Beatles embodies rock-and-roll staying power. They arrived on the scene at a time when music had the power to literally change the world. Artistically, commercially, culturally and spiritually, The Beatles ticked all the boxes. Other key bands such as The Rolling Stones, Led Zeppelin and Pink Floyd have also tested time. With the exception of The Rolling Stones, all of these bands eventually went their own separate ways – at least until the more recent trend towards reunion tours. There is no indication that such a split will be appearing anytime soon in U2. Even in their 'break' between their eighth and ninth (official) albums, they still worked together in some capacity. U2 continue to release an album, on average, just over once in every two years and much of that intervening period is taken up with promotional work and touring. The gap between their last two albums was four years, which seems to be at least in part due to Bono's ever-increasing political and humanitarian roles.

It is sometimes apparent that the main reason this band it still together is that they need each other. They are all involved and they all struggle together. They like the idea that they have been seen as contemporaries of bands such as Oasis, Coldplay and Green Day and they work hard not to be a veteran band. Age has mellowed them … but not too much. Not many people get to twenty-five or more years in a marriage, let alone in an artistic or business partnership. They have made some bad decisions, but they have survived them and learned from mistakes. In doing so, they acted on the words Bono once uttered: 'My heroes are the ones who survived doing it wrong, who made mistakes, but recovered from them.' They have gone through personal loss, addictions and arguments and yet are still together. Aside from their music, it has been their personal closeness, combined with an ability to give each other space when needed, which has kept them going and enabled them to survive for so long. It is a very elegant and fruitful co-dependency.

So What Next?

The music industry has changed utterly since the last album. Bands like the Arctic Monkeys, Radiohead and Coldplay are at the cutting edge of changing the business model within the music industry. The advent of social networking has meant that many bands are taking a more active role in managing directly all aspects of musical activities. Record producers and companies are treading carefully in this rapidly reconfiguring industry, where potential greater commercial success can be achieved via aggressive online music campaigns with the commercially strong strategic partners than chasing CD single sales in different countries. The development of iPods, MP3 players and further device convergence between music players, mobile phones and laptops has the potential to open up new and more profitable distribution channels for bands. In addition, shows like the X Factor and American Idol have added another dimension to sourcing musical talent that has potential mass audience appeal. Such a rapidly changing industry context will provide a challenging commercial and musical backdrop to their next album. According to Bono, there were thirteen songs left over after the sessions for *How to Dismantle an Atomic Bomb*. There are also suggestions that the band may re-record 1997's *Pop* as they were not completely happy with what came out first time around.

Any rumours of their demise are certainly overstated – U2 is far from finished and continue to reinvent and refresh. And what of the future? As early as 1997, Paul McGuinness was already forecasting much of what is happening within the music industry today:

> I don't think retail is going to disappear quite as quickly as some people imagine. I don't think it will disappear at all. But we all have to get more imaginative about how to market and deliver music in the future. I believe that the consumer is a far more complex animal than the record business sometimes

gives him credit for. I know plenty of people who listen to rock and roll and opera and world music. People go to different kinds of movies and so why do we expect for them to buy only one kind of record? Niche marketing and retailing is going to be very significant. Record stores will have to become more friendly environments for the consumer.

During the Vertigo Tour, they delighted fans by including some of their earlier works from albums such as *Boy*. There is a direct link between these earlier songs and *How to Dismantle an Atomic Bomb*, with old songs feeling very current and standing the test of time.[6] The release of U2 3D film using revolutionary digital 3D technology used in sporting events is another sign of U2's ability to harness music and technology to enhance the band's appeal and longevity. Thirty years on from Larry Mullen's school notice board advert, U2 remain at the top of their game and have no intention of passing on the rock-and-roll crown anytime soon.

Appendix 12.1: U2 Recordings and Tours

U2-3 (1979) (independently produced as a three-song EP)
Boy (1980)
Boy Tour (1981)
October (1981)
October Tour (1981)
War (1983)
War Tour (1983)
Under a Blood Red Sky (a live 1983 set)
The Unforgettable Fire (1984)
The Unforgettable Fire Tour (1984)
Wide Awake in America (1985 EP)
Live Aid Concert (1985), London
Self Aid Concert (1986), Ireland
Conspiracy of Hope Tour (1986) (Amnesty International)
The Joshua Tree (1987)
The Joshua Tree Tour (1987)
Rattle and Rum (1988)
Love Town Tour (1989) (Australia, New Zealand and Japan)
The Point Depot, Ireland
Achtung Baby (1991)

---

[6] See <http://www.u2tours.com/news/article.src?ID=1124>.

Zoo TV Tour (1992)
Zooropa (1993)
More Melon (a 1995 bootleg)
Original Soundtracks No. 1 (1995) (as 'Passengers' with Brian Eno)
Batman Forever soundtrack
Mission: Impossible soundtrack
Goldeneye soundtrack
Pop (1997)
PopMart World Tour (1997)
The Best of 1980–1990 (1998)
All That You Can't Leave Behind (2000)
Elevation Tour (2001)
The Best of 1990–2000 (2002)
How to Dismantle an Atomic Bomb (2004)
Live 8 Concert (2005), Hyde Park
Vertigo Tour (2005)

Appendix 12.2: Band Member Biographies

Larry Mullen, Jr

Larry Jr was born to Maureen and Larry Mullen in Dublin, Ireland, in 1961. He had two sisters, Mary and Cecelia. Mary died tragically in 1973. His love for music started with the piano, but eventually he switched to drums. His first drum set was given to him by his elder sister Cecelia. During his youth, Larry was a member of the renowned Artane Boys Band. However, their rules concerning long hair hastened his departure. Mullen attended several schools, including Scoil Colmcille School of Music, Chatham Row and finally Mount Temple, where he posted a note about getting a band together. The 'junior' was added to his name to prevent his tax bills from going to his father. He lives in Dublin with his partner Ann Acheson and their three children. Musically, Mullen is a fan of country and western music and Elvis Presley. Within the band, Larry takes a keen interest in the merchandising aspect and oversees the items to be sold during each tour. Of all of the band members, he is the most private.

Paul 'Bono Vox' Hewson

Paul David Hewson was born on 10 May 1960 to a Catholic father (Bobby) and Protestant mother (Iris). Paul was brought up as a member of the Church of Ireland, but as he has said, 'I always felt like I was sitting on the fence.' His mother's death in 1974 affected him badly and saw him becoming more rebellious.[7] Bono's initial role in the group seemed to be more as the organiser, as his singing in the early stages was not up to the standard needed. His ability to write poetry evolved into his being the main songwriter. At concerts, he formed the natural link between the band and the audience – he is a showman, sometimes to the extreme. He also used their concerts as a means of preaching his beliefs and opinions to those who would listen – a precursor of the way he, today, preaches to international leaders. Humanitarian issues are as important, if not more important, to Bono than the music has ever been. In 2002, he said, 'I'm tired of dreaming. I'm into doing at the moment. U2 is about the impossible. Politics is the art of the possible. They're very different and I'm resigned to that now.' He played a key role in the organisation of 2005's Live 8 concerts (Associated Press 2005*a*), at which U2 performed. Many believed that Bono had an outside chance to be elected as president of the World Bank (Associated Press March 2005), but this did not come to pass. He was also a nominee for the 2005 Nobel Peace Prize, but lost out to Mohamed ElBaradei and the International Atomic Energy Agency. It is unlikely that this will be his last chance to win this award as his fight continues relentlessly. His influence is far-reaching and hugely influential and his ability to be a rock star that people in power take seriously is essential: 'I can do better by just getting into the White House and talking to a man who I believe listens, wants to listen, on these subjects.' Bono is married to Ali Stewart and they have four children.

David 'The Edge' Howell Evans

Dave 'The Edge' Evans was born in Barking, Essex in 1961 to parents of Welsh descent, Gwenda and Garvin Evans.[8] When he was one year old, the family moved to Dublin, where he has lived ever since. There he grew up as a quiet kid, a loner and very intelligent. He did well in school, and up until before he met those who would be his future band mates, he wanted to go to university and become a doctor. When he left school, he informed his parents that he would take a year off from studying to see how the band would get on. Evans' guitar playing is world

---

[7] Byrne, Kevin, 'Biography: Bono', available at: <http://www.atu2.com/band/bono/>.
[8] Santana, Mariana and McGee, Matt, 'Biography: The Edge', available at: <http://www.atu2.com/band/edge/>.

renowned – he occupied twenty-fourth place on *Rolling Stone* magazine's list of 'The 100 Greatest Guitarists of All Time', ahead of Mark Knopfler and Brian May. He also provides the (often) dramatic backing vocals on many of the group's best known releases and, on a few occasions, has provided the lead vocals. The Edge has also recorded with Johnny Cash, Tina Turner and Ron Wood. In 1996, he was the first recipient of the Rory Gallagher Rock Musician Award (Larry Mullen was awarded one the following year). In 1983, Evans married Aislinn O'Sullivan, with whom he remained for seven years and had three daughters: Holly (1985), Arun (1986) and Blue Angel (1989). In 1990 they separated and in 1996 were legally divorced. He now has a daughter, Sian, and a son, Levi, with Morleigh Steinberg, the belly dancer and choreographer from the Zoo TV Tour, whom he started dating in 1993. The two were officially married in June 2002.

Adam Clayton

The first son of Jo and Brian Clayton, Adam (sometimes called 'Sparky') was born in 1960 in Oxfordshire, England. Brian was an RAF pilot[9] and moved to Ireland in 1965 to work for Aer Lingus. Adam spent many of his school years as a boarder, something he resented and rebelled against as he grew older. His first bass guitar was bought by his mother in 1975 for £52, though it was not until 1996 that he received formal training. In 1978, he was (because of disciplinary problems) asked to leave Mount Temple High School. His early role in the band, as well as bass player, was effectively as manager – this basically involved pestering anyone with a connection in the business for help. Adam is not as openly religious as the other band members. He has worked with other artists such as Nanci Griffiths and Robbie Robertson and, while not noted as a singer, he provided vocals on the song 'Your Blue Room' from *Original Soundtracks No. 1*, a spoken piece. Clayton was awarded the Bassist of the Year award at the Gibson Guitar Awards in 2000. He remains unmarried.

References

Ali, Lorraine (2005), 'Don't Push Me 'Cause I'm Close to the Edge', *Newsweek*, 26 December.

---

9 See <http://www.threechordsandthetruth.net/u2bios/u2adambio.htm>.

Associated Press (2005), 'Bono Visits Bush at the White House', 19 October.

Associated Press (2005*a*), 'Rock, Rap, Reunions at Live 8 Concerts', 3 July.

Associated Press (2005*b*), 'Bono Seen on Short List for World Bank Chief', 6 March.

Carr, D. (2005), 'Media Age Business Tips From U2', *New York Times*, 28 November.

Collins, J. (2007), 'Elevating Business for Bono', *Irish Times*, 8 June.

Eliraz, M. (2006), *Band Together: Internal Dynamics in U2, REM, Radiohead and the Red Hot Chili Peppers*, North Carolina: McFarland & Co.

Goldsmith, M. (2007), 'My Dinner with Bono: Bono's Journey from Rock Star to Humanitarian', *BusinessWeek*, 26 April.

Heffernan, B. (2006), 'U2's Tax Move Is Defended by Band's Manager', *Irish Independent*, 21 September.

Irish Times (2007), 'Elevating Business for Bono', 8 June.

McCormick, N. (2006), *U2 by U2*, London: Harper Collins.

Mullins, R. (2004), 'Beautiful Day for Apple, U2', *Silicon Valley/San Jose Business Journal*, 26 October.

Olsen, P. (2005), 'Managing the Edge (and Bono)', *New York Times*, 12 June.

Santana, M. and McGee, M., 'Biography: The Edge', available at: <http:// www.atu2.com/band/edge>.

Taylor, T. (1997), 'U2's Paul McGuinness – A Manager and a Gentleman', *National Association of Record Industry Professionals*, 1 June.

Tyrangiel, J. (2002), 'Bono's Mission', *Time Magazine*, 23 February.

Wenner, J. (2005), 'Bono – The Rolling Stone Interview', *Rolling Stone*, 20 October.

CHAPTER 13

O2 Communications Ireland

Gordon Lynn, Theo Lynn, Malcolm Brady and Paul Davis[1]
Dublin City University Business School, Dublin City University

Danuta Gray, chief executive officer of O2 Ireland, stood in front of a gathering of Ireland's national media in October 2006 and announced the launch of mobile TV for O2 customers:

> O2 are delighted to be first in Ireland to trial live broadcast television to customers on their mobile phones. This latest innovation in the wider communications sector is set to play a key role in the future of mobile technology. Mobile television will greatly enhance the range of services to users and is an exciting progression towards the mobile phone becoming a more advanced, multi-faceted communications tool. The convergence of mobile phones and broadcast media also offers business opportunities for the organisations involved in both sectors and will no doubt lead to exciting initiatives in the future.

At that announcement, O2 Ireland became the first mobile operator in Ireland to bring to trial broadcast mobile TV, commencing with an initial technology trial in December 2006. In January 2007, the trial expanded to include 400 O2 Ireland customers in the greater Dublin area who experienced broadcast TV on their mobile phones for an eight-month period, allowing users to flick between TV channels on their mobile, just as they would do if watching TV at home.

Two months later, O2 Ireland again expanded into new territory, this time the music industry, with another announcement for the national media on the official launch of Napster Mobile. Commenting on the launch, Gerry McQuaid, O2's new business director said:

---

[1] The authors wish to acknowledge O2 for its support in compiling this case study. Information in the study is based on publically available press releases, and relates to O2's position up to 2007. This case study is intended solely as a basis for class discussion. It is not intended to illustrate either effective or ineffective management.

We are delighted to be the first mobile operator in Europe to launch Napster Mobile. The Napster brand is instantly recognisable as one of the world's biggest music brands with 2.2 million tracks available immediately for our i-Mode customers. Our customers have asked us for online music brands and we are delighted to provide the Napster catalogue as part of our service. The Napster announcement today forms part of an overall music strategy, coordinated closely with the director of music in Telefónica.

O2 Ireland became the first mobile operator in Europe to offer Napster Mobile with its 3G i-Mode handsets. Napster Mobile allows O2 Ireland customers with 3G access to search, browse, preview and purchase content from Napster's immense music catalogue of over two million songs. In addition to the service, O2 Ireland customers are also able to access a copy of their mobile downloads on their personal computers, giving them the flexibility of listening to their music both on the go and at the PC, all from one universally recognised music brand.

Modern-day mobile phone technology has evolved greatly from its original form. New product and service offerings are breaking down traditional boundaries of the mobile device as a conversational tool. The entire mobile industry is adapting to the rapidly evolving lifestyle changes that have been driven by technology advancements. Over the past twenty years, true handheld mobility has developed and displaced all earlier forms of mobile communications for consumers. Along with the dramatic shifts in demographics and evolution in mobile technology, many technical and commercial pressures face mobile network service providers today. With markets moving towards saturation, revenue growth can no longer be equated to subscriber growth. Instead, revenue growth must now come from increased usage of the existing services (e.g. voice service) and from the use of new innovative data services. The Irish telecommunications industry is no exception to this, as record levels of mobile phone subscribers and increased competition in the form of new market entrants have saturated the market and slowed revenue growth.

Trends in the Irish Mobile Market

Market Penetration

At the end of March 2007, ComReg reported that there were almost 4.7 million 2G and 3G mobile subscribers in Ireland with mobile penetration of 112 per cent (based on the number of active SIM cards per 100 of the population). Irish mobile penetration is close to the European average. Considering mobile phone penetration in Ireland was only 79 per cent at the end of 2004, this trend represents massive growth.

Market Share

The Irish mobile market is dominated by three companies: Vodafone, O2 and Meteor. The market share between the existing operators can be broken down by subscriber numbers and retail revenue. Vodafone and O2 dominate the market with over 82.1 per cent market share of subscribers and 86.4 per cent of revenues between them. Over the past three years there have been trend changes in the market share of the top three operators, with Meteor gaining market share at the expense of Vodafone and O2. According to ComReg, Meteor has 17.9 per cent of mobile subscriptions, but has a smaller market revenue share of 13.6 per cent. It should be noted that ComReg will only commence reporting on the mobile network '3''s market penetration in September 2007.

Market Revenues

The mobile market revenue is measured by average revenue per user (ARPU), an indicator of the average monthly revenue generated by a mobile subscriber. Revenue can be generated from voice and data usage of the mobile. ComReg estimated mobile ARPU in Ireland at €44.48 per month in the first quarter of 2007, a 5 per cent decline since the last quarter, and a 5.8 per cent decline in ARPU since the first quarter of 2006 when ARPU in Ireland was €47.20. This is consistent with a wider European decline in mobile ARPU and Ireland's mobile ARPU still remains the highest among the EU member states monitored and substantially higher than the EU average of €29.63.

Interestingly, a breakdown of voice and data revenues suggests that there is an increase in data service usage and revenue. Data services would include the use of multimedia messaging services (MMS), general packet radio services (GPRS) and 3G data services. ComReg (2007) reports that, in Europe, Irish mobile operators have the second highest level of data revenue as a percentage of their total mobile revenues (22 per cent).

As the Irish mobile market develops, standard voice and data products and services have become more commoditised, with revenue and margins falling over time. Competition and regulation have driven down the cost of these services. Thus, the emphasis on mobile operators like O2 Ireland is to drive down the cost of standard products and services and derive greater incremental revenue and profitability from new data and value-added services, including services outside the communications universe, e.g. Internet.

The Evolution of O2 Ireland

Esat Digifone was founded in 1995 as a joint venture between the Esat Telecom Group and Norwegian telecommunications entity Telenor. At the time the Esat Group was headed up by entrepreneur Denis O'Brien, who commented on the launch: 'Today only 3 per cent of [Irish] people have mobile phones, they are perceived as a high cost luxury item. I have to change that otherwise I won't have a successful business.'

Late in 1996, Esat Digifone was awarded the second GSM mobile network licence by Irish telecommunications regulatory body ComReg. This allowed Esat Digifone to compete against 'first to market' rival Eircell (now Vodafone Ireland). Esat Digifone's vision was 'to be the number one mobile network provider in Ireland' and with no time to spare they began aggressively rolling out a national network and providing services to post-paying (i.e. monthly bill) and pre-paying (i.e. top-up card) customers in Ireland.

Strong results and massive growth soon followed and, by 1998, Esat Digifone commanded up to 44 per cent of the mobile market share. Many factors paved the way, but particularly important to its success were the employees' focus on the customer and the quality of the fast expanding mobile network. These trends continued over the following years and significant investments in technology positioned Esat Digifone on track to achieve their vision. The employee base grew to over 800 people, based in Dublin, Cork, Limerick and Galway.

From Esat Digifone to O2

It did not take long for Esat Digifone to attract the attention of foreign investors. In 2000, as part of the Esat Telecom Group restructure, Esat Digifone was sold to the British Telecom Group (BT) for £2 billion. The company continued to operate as Esat Digifone until early 2001 when BT Wireless de-merged from the BT Group. It took with them Esat Digifone in Ireland, Viag Telecom in Germany, Telefort in Holland, Manx in the Isle of Man, and Genie ISP and BT Wireless in the UK. These companies were then re-branded under the umbrella of the newly created holding company, mmO2 plc. The strategy was to create a single brand that would be recognised across Europe. This brand became O2.

Telefónica Takeover

Up until February 2006, O2 Ireland was a wholly owned subsidiary of O2 plc. In mid-February 2006, a takeover bid of O2 plc by Telefónica

SA, the Spanish telephone operator, was approved by shareholders. On 7 March 2006, O2 plc de-listed from the London Stock Exchange.

O2 is now a wholly owned subsidiary of Telefónica SA, which comprises mobile network operators in the UK and Ireland, along with integrated fixed/mobile businesses in Germany, the Czech Republic (Telefónica O2 Czech Republic) and the Isle of Man (Manx Telecom). It also owns 50 per cent of the Tesco Mobile and Tchibo Mobilfunk joint venture businesses in the UK and Germany, respectively. As part of an enlarged company, O2 built on its track record of operational delivery, brand strength and the momentum it has established in its markets. O2 and Telefónica brought together two strong, successful, growth-orientated companies creating a major pan-European/global telecoms player. The combined entity is now the second largest global wireless operator outside of China. It has more than 116 million mobile customers and the combined group is the world's second most valuable telecom operator with an enterprise value of €120 billion. A summary of the financial data for O2 is provided in Appendix 13.1.

It is evident that O2 Ireland has come a long way since 1996. O2 Ireland cites two key success factors – its continuing investment in the O2 network and its culture and people.

The O2 Network

O2 believes success in the highly competitive Irish mobile market is shaped around maintaining a superior quality network. This means:

- Ensuring that customers receive the best possible service and network quality.
- Continued investment in the network, ensuring ongoing and consistent improvements to O2 products and services.
- Reducing the costs of using mobile technology over the network.
- Consistency of service 24/7, 365 days a year.

Since 1997, O2 has invested heavily in the O2 network, the communications infrastructure that underlies O2's business. The O2 network is considered to be one of the best mobile networks in the world with an ongoing investment of €200 million per annum.

Mobile phone technology is constantly evolving, providing opportunities for the existing competition and new market entrants to offer new services with lower-cost infrastructures. As such, continuous evolution and fast adaptation to technological change is essential for companies like O2, while representing substantial risk and investment from both a technology platform and people perspective. New platforms may not be adopted in the forecast timeframe or indeed at all, and each new technology introduction requires a significant investment in training and support processes. In November 2002, Danuta Gray invited Cap Gemini consultants to analyse the existing methods of managing the technology element of delivering products and services into the marketplace. Following radical environmental analysis of the company over a seven-month period, the consultants recommended a radical change strategy to the existing functional structure and design. The advice to the CEO was that 'silo' mentality (single inwardly looking organisation) could be removed by restructuring the IT and technical department into a single technology department. A change team was appointed in May 2002, and following months of organisational change workshops, the technology department was launched on 1 December 2003. This radical restructuring laid the foundation for further product and service enhancement on the technology front.

The continuous evolution of mobile phone technology was embraced by O2 and their technology function. Following the purchase of one of the four 3G licences from ComReg in 2002, O2 Ireland positioned itself to meet the future demands of customers. Having a 3G licence meant that O2 could build a larger network (predominantly on to the existing 2G network) to allow larger amounts of voice and data services to be transported and downloaded on mobile phones up to four times faster than the speeds offered by second generation handsets. The launch of O2's 3G network was postponed, as industry rivals Vodafone were first to market in 2003. The decision to delay the launch was based on not substituting quality of network standards at the expense of the customer experience.

In May 2005, O2 announced the commercial launch of i-Mode. i-Mode is the world's most widely used mobile Internet service, developed by NTT DoCoMo (Japan's largest mobile communications provider). i-Mode became available exclusively to O2 in Ireland and offered mobile Internet services to both pre-pay and post-pay customers. i-Mode greatly enhanced O2's position in an increasingly competitive Irish mobile landscape and serves as a strong differentiator on mobile data services provided by operators. i-Mode was developed as an inexpensive method of packet-switched, high-speed communication. Packet switched means that i-Mode communications are 'always on', unlike voice calls that are 'circuit based' and only functional after dial-up. i-Mode offers access to thousands of websites for a wide range of purposes, including eBay for shopping, MyHome.ie for househunting, IrishJobs.ie for job-seeking and Napster.com for music.

Late in 2006, O2 Ireland announced a radical network swap-out programme called Enigma. Project Enigma involved a multi-million euro partnership with Ericsson Ireland to face-lift the O2 network from the existing combined Nortel/Nokia hardware to Ericsson equipment. The two-year programme is designed to future-proof the O2 network with increased levels of quality and capacity for the existing technology and for future offerings, such as HSDPA and 4G.

O2 People, Customers and Community

In March 2006, O2 Ireland was named the overall Best Company to Work For in Ireland by the Great Place to Work Institute and the *Irish Independent* newspaper. For the second year running, O2 was also awarded Best Company to Work For in the 'over 1,000 employees' category. Commenting at the awards ceremony, Danuta Gray said:

> Our aim is to create a friendly working environment where people take pride in their jobs, in their teams and in the company, and where employees feel that they can be themselves. It's only by getting it right for our people that we can get it right for our customers.

The people of O2 have always played a major role in the organisation's success, from the first 'start-up' employees in 1995 to the 1,700 employees in 2007. From day one, the people values of the organisation have focused on customers, a focus that has remained since integration with the mmO2 group whose corporate values include being bold, clear, open and trusted. The prevailing culture in O2 has been there since inception and stems from the entrepreneurial attitudes that grew the company to where it is today.

This unique culture is a means of creating competitive advantage and has been fully integrated into the existing strategy. The strategic targets are based on adopting the philosophy of having 'the most satisfied employees', which in turn will lead to greater levels of customer service, thus gaining 'the most loyal customers' who in turn will achieve new levels of loyalty, service, revenue and profits for O2.

In late 2005, the launch of the 'O2 Customer Promise' provided a vision of how O2 planned to meet the strategic objectives of having the most loyal customers. The Customer Promise was founded following a series of customer insight and research initiatives, where O2 customers described what they really valued. The promise comprises six simple statements:

1. We make it easy to do business with us.
2. We treat you personally.
3. We reward loyalty.
4. We give great value for money.
5. We get the basics right first time.
6. We are passionate about service excellence.

These statements have been adopted into an array of service offerings that aim to provide unprecedented levels of service; this will differentiate O2 from its industry rivals, thereby providing a competitive advantage for O2.

To facilitate and embed the Customer Promise into the culture of O2, a series of group-wide training programmes called 'Making It Happen' was introduced in 2006. 'Making It Happen' concentrated on creating higher levels of customer service and loyalty and giving employees a strong understanding of the business, customer segment profiles and the impact of each employee's role on the bottom line. With over 95 per cent attendance, the programme has been successfully rolled out throughout O2 Ireland.

O2 recognise that they not only have a corporate responsibility to their employees and customers, but also to the wider community. Addressing the publication of the Telefónica O2 Corporate Responsibility Report 2006, Peter Erskine, chairman and CEO of Telefónica O2 Europe plc, addressed this issue directly:

> All elements of society are interdependent.... By building partnerships and alliances with people inside and outside of O2, our business is a better one – creating jobs, value, wealth, environmental progress, fair products and a sustainable business that listens and learns from others.

Corporate social responsibility is represented in many programmes that O2 Ireland has initiated or participated in. It has been active in initiating and developing environmental programmes including the use of renewable energy and collecting redundant handsets for recycling. In addition to supporting fundraising initiatives and sponsoring projects, such as the O2 Ability Awards, Business in the Community's Schools' Business Partnership and the CITY project in Ballymun, O2 has used its technology capabilities to launch new specially designed handsets with the National Council for the Blind to support visually impaired users. As mobile penetration increases, O2 is faced with new risks and challenges that result from the business it is in. For example, it has recently launched a number of child protection and health research initiatives relating to mobile communications.

Competition in the Irish Mobile Telecommunications Industry

The Irish mobile telecommunications industry has changed considerably in the ten years since O2 Ireland was first launched (see Table 13.1). The industry has experienced rapid growth, especially in recent years. The industry players have doubled in number and increased in size, with new market entrants like '3', Smart Telecom and a series of potential mobile virtual network operators (MVNOs), for example, Clever Communications. Many of these new competitors have significant financial backing.

Table 13.1: The Competitive Landscape of the Irish Mobile Telecommunications Industry has Changed Dramatically Since 2004

2004	2006
• Three players – Vodafone, O2 and Meteor (O2 and Vodafone with 90 per cent market share)	• '3' entered the market with aggressive growth plans
• Second highest ARPU in Europe	• Eircom plans to grow Meteor by exploiting synergies
• Eight per cent market revenue growth	• Smart win, then lose the fourth 3G licence
• Penetration hits 100 per cent	• MVNOs to enter the market

Vodafone Ireland

Vodafone is Ireland's leading mobile phone operator, with a customer base of over 1.8 million and a total of 1,500 employees. The company was established in 1984 by Telecom Éireann and operated Ireland's first mobile phone service as a separate brand, Eircell. In May 2001, Eircell was acquired by Vodafone. At the end of March 2007, Vodafone had a 46.9 per cent market share based on subscriptions and a 45.8 per cent market share based on revenues, representing a decrease of approximately 3.6 and 3.5 per cent respectively over a two-year period.

Vodafone's vision is to be the world's mobile communications leader. In Ireland, Vodafone operates both a 2G and a 3G network; the former uses a digital GSM 900 mobile phone system and the latter a universal mobile telecommunications system (UMTS) (the first such 3G system in the Republic of Ireland). As Ireland's first mobile phone service, Eircell enjoyed rapid growth. In October 1997, Eircell introduced the world's first 'pay as you go' system under the Ready to Go brand, turning mobile communications in Ireland into a mass-market product. Vodafone Ireland introduced UMTS services (branded 'Vodafone live! With 3G') in 2004, launching the first handsets in November ahead of O2 Ireland and '3'. Initially restricted to bill-pay customers, Vodafone extended UMTS to pre-pay customers in June 2005.

Meteor Communications

Launched on 22 February 2001, Meteor became the third mobile operator in Ireland and gradually gained a 10 per cent share of the Irish market. In 2004, Western Wireless (the then parent company) bought out the remaining minority shareholders in the consortium, and it became a wholly owned subsidiary of that company. In July 2005, Eircom acquired Meteor for €420 million; it is now a wholly owned subsidiary of Eircom Group plc. At the end of March 2007, Meteor had a 17.9 per cent market share based on subscriptions and a 13.6 per cent market share based on revenues, representing an increase of approximately 8.1 per cent and 7.5 per cent over a two-year period.

Meteor has gained a significant share of the pre-paid teenage and international markets by focusing on high-value, low-cost service offerings. These service offerings include free Meteor to Meteor calls and texts for life for post-pay customers, and 5c calls or free texts for life for pay-as-you-go customers. Recently, Meteor added an innovative 'call a friend for free' tariff for pay-as-you-go customers who 'top up' by €20 in one go per month. Meteor is now activating as many bill pay (post-paid) customers as its competitors.

Meteor holds a UMTS licence and offers 3G services such as video calling to their customers. Although a late entrant into the GPRS (2.5G) segment, they now offer these services. Most recently, Meteor won a bid for the final 3G licence after Smart Mobile, who was initially offered the licence, withdrew. Meteor is now obliged to have 33 per cent of the population covered by 3G before September 2008. Meteor have also recently signed a deal with T-Mobile UK, which will see T-Mobile UK contract customers being offered a flat rate of £0.25 for calls made while roaming on the Meteor network in Ireland. Meteor has 38 stores throughout Ireland and over 7,000 top-up outlets.

'3' Ireland

Hutchison 3G Ireland Ltd is the fourth mobile phone company in the Republic of Ireland. A subsidiary of Hutchinson 3G, it trades in Ireland under the brand '3'. The company holds a UMTS mobile telecommunications licence from ComReg, which was granted in June 2002. In 2004 it began testing its network with major corporate clients and in May 2005 began running commercials on Irish television, fuelling speculation that it was to launch shortly. However, it was not until July 2005 that the network was launched and became available to the public.

'3' operates on a UMTS (3G) network only using the subscriber trunk dialling (STD) code of 083. In May 2006, '3' launched its pre-paid service, 3Pay, and, as of March 2007, 3 Ireland had 77,000 subscribers, 1.6 per cent of the Irish mobile market. It is presently making much of its video capabilities, providing free video content including news from Independent Television News, FA Premier League video clips and movie trailers. In October 2006, '3' Ireland announced they would have twenty-eight shops opened by the end of 2007 and a further eight opened by the end of 2008.

MVNOs

Regulatory pressures from ComReg have forced changes in the mobile industry and have paved the way for mobile virtual network operators (MVNOs) to enter the Irish marketplace. MVNOs traditionally tend to use low price strategies to win market share, which attracts the lower value end of the market more so than small to medium enterprises or corporate customers. Leveraging off the success in the UK with Tesco Mobile, at the end of October 2007 Tesco Mobile launched in Ireland, using O2's network via a 089 prefix.

Emerging Trends in Telecommunications

Mobile Content

Increasing mobile phone ownership, usage and dependency has stimulated increased demand for a whole range of content while on the move. The global market for mobile content has grown significantly since the late 1990s. A recent report published by the Yankee Group has shown a gradual increase in the total revenue generated by non-voice services in Western Europe, up from 17 per cent in 2005 to 19 per cent in 2006. The breakdown of mobile content services is shown in Figure 13.1.

Figure 13.1: Mobile Content Services usage in Europe

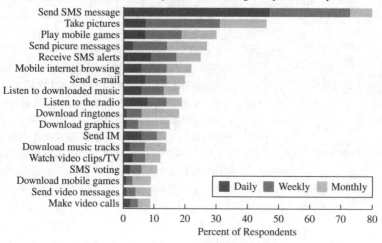

How often do you do the following with your mobile phone?

Source: Yankee Group 2006 European Mobile Multimedia Survey

Mobile content services in Ireland is developing rapidly as all four mobile operators offer a variety of services like Vodafone Live, Meteor Stuff, O2 Active and i-Mode, and What's on 3. In a recently published ComReg Amárach Trends survey, Irish mobile users were asked about the range of services they performed on their mobiles. An analysis based on age profiles suggests that younger users are driving mobile content usage, downloading ringtones (33 per cent), games (18 per cent) and music (11 per cent). A 2007 Yankee Group report concurs, stating that revenue generated by mobile content has largely been from ringtones and games, and advises that operators make a concerted attempt to extend appeal beyond the core group currently subscribing to these services. They anticipate that further growth will be driven by increased demand for broader mobile content services, particularly mobile TV and Internet browsing.

VoIP

As a technology, VoIP, or voice-over-Internet protocol, is a clever 'reinvention of the wheel'. Yet it is a technology that has the potential to redefine the way the world communicates. VoIP is a method of taking analogue audio signals, the ones currently used in phones, and turning them into digital data to be transmitted over the Internet. The practical upshot of this is that, by using free VoIP software, callers can entirely bypass phone companies and their charges. Unsurprisingly, demand is growing greatly. Consumers are shifting to VoIP due to the flexibility it offers. With VoIP, a call can be made wherever there is a broadband connection. Industry observers IDC believe that users of VoIP (including Skype) will grow from three million currently to over twenty-seven million by the year 2009. Instat believes that, by 2009, 12 per cent of all the cellular subscribers will have wireless local area network (WLAN) on their devices and the number using it for voice will be higher than the number using it for data only. Leading VoIP provider Skype claims that it has 33 million registered users and adds 155,000 new users a day.

Despite this growing interest in Internet-based telephony, the technology is still in its infancy. Just a few years ago, only a handful of companies were offering VoIP services and then only to business customers. The Irish consumer is not that well educated in this area yet. While there is growing penetration of Skype, it is based on fixed personal computers and used for long-distance calling. Outside of the high-tech early adopter group, there is little current desire due to security fears and general lack of awareness. However, as broadband penetration grows, there will be a larger penetration of VoIP solutions. Currently in Ireland, Skype provides about 64 per cent savings on domestic calls and 88 per cent on international calls.

Wi-Fi Broadband

Broadband penetration in Ireland falls somewhat behind its EU counterparts and the EU average of 15.6 per cent as shown in Figure 13.2. Amárach Consulting (2007) reports that 76 per cent of Irish people are aware of broadband services, but only 53 per cent are aware of broadband wireless (Wi-Fi) and 54 per cent of 3G (see Appendix 13.2).

Wi-Fi allows individuals to access the Internet from Wi-Fi hotspots without the need for wires. In Ireland Wi-Fi hotspots, or areas that offer Wi-Fi access, can be found in selected locations such as libraries, hotels, conference centres, cafés and public buildings. In most cases, the user pays for high-speed Internet access at an access point, based either on a voucher payment for a specific amount of time or a monthly subscription. Despite having a lower broadband penetration than EU counterparts, plans were announced in January 2007 by Dublin City Council to launch a Wi-Fi Internet service allowing Dubliners free access to the Internet anywhere in the capital. It is projected that building such a Wi-Fi network for a city the size of Dublin could cost between €12 million and €20

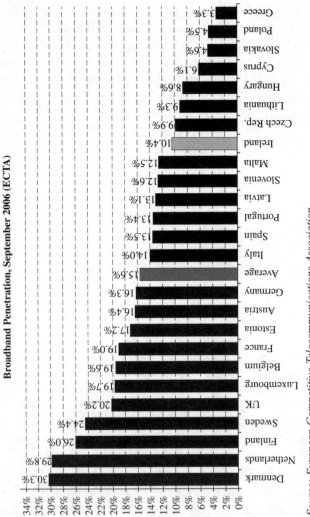

Figure 13.2: Broadband Penetration in the EU

Broadband Penetration, September 2006 (ECTA)

Denmark	30.3%
Netherlands	29.8%
Finland	26.0%
Sweden	24.4%
UK	20.2%
Luxembourg	19.7%
Belgium	19.6%
France	19.0%
Estonia	17.2%
Austria	16.4%
Germany	16.3%
Average	15.6%
Italy	14.0%
Spain	13.5%
Portugal	13.4%
Latvia	13.1%
Slovenia	12.6%
Malta	12.5%
Ireland	10.4%
Czech Rep.	9.9%
Lithuania	9.3%
Hungary	8.6%
Cyprus	6.1%
Slovakia	4.6%
Poland	4.5%
Greece	3.3%

Source: European Competitive Telecommunications Association million. In addition to Dublin residents, the service could be accessed by tourists, business people visiting the city, mobile workers and the voluntary sector.

O2 in 2007 and Beyond

Irish mobile telecommunications have evolved at a considerably rapid pace since O2 launched as Esat Digifone in the late 1990s. Now, with record levels of mobile subscriptions, the marketplace is saturated. Regulatory body ComReg has created an industry where additional competition has entered with significant impact on incumbent firm revenue streams. Add to the mix the increasing demand and expectations from a more technologically advanced consumer who seeks a range of services on the move, superior network quality, excellent customer service and best in market value. Not only has consumer demand changed, but also the technology itself is transforming to meet demand. Traditional boundaries are been broken with mobiles moving into Internet services and Internet services moving into telephony. Never before have there been such pressures on a mobile operator to evolve to meet a changing environment.

O2 Ireland's customer base at the end of December 2006 was 1.632 million, its highest ever level; however, it suffered a decline in service revenue of 1.5 per cent year on year. Can Danuta Gray and her management team return to the path of revenue growth in such a competitive market? And, if so, how?

Appendix 13.1: Summary of O2 Financial Statements 2006–2003

	2006* €'000	2005 €'000	2004 €'000	2003 €'000
Revenue	756,746	858,617	762,013	686,487
Cost of sales	305,852	301,439	216,848	237,734
Depreciation of network assets	N/P	73,402	74,224	68,468
Gross profit	450,894	483,776	470,941	380,285
Administrative expenses	267,520	262,341	280,578	252,781
Operating profit	183,374	221,435	190,363	127,504
Profit before taxation	176,000	214,547	199,228	107,824

ten months
Source: O2

Appendix 13.2: Amárach Consulting Survey Reporting on Broadband Awareness in Ireland 2007

Are you aware of a service which is available called broadband internet access?

Percentage who said Yes:	
Gender	
Male	77%
Female	74%
Age	
15-24	87%
25-44	87%
45-64	66%
65-74	31%
Region	
Dublin	68%
ROL	76%
Munster	77%
Conn/Ulster	86%

Yes 76%

No 24%

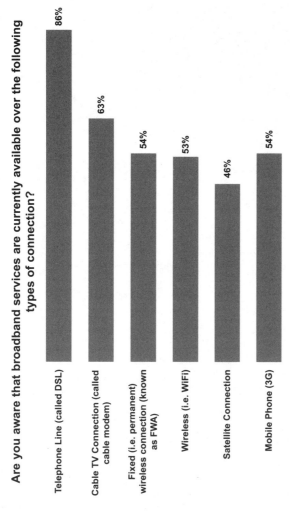

Appendix 13.2: (*Continued*)

Are you aware that broadband services are currently available over the following types of connection?

Telephone Line (called DSL) — 86%

Cable TV Connection (called cable modem) — 63%

Fixed (i.e. permanent) wireless connection (known as FWA) — 54%

Wireless (i.e. WiFi) — 53%

Satellite Connection — 46%

Mobile Phone (3G) — 54%

Source: Amárach Consulting, 2007

CHAPTER 14

Managing Relationships for Innovation in the Food Industry

Patrick Lynch and Thomas O'Toole[1]
School of Business, Waterford Institute of Technology

The late February board meeting had been exhaustive and extremely argumentative. Long after everyone had left work for the day, Carl Young, the managing director of Farmfresh,[2] sat behind his mahogany desk and reflected on the day's meeting and the heated debate concerning Packfex, one of their plastic film suppliers. Five months ago, in two of Farmfresh's production facilities, Packfex's film (Chubb X1) was uncharacteristically causing significant wastage, approximately 33 per cent in their pudding range of products. In production terms, the golden rule is that production wastage running into double figures is totally unacceptable. Over the five-month period, Farmfresh had absorbed substantial costs while both companies attempted to rectify the errors in the film and the production process. Besides the ever-increasing costs and shrinking profit margins, the inconsistency in production meant that delivery of their pudding product range was unreliable. Indeed, pressure was mounting from numerous customers, especially the large retailers, to sort the distribution problem. Members of Farmfresh's board were worried about loss of reputation and potentially even market share. In the interim, Young had given his personal assurance to their customers that the situation was under control and that product made to the highest quality would be delivered on time.

[1] The authors wish to acknowledge the case companies and in particular the interviewees for their time, help, guidance and support while researching and compiling this case study. Information in the case study is based on fifteen interviews carried out over a seven-month period between October 2005 and April 2006. This case study is intended solely as a basis for class discussion. It is not intended to illustrate either effective or ineffective management.
[2] Due to the sensitivity of the material contained within this case, company names and individual names have been altered to adhere to confidentiality agreements.

Packfex had guaranteed Farmfresh that a new film would work. However, when the new film was uploaded, the production wastage from Chubb X2 was higher than ever before, approximately 50 per cent. Immediately, the tension between representatives from both companies was intense, with some very aggressive language being expressed by Young's own senior staff towards Packfex managers. Under pressure from the engineering and production departments, the corporate buyer had informed Packfex that they were being de-listed due to the ongoing quality issue with their film.

The next day, Young had organised a board meeting to discuss how the issue was going to be resolved. He was worried that the big retailers would not tolerate another slip-up in distribution, especially over any extended length of time. He knew that competitors would love the opportunity to seize market share on a range of their top selling branded products. However, at the meeting, internal conflict broke out between departments over the issue of who was to blame and whether Packfex should be de-listed. Most blame and criticism was directed at the incompetence of the production and engineering departments, who in turn blamed the incompetence of Packfex. The financial controller had quipped that the money was literally flowing out the company doors and it wasn't his fault. The meeting had become so conflictual that Young had called a halt to the board meeting until the following day.

The Irish Agri-Food Industry

The contribution of the Irish agri-food industry to the Irish economy is very significant in terms of manufacturing output, exports, employment and also through the purchase of raw materials and services. The total value of the Irish agri-food industry in 2006 was over €12 billion or 8.1 per cent of GDP. Exports of the industry amounted to €8.1 billion, with the UK being the main destination for Irish agri-food exports. In 2005, the UK accounted for 48 per cent of all exports and 30 per cent went to continental European markets, while the remaining 22 per cent went to international markets.[3] According to the Census of Industrial Production (2002),[4] 696 companies are engaged in the agri-food industry, providing approximately 163,400 jobs or 8.1 per cent of total employment.

---

[3] Bord Bia: <http:\\www.bordbia.ie >.
[4] Central Statistics Office: <http:\\www.cso.ie/census>.

Nevertheless, in recent years, pressure has intensified on Ireland's agri-food industry due to European Commission price cuts on commodities, as well as an increasingly competitive export market (Department of Food and Agriculture 2004). Indeed, in 2006 some agri-food companies faced troublesome times when the price of their products sold on international markets was lower than the cost of producing them. Another factor is that consumer tastes, market trends and international trade are changing at an ever rapid pace. In addition, Irish agri-food companies are being squeezed by very large European retailers, who control around 50 per cent of the food retail market.[5]

These changes are creating much more competitive EU and world commodity markets, and ever more complex and innovative food product markets (Department of Food and Agriculture 2004). New product development is essential and, according to Ireland's former Minister for Agriculture and Food Mary Coughlan, 'without increased investment in R&D, Ireland's food industry will be outstripped and out-paced by others who already possess the necessary research capability' (ElAmin 2005). The lack of an innovative focus has been identified in the Irish agri-food industry as a major failing. The Irish food industry's expenditure on R&D at 0.3 per cent of sales is lower than in other sectors of the economy. This is in part because it comprises a large number of small and medium enterprises (SMEs), which do not have the capability or expertise to engage in R&D and which, in any event, do not originate from such a background or culture. There is a general consensus at government and industry level that all agri-food companies face a challenge to produce more added value products in coming years and so there is a need to invest more time and resources in R&D to generate a culture of innovation and risk taking in the market (Department of Agriculture and Food 2004).

Pudding and Its Relationship to Plastic Packaging

Pudding can either be white or black. In contrast to the former, black pudding or blood pudding is a sausage made by cooking blood with a filler until it is thick enough to congeal when cooled. Blood sausage is a more recent North American term for the same as well as a useful term for similar blood-based solid foods around the world. In Ireland, pig blood is most often used. Consequently, the pudding consists of pork meat and

---

[5] Bord Bia: <http:\\www.bordbia.ie >.

fat, suet, bread and oatmeal formed into the shape of a large sausage. The importance of the plastic film is that the pudding is cooked in the packaging. Indeed, the plastic becomes the cooking vessel, in that the raw meat enters the packaging and is cooked. The packaging pasteurises and modularises all the cooking process. Moreover, the plastic interacts with the meat, depending on how much blood is in it, and controls the way the proteins and fats interact. When cooking, the meat swells to four times its thickness and the film has to be able to expand and then shrink back during the cooling process. Also the print has to be readable after the expansion and the shrinking. The shrink characteristics of the plastic gives a skin-like appearance to the pudding after cooking. This is a patented application of Packfex and only a few plastic manufacturers have managed to some degree to replicate the process and none to the quality offered by Packfex.

Background of the Two Companies

Farmfresh

Farmfresh is a medium-sized food and agricultural business in Ireland. Its range of businesses includes dairy and meat processing, liquid milk production and the provision of a comprehensive range of farm services, including animal breeding and livestock marketing. The company's products are marketed nationally and internationally. Its most important dairy brand name is Farmfresh, but it also sells products under several other national and international brand names. Farmfresh employs approximately 650 people and has an annual turnover in excess of €200 million.

For many years, Farmfresh operated in a tightly regulated market, which in essence created a comfort zone and allowed the company to survive while operating less efficiently in comparison to the world-class standards of some of its competitors. In addition, Farmfresh had an extremely wide and diverse product range which meant that the company was competing against an equally diverse set of leading competitors, and this was a major factor in its rising costs. In 2002, the company made a loss of €2.5 million and its operating profits dropped by 75 per cent, from just over €20 million to less than €5 million. It had been estimated that the company could lose over €15 million by 2008. In order to combat the loss in profits, the highly competitive nature of the agri-business, the rising production inflation, tighter margins and more sophisticated customers, Farmfresh board of directors appointed an outsider, Carl Young, to the position of managing director. Young, a very experienced CEO, immediately brought his own leadership style to the company, characterised by decisiveness, willingness to confront the issues and assuredness of direction. Unwavering in his vision and leadership style, Farmfresh has undergone significant structural change in the past few years: several plants were closed, over 150 employees were made redundant, the organisational structure was re-organised, business divisions were made operate to specific objectives and more focused business plans, costs have been reduced and product ranges sharpened. There has been specific investment in an innovation centre and a significant change in culture has been attempted.

In essence, under the direction of Carl Young the company moved away from a very formalised approach to a balance between organic and mechanistic structure. While the structure is formalised and processes are in place, as is evidenced by the pursuit of manufacturing excellence and high operational standards, there is also a high degree of flexibility within that structure. For example, autonomous work teams manage and run their functions within the company, and team leaders communicate extensively with management, and vice versa. Meetings are held on a regular basis between management and staff.

However, reflected in its structures, systems and approach to development of corporate strategy is a culture that is very aggressive; people co-operate with one another most of the time in order to survive, but are constantly having power struggles to establish and challenge orders of precedence. Often these struggles take place behind the scenes. There is a strong belief that successful internal processes lead to successful external cooperation and increased profits. In terms of cooperating with external actors, Farmfresh is an experienced collaborator and over the years has engaged in numerous partnerships and product development alliances, both at a national and international level. The company believes that it collaborates well with others. According to Peter Bell, engineering director of Farmfresh, 'We have extensive experience cooperating and interacting with others. We do it on a daily basis ... we are very good at it ...' However, a noticeable feature of Farmfresh's character is that it tends to favour collaboration strategies that provide continuity and security and views divergence from the norm as a threat or an issue of conflict and so reacts aggressively.

Packfex

Founded in 1978, Packfex is a privately owned company specialising in the supply of flexible packaging products to the food and beverage industry and other industrial sectors. These include meat, dairy, confectionery, coffee, fresh and ambient foods, and pet food. The company has gross sales in excess of €15 million per annum. The main production plant is located in Ireland, while a finishing warehouse to customise products for the European market is based in England. However, the ever-increasing number of manufacturers moving their production to cheaper economies has meant that the industry in Ireland has become smaller and many packaging companies have not survived the upheaval. As a consequence, the domestic industry has become highly competitive and most packaging companies, including Packfex, rely on European and American sales for their continuing survival. The highly competitive nature of the industry has meant that the degree of innovation amongst Irish packaging companies is prolific.

Indicative of a company whose origin began as a small family-run business, which evolved into a global manufacturer employing over seventy people in formalised departments, Packfex's organisational structure is a balance between an organic and mechanistic framework: the company holds on to its family values but, as the business has grown, it has been formalised to a degree. According to Eamon Coleman, technical director, 'Our processes are in place, yet there is an informality about us as well. We are doing things in real time so the structure has to be there but there also has to be the case where … informal structures can solve the issue.'

Supporting this balance in organisational structure is a culture centred on the image of the family: 'We have a closeness. There is a community here. In one way there aren't any secrets in our company, everyone knows everyone else's business, it is very much like a family. The formal structures are in place, but we also have the informality around it and then this is also embedded in an innovative culture' (Eamon Coleman). Indeed, there is a strong cultural norm within Packfex to establish and maintain a sense of innovativeness throughout the company and it strives to become a learning organisation. As Eamon Coleman states:

> Innovation creates profits, that is profit to innovate and so innovation has to be the responsibility of everyone in the company. The real trick that we are trying to do is to train our people up so that they will replace you, that they will challenge your position. We reward performance here at Packfex. We train people and we engage them to be more than they initially thought that they could do.

Consistent with its organisational structure and its embedded family culture, Packfex has both formal and informal communication structures in place. Due to the mechanistic processes in place, formal communication is a requirement. Yet, there is a very strong informal communication structure in the company. Packfex adopts an open plan office and actively encourages informal interaction and communication between all levels of the organisation. This balance between formal and informal is eloquently described in the following statement from Coleman: 'There is a lot of formality and informality about our company. They are intertwined. Informal communication generates innovation, it allows people to talk over coffee, ideas are created and shared, yet the formality facilitates the dissemination of that idea in a structured way.'

In terms of engaging in collaborative development projects, Packfex is an experienced collaborator and involves the user throughout the development process. According to Eamon Coleman: 'In order to survive in this industry, we needed partnerships and connections with other companies. We are not afraid to collaborate and share our knowledge with others. We want to learn from them. In the long run it has been the key to our success'. In attempting to enhance its collaborative potential, Packfex have established a team of individuals possessing what Packfex refer to as 'polyphonic' characteristics. Coleman states:

> What that means is that you have several specialities in different areas and as a result of that profile type, you can hold conversations and appreciate what is being said by people in different areas of the company, that is marketing, production, quality, etc. Because our people are polyphonics they create multiple relationships across disciplines. It is very important that you have more than one relationship because if things go wrong you still have connections.

Over the years, Packfex has developed a number of patented innovations from collaboration with other companies. Table 14.1 details a comparative profile of both companies.

Relationship Between the Two Companies

The relationship began in 1985, when Packfex received an order from Farmfresh to supply a standard base-line packaging film. This relationship between the two companies was said to be very good and, as a result, in late 1985, Farmfresh approached Packfex with a request to assist them in the development of a new packaging. Farmfresh wanted to make one of their salami products more attractive to customers and their production process more effective. The problem that Farmfresh was having with the traditional packaging was that when the meat entered the packaging it

Table 14.1: Case Profile Analysis

		Farmfresh	Packfex
Industry	*Sector*	Agri-business	Packaging
	Competitiveness	High	High
Company size	*Employee numbers*	650 employees	70 employees
	International dimension	Yes	Yes
Business strategy	*Formal planning*	Yes	Yes
	Vision	Clearly articulated/focused	Clearly articulated/focused
	Owner proximity	High	High
Organisational structure	*Type*	Simple/mechanistic	Simple
Organisational culture	*Type*	Aggressive	Family/ intrapreneurship
Communication	*Type*	Formal/informal	Formal/informal
Packaging film knowledge	*Experience with film*	Extensive	Extensive
	Technical knowledge	High	High
Collaborative knowledge	*Perceived need for intensive interaction*	High	High
	Prior collaborative experience	Extensive	Extensive

was hot, but when the meat cooled it shrank, leaving the packaging in a distorted state, which was very unappealing to customers.

The production wastage was very high as a result of defective packaging. In addition, the shelf life of the product was too short, further increasing waste on returns. The only potential supplier at the time was a Japanese company; however, the cost logistics of importing the packaging from Japan was prohibitive and so Farmfresh turned to its Irish suppliers for a solution. In contrast to other packaging companies at the time, Packfex was confident that the packaging could be developed and the two companies entered a collaborative agreement to develop the new packaging in late 1985. For Packfex, who at the time were a micro-packaging company with a few employees, the potential rewards of a successful collaborative development project with Farmfresh were high. Indeed, if the project was a success, Packfex would not only acquire a large contract, it would also have a new innovative product with vast market potential.

During the development project, the interaction between the two companies was said to be very frequent and intense. Proprietary information was shared by both companies and, after a number of failed attempts, a revolutionary and unique product specific to Farmfresh's production process was developed towards the end of 1986. The Chubb X1 film was highly innovative and replaced the traditional shirred casing for sausage type packs. Indeed, the innovativeness of the packaging is still evident today as only a few companies have been able to produce a similar film. Presently Chubb X1 is Packfex's biggest selling product and, as Packfex is currently becoming more global, new applications for the plastic are emerging, such as plastic covering for army artillery, and sales of the film in 2006–2007 are expected to increase exponentially.

Over the past twenty-one years, the relationship between Packfex and Farmfresh has become close and many iterations of Chubb X1 have been developed. At an inter-organisational level, the relationship between the two companies is characterised as being highly integrative, with high levels of trust, commitment and cooperation. Indeed, communication between the two companies is regarded by both as being high, with a considerable amount of information sharing. Due to the length of the relationship and the strategic importance of Farmfresh as a customer of Packfex, multiple relationships between both companies have been established at many different levels. Indeed, there are a number of close professional and interpersonal relationships between individuals in both companies (see Figure 14.1).

Of particular relevance to this case is the relationship between Farmfresh's engineering director (Peter Bell) and Packfex's technical director (Eamon Coleman). Both gentlemen are highly experienced executives with extensive backgrounds in engineering and new product development, and had developed a sound working and interpersonal relationship over the years. However, that interpersonal relationship and 21-year-old inter-company relationship was put under considerable pressure because of the high wastage attributed to Packfex's packaging film. Indeed, as detailed earlier, tensions between both companies intensified when the new packaging film created even higher wastage than before, culminating in Packfex being de-listed. The following section traces the quality crisis that occurred between Farmfresh and Packfex over a five-month period. Table 14.2 presents a chronological summary of that interaction, detailing both actions and perceptions of each company.

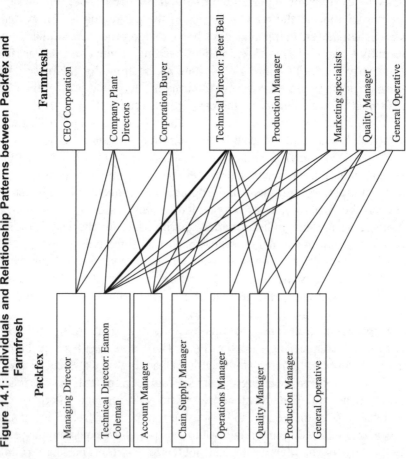

Figure 14.1: Individuals and Relationship Patterns between Packfex and Farmfresh

Quality Crisis Over a Five-Month Period: Perspectives from Farmfresh and Packfex

Table 14.2: Chronological Summary

Timeline	Farmfresh	Packfex
October	➤ Communicated problem.	➤ Assurances were given to Farmfresh that the problem would be dealt with; this did not materialise.
	➤ Not happy with lack of response.	➤ Site visit allowed team to observe the production process in real time.
	➤ Blame plastic film for high wastage.	➤ Blamed a catalogue of mechanical errors with the packaging machines for wastage.
	➤ Frustrated at Packfex assessment of machines and their production process.	➤ Adamant that the mechanical issues had to be dealt with before any product alterations were contemplated.
	➤ Internal conflict emerges over machine issues.	➤ Worked out a methodology to fix the technical faults in the fastest time.
	➤ Is appreciative of Packfex assistance in machine corrections.	➤ Problem with film now evident; agreed that the film had to be altered.
	➤ Ecstatic at lower wastage levels.	
	➤ Problem with film now evident: agreed that the film had to be altered.	
November	➤ Entered the first development meeting with the assumption of a relatively easy task.	➤ Entered the first development meeting with the assumption of a relatively easy task.
	➤ Short timeframe expected.	➤ Short timeframe expected.
	➤ Nervous over high wastage – patience.	➤ Fear over potential consequential loss claim for the wastage.
	➤ Saw Packfex as a partner, close relationship.	➤ Saw Farmfresh as partner, close ties.
	➤ Level of engagement is high.	➤ Level of engagement high.
	➤ Meaningful communication.	➤ Up-lifted film.
	➤ Perceived up-lift as an illustration of commitment.	➤ Intensive interaction.
		➤ Bilateral communication of ideas.
December	➤ Problem not easily identified.	➤ Problem not easily identified.
	➤ Expectations suffer.	➤ Expectations suffer.

Table 14.2 (*Continued*)

Timeline	Farmfresh	Packfex
	➤ Perceive Packfex has let them down. ➤ Frustrated at lack of progress. ➤ Tensions are high.	➤ Realises that interaction is going to be more difficult than previously expected. ➤ Concern over consequential loss. ➤ Tensions are high. ➤ Made some adjustments to film to reduce the wastage slightly. ➤ Reassurances given that problem will be resolved.
January	➤ Frustrated at the lack of progress. ➤ Becomes worried at the degree of difficulty. ➤ Concern at the mounting cost. ➤ Questions whether Packfex appreciated the cost endured. ➤ Felt that Packfex's reaction times could be quicker. ➤ Increasingly becoming worried that the problem could not be solved. ➤ Discontent communicated.	➤ Problem larger than expected – supplier refuses to help. ➤ Realises the difficulty involved and communicates situation to Farmfresh. ➤ Empathises with Farmfresh's situation. ➤ Concern over lack of progress. ➤ Concern over the threat of consequential loss. ➤ Time pressure is critical.
February	➤ Engaged in brainstorming sessions. ➤ Intensive interaction and communication. ➤ Sense of relief and euphoria. ➤ Expect cost and wastage to decrease. ➤ Sense of relational closeness with Packfex. ➤ Chubb X2 fails. Expectations suffer. ➤ Peter Bell felt that Packfex and Eamon Coleman had let him down and had made him look bad within Farmfresh. ➤ Production and engineering feel that Packfex should be delisted. They stop communication with Packfex. ➤ Internal conflict emerges over de-listing.	➤ Interaction is extensive, brainstorming sessions. ➤ Intensive communication. ➤ Past history facilities efficiency. ➤ No relational ambiguity. ➤ Sense of relief over threat of consequential loss being removed. ➤ Sense of closeness with Farmfresh. ➤ Chubb X2 fails. Expectations suffer. ➤ Concerned over tensions. ➤ Communication from Farmfresh is aggressive. ➤ Concerned about the future of the relationship. ➤ Key players refuse to communicate.

October

The high wastage problem that was occurring in two of Farmfresh's plants was communicated when one of the Farmfresh plant directors contacted the managing director of Packfex and demanded that someone come down to their plant and rectify the situation, as it was costing a significant amount of money. The aggressive nature in which Farmfresh's plant director communicated the problem caused an argument to ensue between the two men. Nevertheless, assurances were given that the problem would be dealt with. However, this did not materialise and Farmfresh got extremely upset at the lack of response from Packfex. Tension between the two companies was evident when Engineering Director Peter Bell contacted Packfex and demanded that some of its staff come down to the plant at 6.00 a.m. the following morning to witness the wastage first hand for themselves and to meet with Farmfresh's management board after the production run to discuss how this quality issue was going to be solved.

Peter Bell of Farmfresh stated: 'I wasn't happy overall … there were a lot of questions being asked [about Packfex], like what's happening now. There could have been a quicker reaction time.'

According to Packfex's Eamon Coleman:

> When Farmfresh rang up and said that we are going to run at 6.00 a.m. tomorrow morning and as unreasonable as it sounds and in relation to what other appointment or meeting you have got, I had to jump in and bite the bullet, because they would not be interested in talking to us if we didn't turn up. If we didn't turn up, Farmfresh would have thought that there was no commitment from us to solve the issue we were having.

When the representatives of Packfex's management went to the site the next morning at the agreed time, the first thing that they noticed was that none of Farmfresh's management team was present. In fact, they did not arrive till 9.00 a.m., three hours later. For Packfex, that was quite an amazing statement. They felt that Farmfresh were trying to show Packfex that it was the dominant actor in this relationship. However, the Packfex representatives did not mind being left on the factory floor with Farmfresh's operatives, because it allowed them to observe the production process in real time. It also allowed them to interact with the operatives and to get first hand illustrations and explanations of the problems that were occurring in the production process. When Farmfresh's management came in at 9.00 a.m. a conflict immediately ensued between Peter Bell and Eamon Coleman, the former blaming the film for the high wastage and the latter blaming a catalogue of mechanical errors with the packaging machines.

Eamon Coleman recalls:

> We stated to them that their machines had a catalogue of mechanical problems. At this particular point the engineering director was angry because here am I going through the issues, the problems with his machines. He had worked on these machines for the last seven years trying to get wastage down and here I was jumping all over his toes. And the conflict at this particular point was intense. The anger and the facial expressions in his face as I was going through this was really visible ... The tension at that moment was very high. We were standing on his territory, discussing his machines in such a manner that he was going to find it extremely aggressive. The only way to describe that interaction is that the guy took a pasting from me.

At the formal meeting between the two companies, Farmfresh immediately demanded that the problem with the film be rectified. However, Packfex reiterated the technical faults that they had discovered with the machines and stated that no alterations to their plastic film would be made without these mechanical issues being fixed. Within Farmfresh, the production and engineering departments were not happy with Packfex's assessment of their machines and their production process because it meant that production would have to be stopped and there was now an internal conflict from other departments demanding to know why these technical issues were not already resolved. However, Farmfresh's Engineering Director Peter Bell was claiming that it had to be Packfex's film since other packing ran on the machine with no faults.

According to Eamon Coleman:

> When we went into the meeting, we stated that before any changes were to be made to the product, they had to fix the machines and we gave them five faults that needed to be corrected before we would get involved. Peter Bell did not agree with us and stated that the machine manufacturer had been there last week and that the machines were in pristine condition. They were telling us that our film had faults and that when they put on our roll they got 33 per cent wastage. However, whenever they put on other rolls they were getting none. First of all, alarm bells were ringing. We knew we were not being told the truth. We knew the wastage was high on the other rolls as well. So we told them that there were five faults with the machines and that they needed to be corrected before we would even contemplate adjustments to the product.

Farmfresh was not happy with this scenario because it meant that a full diagnostic on the machines would have to be conducted, which would entail a lot of money being spent on changing parts. There were also time and labour costs and the production would have to stop. To resolve some of the tension between the companies, Peter Bell and Eamon Coleman worked out a methodology to fix the technical faults in the fastest time possible so as not to delay production. As a result of the corrections to the machines, the wastage level on Packfex's film dropped from 33 to 15 per cent. Packfex was also informed that wastage on competitors' films had also significantly been reduced and was now running at approximately 9 per cent. Despite the ongoing wastage issue, Farmfresh was ecstatic. They had a significant drop in wastage, not only on Packfex's film but also on other suppliers'. At this point, Packfex knew there was a problem with the film. At 15 per cent, the waste figure was very high and the fault was no longer with Farmfresh's machines.

According to Farmfresh's Peter Bell:

> In the beginning there were machine issues and a film issue. When the machine issues got sorted, the film was still causing unacceptable levels of wastage. So, for a while, there was a grey area there when there was not a definitive problem with the film ... however when the machines were fixed we knew there was something wrong with the film.

Packfex travelled to Farmfresh's factory floor to witness the wastage. They saw that the packaging film got filled, then sealed, clipped, cooked and chilled. It was during the chilling stage, at the very end of the process, that the fault appeared: the film actually split. Since the film was in Farmfresh's cooking process for four days when the packaging split, it caused not only high wastage and the extra production time needed to compensate, but it also meant serious time delays in Farmfresh's delivery of its product to customers.

Eamon Coleman of Packfex recalls:

> So the second time we went back. Peter Bell had now fixed the machines and got less than 9 per cent wastage with other films on the machine and we were still getting 15 20 per cent. Peter Bell put the roll on and we saw it run. It was quite clear now, black and white, that it was a film issue. Now the situation changed the other way around and Peter Bell was saying that there was something definitely wrong with the film and that he had accepted everything I said about his machines and so what was going to be done about the film.

Both Peter Bell and Eamon Coleman agreed that the film had to be altered and a co-development meeting was scheduled.

November

Both companies entered the first development meeting with the expectation that the adjustment to Chubb X1 would be rectified within a relatively short period of time, approximately a week. The urgency to rectify the problem stemmed from two main rationales: first, Packfex faced a potential consequential loss claim for the wastage, which could amount to ten times the cost of manufacturing the film; second, Farmfresh were in a situation where they had to use the faulty film until the problem could be rectified and the film up-lifted and replaced. For Farmfresh, this meant a period of high wastage, delayed production and unsatisfied customers, and they were willing to accept this while the problem was being corrected. According to Peter Bell:

> Part of the problem was the film had to be fixed, but we still had to produce. It meant that we had to work more to reach our quotas. We really had to have great patience. The wastage was still going on while the film was been fixed.

As a show of commitment, Packfex agreed to take corrective action and sent a team to Farmfresh to go through their stock of Chubb X1 film, and any product that was deemed not fit for process was removed.

December

However, the initial goal of a quick product improvement was diminished as the problem with the film was not easily identifiable. Packfex's Eamon Coleman states:

> We thought perhaps a week ...What we did was we broke down the film and did a technical analysis on it. The problem is that there are about five million parts to a film and locating what is specifically wrong is very difficult ... but when we did the analysis on the film we knew that this was not a simple problem and we had to confirm to Farmfresh that to get a resolution would take a minimum of four weeks.

The tension between the two companies was very high. Farmfresh had an expectation that fault with the film would be resolved in a quick period of time and from their perspective, Packfex had let them down. Farmfresh were extremely frustrated as it meant that the high wastage and the costs associated with it would continue into the near future. According to Coleman:

> Farmfresh were saying to us that had they known that the problem could not be solved quickly, that they would have gone to another supplier.

To alleviate some of the conflict, Packfex did make some adjustments to the film that would reduce the wastage slightly; however, the film could not be up-lifted, as there was nothing to replace it with. This meant that Farmfresh had to keep using the existing film, while the solution was being developed. At this stage, the tension and the conflict between both companies were extremely dense. Coleman states:

> There appeared to be no progress, we were still getting the same film, the same wastage. There just wasn't any progress. Whatever way you look at it, I don't think Packfex came across this problem before and so there was a good bit of confusion. The process for figuring out what was wrong with the film was a bit all over the place. I don't think that they were following any real guidelines in identifying the problem.

Moreover, from Packfex's perspective, the threat of consequential loss was ever present.

January

The analysis uncovered that one of Packfex's suppliers were guaranteeing that their raw material would meet particular sealing requirements but that this was not the case: 'It worked out that one of our suppliers changed an ingredient in the formula without actually informing us. Once we got into it we identified the problem within twenty-four hours' (Eamon Coleman).

Having identified the problem, the supplier was contacted and assurance was given that the requirements would be met. Both Packfex and Farmfresh felt that, within a relatively shorter period of time, the film would be rectified and the production issues at Farmfresh would be eliminated. However, it was soon realised that the problem was far greater than was anticipated. First, the supplier refused to admit that it made any alterations to the sealing layer and refused to engage in any discussion on the matter, mainly due to the possibility of consequential loss on their part. This dramatically delayed the progress, as it meant that Packfex had to analyse its supplier's product to identify which ingredient was altered.

Having identified the ingredient, it was then discovered that new regulations prohibited the ingredient from being utilised in a sealing layer, and hence the reason why the supplier had removed the ingredient from its product in the first place. However, this finding caused a significant problem in that an alternative supplier and alternative ingredient to the formula had to be located. What was more, tensions began to mount significantly between Farmfresh and Packfex due to the ever-increasing catalogue of setbacks that had been experienced on the project. Farmfresh were getting frustrated at what appeared to be the lack of progress. They felt that the film should have been rectified by now and that perhaps Packfex did not fully appreciate the cost to Farmfresh, which was clearly expressed through several communication mediums at that point. While consequential loss was not explicitly threatened, it was nevertheless implicitly implied. Farmfresh was increasingly becoming worried that the problem could not be solved.

February

Through a series of formal and informal brainstorming sessions between Farmfresh and Packfex, an innovative solution to the problem was devised and tested for requirements. It was felt by both parties that the problem had been solved. Indeed, there was a sense of euphoria amongst the people involved and the relationship between the two companies was said to get even tighter. Moreover, there was a sense of relief for both Packfex and Farmfresh. The threat of consequential loss was removed for Packfex and Farmfresh and the high cost and wastage would be reduced. Eamon Coleman states:

> What we did in Farmfresh was very controversial. We changed the sealing layer completely away from traditional practice to what it is now – yy. What happened was that we created a brand new product. So what we did was we took that old product apart and rebuilt it as if it were the ideal utopian product for Farmfresh. Rather than using xx as a sealing layer we used yy. The idea for using yy instead of xx came as a result of new product that we were developing with a European manufacturer and in the course of testing suitable ingredients we discovered that one of the properties of yy was that it was a good sealing layer.

However, when the film ran in Farmfresh's cooking process, the wastage, at approximately 50 per cent, was higher than ever before. Although Chubb X2 had resolved the sealing issue, another problem materialised as a result of the changes to the sealing formula. In essence, the new film was thicker and not as smooth as the original; as a consequence, the film moved slower through the packaging machine causing it to be misplaced. Coleman states:

> What happened was that when we sorted out the sealing issue, because we changed the formula, we found a completely different problem materialised. We sorted out the sealing issue but now there was a problem with the slip … they [the films] were out of place, the product was misplaced – it was not where it should have been. We did alter the feel of their product.

The tension between the two companies and the key individuals, Peter Bell and Eamon Coleman, escalated to an extreme intensity. The communication between the two companies was said to be very aggressive and threatening. As far as Peter Bell was concerned, Packfex and Eamon Coleman had let him down and, worse, had made him look bad within Farmfresh. Indeed, both Peter Bell and the production director were under fierce internal pressure for the failure of Chubb X2. The animosity between the key individuals was clearly evident when both Peter Bell and the production director would not even communicate with Eamon Coleman in relation to rectifying the new problem; as far as they were concerned, Packfex should be de-listed.

Eamon Coleman recalls:

> In relation to the failure of Chubb X2, it was really hard because we had to go back to Farmfresh and pick them up off the floor and there was also a loss of faith in us. At this particular point we are trying to positively reinforce the relationship, no negativity at all ... but Peter Bell was telling me that there was no reason for me to be phoning him, we had our chance, we would be de-listed and that I was wasting his time. I told him that innovation is an iterative process and that this was an engineering situation.

According to Peter Bell:

> It was like we had made no progress at all. There was a lot of patience on our part when the problem with the film was been sorted ... because of the fault we had a lot of waste ... there just wasn't any progress and that is the way we looked at it. It really wasn't what we expected.

However, internal conflict broke out between other departments in Farmfresh, when engineering and production put pressure on the corporate buyer to de-list Packfex. As was detailed earlier, Packfex had multiple working and personal relationships in different areas of Farmfresh, and now they relied upon those multiple relationships to stem the conflict from engineering and production.

Eamon Coleman comments:

> They were flexing their muscles, showing their mettle, it is all about pecking order and we knew that ... We knew that our product was very unique to Farmfresh and that they would have a hard job replacing us ... we had to be patient. They couldn't de-list us, but they had not realised that yet.

The Future

As Carl Young sat in his office he knew that the situation needed to be rectified quickly. He was unhappy with the way the board meeting went today, especially the blame mentality of his senior management. He was worried. The large retailers were not going to be happy with any more distribution problems. The internal conflict had to be resolved if they were going to get over this rough patch. In relation to Packfex, Young knew it would be difficult to de-list the plastic company because the film was particularly unique to Farmfresh's production process, and locating another supplier would be easier said than done. In addition, if they decided not to de-list the plastic supplier he needed the inter-company conflict to be resolved and especially the interpersonal conflict that was going on between certain boundary spanning members. Young knew that if he did not get his engineering and production directors to sit down with Packfex's technical director the project would fail and the problem would never be rectified. They were the key individuals. Carl Young sat back in his chair and wondered how he was going to handle the situation.

References

Ahmed ElAmin (2005), 'Public R&D Funding Pays off for Ireland's Food Sector', *Dairy Reporter*, 16 June.

Department of Agriculture and Food (2004), *Agrivision 2015*, available at: <http://www.agriculture.gov.ie>.

Section III

Management Reflections

CHAPTER 15

Re-invention from Within:
A New Mandate from Irish Management

George Bennett
IDA Ireland

The evolution of Ireland to a knowledge-based economy has been influenced by many factors, including the remarkable transformation process of Irish-based multinational investors. Ireland is of course not the only country to have been transformed by foreign direct investment (FDI), but its response to the FDI phenomenon is unique.

A re-invention from within has unfolded over the past ten years. The managers of Irish enterprises have actively influenced the transformation of their own lives, those of their employees, their enterprises and the place of their nation in the world.

Profound Impact of Multinational Companies on Irish Management Expertise

The impact of FDI on Ireland is pervasive and runs much deeper than job creation. The positive impact is visible in many key aspects of Irish life. Foreign-owned companies are positioned at the cutting edge of demand for high skills, of advanced management training and of business processes that permeate the wider business community.

Multinational companies (MNCs) have contributed greatly to the broadening of the economic base in Ireland by linking to and fostering entrepreneurial activities and indigenous start-ups aimed at supporting and selling to the FDI community. Combined with our innate enthusiasm for finding new ways of working, the net effect is that Ireland has developed as a recognised centre of management expertise. This is further endorsed by the appointment of Irish managers to very senior leadership positions in multinational companies across the globe.

Managers in Ireland are very much attuned to corporate procedures and practices and have the confidence to develop them. Their instinctive ability to adopt, innovate and communicate has allowed them to use that knowledge constructively, for the benefit of all.

Ireland is now in a leadership position in many of the diverse and key international business segments, including biopharmaceuticals, digital media, information and communications technology (ICT), financial services and medical technologies.

On a less tangible but equally profound basis, FDI, through its presence in Ireland over the past forty years, has contributed greatly to our national confidence and standing in the world.

Deepening and Widening the Corporate Mandate

The competitive global environment in which MNCs operate constantly determines and shapes best operational and business practice. This culture of learning and innovation, combined with Ireland's increasing skills and talents, has prompted investors to transform their operations in Ireland. For many companies, both large and small, this change has been expressed through wide ranging expansions of their original corporate mandates.

Irish managers also responded by outperforming on the set metrics and by exploring methods to widen the mandate of their enterprises in Ireland. This is made easier than it might have been in other countries because Ireland is a largely homogeneous, English-speaking society in which it is easy and natural for managers to set up and explore informal networks.

In addition to following standard corporate channels, they used their characteristic soft skills and abilities to communicate well to influence and convince their parent and sister companies to attract specific elements of the business to Ireland.

Many companies might have commenced with a single mandate, manufacturing for example, but have moved now to take on Europe, the Middle East and Africa (EMEA) and global corporate responsibilities in areas such as sales and marketing, procurement, R&D and technical and customer support.

GlaxoSmithKline (GSK), for example, came to Ireland over thirty years ago with a focus solely on manufacturing. Its mandate has widened to include R&D, manufacturing, sales and marketing, clinical trials and corporate financial shared services. Now it has four sites in Ireland, employing more than 1,600 staff.

Similarly, the Cork facility for Apple was originally established to manufacture the Mac PC. However, over time, the manufacturing site has evolved to become a multi-functional manufacturing and services operation for the EMEA market. The site has moved up the value chain, creating a centre of excellence across a range of business functions, including: advanced manufacturing, financial shared services, supply chain management, customer and technical support, telesales, treasury, software testing and localisation. Apple now employs about 1,800 staff in Cork.

The ripple of change spreads not only upwards in multinational companies, such as GSK and Apple, but also outwards into Irish-based FDI enterprise in general. IDA Ireland has been steadily supporting such developments. This state agency actively encourages enterprises to increase their added value with additional corporate functions, such as establishing European headquarters, as well as concentrating on innovation (such as R&D) and services, logistics and supply chain management functions, alongside advanced manufacturing.

Increasing Research and Innovation

If Ireland is to maintain and develop its competitive status as a leading knowledge-based economy, then it is imperative that a comprehensive framework for the future management of the research and innovative sectors is implemented. In this regard, the creative competence inspired by multinational companies, which infused Irish management in general, also influenced Irish public policy.

The Irish government is making concerted efforts to build a substantial foundation of world-class science and technology in Irish universities and colleges, research institutes and both foreign-owned and indigenous companies and, in particular, to encourage strong business and academic collaborations.

The National Strategy for Science, Technology and Innovation, which sets out a roadmap for these sectors until 2013, aims to bring together – in a unique, no-nonsense and highly pragmatic way – a wide range of national institutions to help create new knowledge and leading-edge research outcomes.

In addition to this clearly defined and ambitious strategy for research and innovation, these sectors have been earmarked for significant increases in investment and financial support in the future.

Integrated Landscape of Vision, Innovation and Management Leadership

Looking at the origins of Ireland's extraordinary achievements between 1993 and 2001, the former Taoiseach Garret FitzGerald has pointed out that output per worker grew three times faster than anywhere else in Europe.

> Undoubtedly a major factor in this was the arrival in Ireland during that eight-year period of almost 300 new mainly high-tech industrial projects … These increased almost fivefold the value of our manufacturing output, trebled the volume of exports, and, most important of all, virtually quadrupled the reported money value of the average industrial worker's output.

Within a relatively short time, in terms of economic development, the advantages that Ireland had as a place of low costs and labour surplus have been substituted by the new distinguishing characteristics: high intellectual agility, flexibility, creativeness and speed. These qualities are attracting a new breed of FDI. For example, Boston Scientific used researchers in Ireland to develop and launch the world's first drug-coated stent. Bristol-Myers Squibb's Swords Laboratories is the launch site for several new health care treatments used to treat hypertension, cancer and HIV/AIDS. Microsoft marked its twentieth Irish anniversary in 2006 by opening a new R&D centre employing 100 highly qualified staff. Intel is engaged in several research collaborations with leading Irish companies. Wyeth has established a bio-therapeutic drug discovery and development research facility at University College Dublin (UCD). The key distinguishing unique selling point (USP) contributing to the transformation is technical, operative and, most critically, management talent.

Irish-based managers have used advanced influencing and networking tools combined with superior delivery performance to encourage their parent companies to place business functions in Ireland that have traditionally remained deeply rooted in their countries of origin.

The current transformation is significant in that it is not so much the replacement of one type of industry by another: it is the transformation of those industries themselves within Ireland. In this sense, the transformation over the past ten years owes much to the direct involvement, connectivity and evolution of Irish management competencies.

CHAPTER 16

Software Sales Forecasting: How to Do It Well

Stephen Allott

Former Executive Chairman, Trinamo Consulting

Operational management skill is a key factor in the success of technology companies. This factor is more significant than is often appreciated. An aspect of operational management skill is sales forecasting. When I joined the London software company Micromuse in September 1995, one of the first questions the owner asked me was, 'What are we going to sell in the December quarter?' Forecasting matters. Is your company going to hit the target or not in this quarter? If your forecast is well ahead of plan, you could accelerate some hires and approve the key investments. If you are falling well short, you have to find out fast what is going wrong and probably impose an expense freeze. Even more drastic action may be needed if things are really bad. European technology companies have a very wide range of approaches to sales forecasting; some are good but many are very poor. Information on best practice approaches to forecasting is generally hard to come by. There appears to be little published literature on the subject. The information that is available is limited to traditional approaches that have serious defects.

Trinamo has developed a comprehensive approach to sales forecasting based on best practice benchmarks. Many UK companies could benefit by adopting the Trinamo approach.

Why Forecasting Matters

Forecasting is central to good management of any technology company. Being good at forecasting will really help you to grow a successful business. Poor skill in forecasting will cause problems. Let us begin by asking why exactly businesses need to forecast accurately. Usually, any business report is produced for a purpose. It should inform a decision. We start by asking what decisions are taken on the basis of a sales forecast.

Generally, there are four separate types of decision that forecasts inform:

- Recruitment and investment decisions: if the company is forecast to perform at or above plan, you can attain planned hires and planned investments. If you are falling short, you may have to defer planned hires and planned investments. What you are trying to find out is, 'How are we doing?' You are looking forwards, not backwards. This is an important shift from management by accounting information, which based on 'How we just did'.
- Priorities on key deals to close: a bottom-up sales forecast that shows, deal by deal, what sales are expected to come in will quickly reveal what deals make up the bulk of the company's forecast and therefore are the priority for management and other key people in the company. Management should spend their time on the deals that have the highest economic yield for the scarce management time invested. The sales forecast is the document that enables management to make this calculation.
- People performance and management: in addition to knowing whether the company is going to hit its target, you will want to know which sales people (or managers or divisions) are forecast to make their targets and which are not. Again, we are looking forwards, not back, so you can take corrective action before things happen rather than after the event.
- Product performance and management: in a business with multiple products, you will want to see what the expected performance by product is going to be, again so that corrective action and investment decisions can be taken. In a manufacturing business, forecasting is even more critical as you have to decide what to build before contracted orders are received.

We Often Find Management Using Poor Approaches

Confusion over Measurement Periods: Monthly, Quarterly or Annual?

Forecasting should fit into the company's performance measurement periods. We suspect that European and British technology companies often under-perform because they do not use quarterly performance measurement. On the other hand, the American quarterly system definitely works. Although we are not in favour of all practices in the US, the quarterly management system is definitely something that Europe should copy. Annual targets with monthly board reports fail on two counts.

Having your targets on an annual basis is too long a time period for most, albeit not all, technology companies, whilst a monthly basis is too short. If you are not convinced, consider the systems dynamics:

- People push harder when they have a deadline. It is simply human nature. A quarterly system has four times as many deadlines as an annual system and therefore more effort is applied.
- Natural selection of successful sales people is a key element of sales management. Natural selection operates four times as fast in producing a fit population in a quarterly system as in an annual system.
- Months are too short a period to forecast performance in most technology companies. Deals can slip from one month to the next. Months are too short a period for sales people to try something new and see if it works. We have seen people using deal tracking software that asks you to predict the month in which a deal will close. While this may be useful in a business for which a monthly system is appropriate (such as a simple distribution business), this prevents many of the benefits of proper forecasting emerging.
- Problems are identified faster with quarterly targets than with annual targets. Much of the business management is about problem identification and solution so accelerating this process is very valuable.

Forecasts Based on the Gross Value of the Sales Pipeline

In addition to confusion over whether to use annual or quarterly targets, we find three typical types of forecasting approaches being used: gross pipeline value, sales stage and run rate extrapolation. We consider that all three approaches suffer from serious defects. Some companies pay close attention to the gross value of the sales pipeline and then derive an expected figure for bookings (i.e. new orders) from that gross value. There may be a steady historic relationship between the gross value and the bookings result that is used to forecast bookings. A reasonably widespread rule of thumb is that the gross value of the pipeline needs to be three times the bookings target.

Care is needed to distinguish between the gross value of deals that might close in the quarter in question and longer-term deals. One would need to set a clear rule on what a deal that might close in this quarter consists of to operate this system effectively. In general, we disapprove of this approach. People use it because the data is easy to collect, there may be too many deals to do a detailed bottom-up analysis and the large numbers of the gross values can look reassuring. A further hazard is that being the fifth bidder on a big deal with a large gross value could seriously distort the figures. We do not doubt that monitoring the gross value of the sales pipeline can be helpful. It can identify trends, but it is not a substitute for proper forecasting.

Factored Forecasts by Sales Stage Percentages

A very popular approach, recommended in many books and by experts, involves generating a factored sales forecast based on the stage of each deal. Sales managers are trained to advance deals from stage to stage: from first meeting to requirements capture, from invitation to tender to quotation, from technical qualification to shortlist and so on. Commonly there are ten stages in a sale and each stage is given a percentage: stage 1 being 10 per cent and stage 9 being 90 per cent, and so on.

We definitely disapprove of this approach when done mechanically. It should be obvious that deals can advance at varying paces depending on different customers. Slavishly using the same factor for deals running at different speeds can seriously distort one's sales forecast. Similarly, a deal could be at an advanced stage (and so at a high percentage factor in this system) and yet be certain not to close in the quarter in question. Consider something at sales stage 6 (of 10) on the last day of the quarter. A mechanical system allocating a percentage probability would give this a 60 per cent weighting, yet the chance of it closing in a day will clearly be nil.

The incumbent sales manager in Micromuse in 1995 used this system, and I simply could not understand why he did. Only now, after more than twelve years of studying this question, I have found the answer. Why is such an analytically flawed approach so widespread? There are several reasons:

- Subjective closing probabilities are discredited. Lazy sales managers have asked their staff to give probabilities of whether individual deals will close in that quarter rather than make their own assessments. This leads to a lack of common standards being applied to the assignment of probability and perverse incentives operating. Poorly performing reps may try and keep their jobs by telling management that a big deal is just around the corner when in fact there is no such thing.
- The search for something to replace the rep assigned has led the industry to an objective use of sales stages. Sales managers are now trained to seek proof from a rep that a sale has advanced to a

particular stage. Why has this been chosen rather than better methods?

- We suspect this is partly because the data is easy to collect. Sales managers routinely monitor the sales stages of their prospects and the deal gross value is always known. When sales managers are asked for a more scientific approach to forecasting than guesswork, using the sales stage has provided them with some sense of analytical rigour. We also suspect that the search for forecasting rigour is most highly developed in larger organisations where a data-driven approach looks appealing.

This forecasting approach is embedded in tools like <http:\\www.sales force.com>, which can lead to inaccurate forecasts being generated. Whilst we like the contact management parts of the mentioned site, we think that the forecasting elements can be dangerous. Oddly, the fact that professional-looking graphs and charts can be produced at the touch of a button encourages sales managers to use this facility to generate board reports, which we think can be misleading. In 2006, Miller Heiman found that 72 per cent of their respondents said their customer relationship management (CRM) system did not provide accurate forecasting.

Forecasts Based on Run Rate Levels of Business

Finance professionals have a different approach to forecasting than that of sales professionals. Whilst a sales professional is more likely to use a bottom-up approach, deal by deal, and perhaps produce a factored amount based on sales stage, finance professionals often rely on historic data, such as sales run rates, perhaps adjusted for seasonality. Again, we would definitely disapprove of this approach.

Trinamo's Recommended Approach to Sales Forecasting

We recommend a simple approach using a factored forecast where the factor is assigned to each deal by the sales manager rather than the sales person. The forecast should be of the expected bookings result for the quarter (see Table 16.1).

The manager should talk to each sales person to understand the state of each of their deals, and therefore will be able to assign the probability of the deal closing in the measurement period. We think it is a good thing that this forces the manager to talk to his or her sales people individually. That is the manager's job. Through this process the manager understands what needs to be done to advance each deal. People ask us what factors

Table 16.1: Sample Quarterly Sales Forecast

Rep	Deal	Gross	Factor (%)	Factored Value
Fred	Arsenal	100	50	50
Fred	Spurs	200	70	140
Bill	Chelsea	60	90	54
Bill	West Ham	100	100	100
Total		460		344

a sales manager should use to determine a deal closing. We believe that a sales manager should use any information they think is relevant which will generally include:

- His or her experience of the rep in question, how accurately that rep forecasts, the rep's track record and the rep's general approach to sales.
- His or her experience of the account in question, its buying behaviour and whether it is an existing customer.
- His or her knowledge of the deal in question, its sales stage, where the company stands in the ranking (first or second choice, etc.), the buying process, whether budget has been assigned and what the buyer has said will be the expected timing of the order. Whether the manager has visited or spoken to the prospect and what other executives in the company have to say about the deal is also important. It should be obvious that a deal at stage 8 where your company is first choice has a better chance of closing than a deal at stage 8 where your company is last choice.

When a company has a single sales manager, it can apply a common approach to forecasting across all reps. When a company grows to having multiple managers, training and workshops for forecasting need to be given.

This probabilistic approach works best when you have a reasonable number of deals. If there is only one deal which is 50 per cent likely, then your forecast would always be wrong. However, this is rarely a significant objection to using the forecast. Analytically, this produces a midpoint prediction in the range of possible outcomes. Given skilful factoring, over time it will accurately predict results.

It also identifies three key figures:

- Minimum result: the sum of deals at 100 per cent – 100 in Table 16.1.
- Probable: the factored value – 344 in Table 16.1.
- Maximum: the gross value – 460 in Table 16.1.

The factored value shows the priority for investment of management time. The Spurs deal with a factored value of 140 is worth three times more than either the Arsenal or Chelsea deals, and therefore it should attract three times as much time. Sorting the table by factored value makes this clearer (see Table 16.2).

Table 16.2: Sample Quarterly Sales Forecast (by Factored Value)

Rep	Deal	Gross	Factor (%)	Factored Value
Fred	Spurs	200	70	140
Bill	West Ham	100	100	100
Bill	Chelsea	60	90	54
Fred	Arsenal	100	50	50
Total		460		344

Consider that accuracy using this method can be monitored by tracking whether the final bookings result matches or beats the forecast result. Forecasting accuracy is valuable to track. Note that accurate forecasting means that one in two 50 per cent deals should close. By definition, any 50 per cent deal will end up as a 100 or a 0 per cent deal so factors, of themselves, cannot be accurate.

When is the Trinamo approach not suitable? If a sales manager has too many deals, how does he or she assess each one individually and what should be done? We think the answer to this question is linked to the measurement period and a manager's span of control. In a quarterly measurement system, each rep may have five or ten deals to close, and each manager should have six to eight reps. This means each manager will have to assign probabilities to between thirty and eighty deals. This is not as burdensome as may appear, given that the core of the manager's job is to discuss each rep's pipeline. If the number of deals climbs much above this level, it may be that deal sizes are small and that a monthly or even weekly measurement system would be better.

Operational management excellence is key to technology company success and is under-developed in Europe. Sales forecasting is an important element of management skill. Irish and European technology companies should review their approaches to sales forecasting and adopt the best practice.

CHAPTER 17

Female Entrepreneurs:
How and Why They Succeed

Margaret Heffernan
Simmons Graduate School of Business, Boston

Ten years ago, I stood in a lift in a Massachusetts office block. The woman next to me looked at me in the face and asked,

'Are you Margaret?'

I had to confess that I was.

'Well, I just wanted to look at you. I've never met a woman CEO before,' was the response.

For a moment, the comment made me feel a bit of a freak. But then I stopped to reflect. I had not met many women CEOs either.

What a difference a decade makes. Since that exchange in the lift, there are now over ten million American women who own their own companies. Women-owned businesses have grown at twice the rate of business as a whole, and their companies now generate two trillion dollars in sales and employ more people than the global Fortune 500 combined. Owning nearly half the private companies in America, these women are strikingly successful; their employment and their revenues have grown faster than the business as a whole and they are more likely than others to stay in business. And every day in America another 420 new women-owned businesses are formed.

This is a tectonic shift, far outstripping in magnitude the frustrating advance of women in traditional corporations. Indeed, it may be that the obstacles women face inside more established companies is one of the drivers of this entrepreneurial explosion. Opportunity to advance may now be equal for men and women under the law, but everyone can see that it is not happening. Recent data from Catalyst shows that the number of companies with one or more women directors is down and the number of companies with women board members is stagnant, at around 15 per cent. At the current rate of change, it will take seventy-three years for corporate American women to reach parity with men – and many of them are not prepared to wait. Cecilia McCloy is just one case in point, but hers is the archetypal story. As a vice president for the research and engineering firm SAIC, she became fed up by her inability to influence the company's direction:

> I quit over dinner. I just got to boiling point and I quit. Walked out of the restaurant, walked back to my hotel room, called my husband and said I'd quit. I said, 'Everyone else has his or her own business. Why not me?'

The single reason most often cited by women to explain why they go into business for themselves is simple: they want independence. They seek control of their own destiny. They do not want to be passive victims of corporations and strategies, and also men who do not value them. The independence they seek is not only professional. Women in high-growth businesses may not put money at the top of their list of motivators, but they do put it second. This is not about fast cars and big houses. For women, financial independence is about not being held hostage to a marriage or a job that no longer satisfies. It is about having choices.

More innovation than we might imagine has its roots in dissatisfaction. Not only does discontent with traditional corporations drive women to start their own businesses; profound frustration with levels of service drives them to design new products and to redefine markets. Anne Heraty's vision for CPL derived, at least in part, from her sense that she could not provide good enough service in the market as it was defined at the time.

> I had been working in a generalist recruitment company and I really felt if I was interviewing a CFO one day and a programmer the next, it was difficult for me to understand and advise them. I was dissatisfied with the way I was doing my own job. My thought was: if I concentrated on just one sector (I had a particular affinity with the technology sector because I'd studied maths and economics at university, and done some computing) I felt I could advise better, in terms of careers, next moves and clients. I could just do a much better job.

Female entrepreneurs are often underestimated because, it is said, they build small companies. In the US, only about 3 per cent of women-owned businesses have revenues over a million dollars. This number loses much of its significance, however, when seen in context: only 6 per cent of *all* American businesses have revenues over a million dollars. Nevertheless, women do tend to be drawn to, or focus on, niche markets. But far from signalling insignificance, this shows profound insight into how the commercial world works. These days, mass market scarcely exists – and it is far too expensive (in marketing terms) for any neophyte entrepreneur to enter. The rise of niche markets has been driven by consumers who are ever more demanding. Serving such customers demands specialised focus, as Anne Heraty intuited when she started her company. Anne says:

> My other belief was that it was important to my business to build a very deep network – and that was harder to do generally. I wanted to get to the stage where anyone in the technology sector would come to me as having deepest knowledge, the best connections, the best insight. You just couldn't do that if you looked at the whole employment market; you had to specialise.

The fact that Heraty started CPL just as the technology market was exploding may not be just a happy coincidence. Another important driver of female success is a visceral sense of the zeitgeist. Psychologists argue that the way that women's brains work makes them better at collecting all the data and patterns that teach them how to read the market. Empathy, they argue, is 'hard-wired' in women and makes them better able to intuit needs. Not everyone believes this argument about hard-wiring. They prefer a historical explanation, arguing that people low in social power – as women, historically, have been – learn to read signals; they have to, for their survival. Lacking institutional protection, their very lives or careers depend on being profoundly in tune with shifts in mood and attitude. Since the only way women have been able to achieve anything has often been by staying *off* the radar screen, it means that they have needed to be very aware of what was on it.

Carol Latham's firm, Thermagon, exemplifies many of these trends. Working for BP as a materials chemist, Carol watched from the sidelines as the personal computing industry took off. What, she wondered, would be its biggest problem? She decided it would be heat. The smaller computers got, the hotter they became. And when they were too hot, they slowed down and stopped. When Carol came up with a solution, BP did not want to know. What, after all, did Carol know about computers? Belittled and frustrated, Carol left BP to prove she was right – and she did so, triumphantly. Carol began serving a highly specialised niche market, but a niche market that was exploding. She could design high-quality products that commanded a high price, and delivered a large margin, because Carol knew her market so well.

Concentrating on niche markets need not mean that a company stays small. When women are accused of aiming low, it is often because they are uncomfortable making grandiose claims at the outset. Doreen Marks set up Otis Technology when she was sixteen. The company makes gun cleaning equipment that is sold all over the world to sportsmen and the military. The company is so innovative that they call in an intellectual property lawyer several times a year to keep track of their patents. And the employment Otis has created has transformed the tiny town in upstate New York where the business is based. But none of this was obvious when Doreen started the company. According to Doreen:

> Big just came to us. I didn't aim big or small – it just happened. I just kept saying: why can't you do it this way? I'd be sitting at the kitchen table, fiddling with a patch and my dad would ask what I was doing. And I'd say, 'Well, why can't you do it this way?' And a few years later, the patent office says it's the biggest advance in gun cleaning they've ever seen!

Every country in the world envies the US rates of female entrepreneurship. In the UK, the Exchequer has estimated that, if women were starting new businesses at the same rate as in the US, 375,000 new companies would emerge, transforming the economy. The problem that the government wrestles with, that all governments have to confront, is how to inspire women with the passion, enthusiasm and courage that entrepreneurship demands. While frustration with existing options may drive women *out* of traditional corporations, what, they wonder, could drive them *into* entrepreneurship?

In the US, culture is key. Entrepreneurs are widely admired, and successful entrepreneurs are celebrated as heroes, leaders and innovators. When I started my first new business, even strangers encouraged me. 'That's wonderful!' they'd say, 'What can I do to help?' They hoped that I might be successful – and, if I was, everyone wanted to share in my success. That coupling of generosity and optimism was pervasive.

In the UK, the story has always been different. There what I met with was scepticism. 'I guess you can't get a real job,' the look on every face seemed to say. These differences are important. Every entrepreneur needs help, from friends and strangers alike. And every new business needs momentum. One sceptical glance can be enough to stop the infant company in its tracks.

Fear of failure is widely touted as a major cause for lower rates of female entrepreneurship throughout Europe. But that is to suggest that Americans are *not* afraid of failure, which, in my experience, would be wrong. Of course, entrepreneurs fear failure and hope for success; otherwise they would not get started at all. But failure in the US is no cause for shame or embarrassment. Rather, it is a qualification for starting the next business. Once you have experienced a business failure, or closed a company, you know a lot more than those who have only ever known success. You remember mistakes forever; you are alert to the alarm bells that certain decisions set off. Risa Edelstein, a successful Canadian entrepreneur, once described the mistakes she made building her first business as 'my MBA'. Those who do not make mistakes, she said, make nothing.

Optimism, generosity and honesty about mistakes are hard things for governments to mandate. Culture – whether in a company or in a country – is fiercely resistant to change. But the federal government in the US did one thing, which has proved to have a tremendous impact on the growth in female-owned businesses: it decided to measure them. Before they were counted, women's companies were regularly dismissed as too few and too small to matter. Once they were counted, perceptions shifted overnight. Finally visible, female entrepreneurs were taken seriously. Presidents started actively to court them, now perceiving that they were economic and political influencers. States legislatures funded Women's Business Centres, seeing now that women could create jobs and wealth. Multinational corporations began to buy from women-owned businesses, hoping to demonstrate that their diversity efforts were more than skin-deep. And state sponsorship of conferences for women accelerated the networking and information-sharing that entrepreneurial environments demand. Statistics may not be sexy but the decision to count the number and value of women-owned businesses is the single most important step any government can take to change perceptions and encourage growth.

Business relationships are the most interactive in the world and they are not just influenced by the culture in which they operate; companies, in their turn, change that culture. *The Economist* recently estimated that, in the developed world, the entry of women into the workforce has had more impact on economic growth than China. As women evolve from workers to owners, their expanded influence can only be imagined. What we know already is that the impact, as seen in the US, is already significant and is likely to become more profound. It seems utterly implausible that, in the future, the female CEO will be much of an oddity.

CHAPTER 18

Building a Customer Responsive Organisation at BMW Group Ireland

Lisa-Nicole Dunne

BMW Group Ireland[1]

Since 2004, BMW Group Ireland has seen growth across all areas of the business. From new and used car sales (BMW and MINI), motorcycles, parts, accessories and after-sales service, a series of goals have been achieved and records are broken. This piece reflects on how the BMW strategy at top functional and business levels has helped to achieve this outstanding performance in just three years.

While there are said to be four building blocks to gaining competitive advantage, BMW Group Ireland have focused on achieving superior customer responsiveness to achieve premium marquee sector leadership in the automotive industry (Hill and Jones 2001).

Background

BMW Group established a wholly owned subsidiary in Ireland, BMW Automotive (Ireland) Limited (BMW Group Ireland) on 1 October 2003. This company is responsible for the sales and aftersales of BMW cars, motorcycles and MINI cars in the Republic of Ireland through building and managing a successful dealer network. In 2004, BMW Group Ireland vertically integrated entering a cooperation agreement with Permanent TSB Finance offering BMW Financial Services to support the sale of new and used vehicles. In 2007, a further partnership with Zurich Financial Services has seen the introduction of BMW Insurance to Ireland, providing a new source of profitable revenue.

---

[1] Lisa-Nicole Dunne has since taken up the post of customer management director with The Carphone Warehouse plc.

The business level strategy has remained focused on the customer in all the areas. BMW officially introduced CRM into its strategy in 2001, as an integrated approach to identifying, acquiring and retaining customers. Using customer relationship management (CRM) principles and software, BMW gains customer insights, attracts new customers and strengthens loyalty. The main trigger for introducing CRM was acknowledging customers' increasing expectations, and that individual communications and service are the key elements of the brand experience required to win and keep the customers.

Approach

Many functions play a role in achieving superior customer responsiveness, from marketing to human resources, production to leadership. BMW differentiates by designing services and customer-facing processes above the expectations of competitors and customers. Major investments were made to improve the standards of dealerships and in developing a workforce that is indispensable in the execution of this strategy. The model range now available has increased, allowing customisations by customers through extending the flexible manufacturing process to Ireland.

CRM is an integral part of the group strategy as it extends sales potential and ensures engagement with customers at every touch point, therefore developing a relationship with customers. To do this, the mindset and culture of an organisation must be all about customer orientation and the delivery of an 'ultimate' customer experience. Alongside national dealer development strategies, a strong product offensive and rigorous brand management, a true belief in creating a customer experience beyond their expectations has strongly contributed to the success of BMW and MINI in Ireland.

Implementation

This success results from a three-pronged approach to establishing a customer focus, beginning with leadership and a vision. The core objective clearly stated by the managing director in year one was 'achieving customer service excellence, becoming the leader with the most desirable brands, most successful retail network and most satisfied customers'. This focus at the top level was critical to the success of the strategy, as it ensured that the entire team was motivated towards the same goal and that the appropriate budget was allocated to execute all the defined CRM activities.

The second step was filtering this vision to employee attitudes through training, and the creation of a programme that measures and rewards employees and dealerships for superior levels of customer service and satisfaction. This mechanism simultaneously provides a platform to listen to customers and therefore to 'know thy customer'. The third step in our approach is for customer focus (Hill and Jones 2001).

Know thy customer: customer communications at BMW are primarily event driven, closely managed and appropriate to the customer. This allows BMW to ask about their customers' needs, satisfaction levels and more about themselves. All information is recorded and used to tailor future communication and service to a customer's preferences. BMW have a policy of permission marketing and treat customers as individuals.

Joint sales, aftersales and financial services ventures rolled out the CRM system, set up a customer interaction centre and satisfaction programmes guaranteeing one touch point. Although integrations like this are challenging to co-ordinate and to get buy-in on all sides, they are essential for true customer focus.

Key Managerial Lessons

The key lesson learned from the BMW experience is as follows: a clear vision focused on the customer that pervades an organisation helps internal cooperation. When establishing new integrated functions in a start-up environment, communication must be crystal clear.

Brand behaviour management is a key strategic objective for customer responsiveness. This means recognising every moment of truth and ensuring all employees know the expected BMW behaviour. All staff and outsource partners must be trained to ensure that a suitable brand experience is provided. Customers do not just experience a brand through its products, so the behaviour of every employee or 'face to the customer' is fundamental (BMW Brand Management 2006).

BMW monitors the performance of our retail network, partners and agencies and provides the ongoing customer feedback. Our customer satisfaction programme is directly linked to a bonus system, ensuring the appropriate focus on customer responsiveness. BMW continues to offer customer-focused service packages and products (such as service inclusive) and models (such as the BMW 316i ES Saloon), after listening to customers.

Astute business process engineering and project management are increasingly important, with endless new projects and initiatives to manage. It is better to focus on a few new initiatives at a time, so priority management is imperative. Similarly, obtaining data that is not used is unproductive. Information systems must provide easy access to all information a customer or agent may require and agents must be empowered to make decisions.

BMW benefited from being new, therefore not having the history of units working completely independent of each other, so we could set up joint initiatives all set around delivering customer service excellence (Gulati 2007).

Overall, the essential ingredient for BMW success to date has been the buy-in and integration of wholesale and retail level in acknowledging that the 'customer is king'. This is in line with the BMW Group CRM mission statement:

> Building premium cars is our vocation, building premium customer relationships is what drives us.

References

Central Marketing and Brand Management Department (2006), *Creating a BMW Pre-sales Experience: Exhibitions and Events*, Munich: BMW.

Ford, D. *et al.* (1998), *Managing Business Relationships*, West Sussex: John Wiley & Sons Ltd.

Griffin, J. (1995), *Customer Loyalty: How to Earn It, How to Keep It*, New York: Lexington Books.

Gulati, R. (2007), 'Customer Focus – Silo Busting: How to Execute on the Promise of Customer Focus', *Harvard Business Review*, May, 98.

Hill, W.L. and Jones, G.R. (2001), *Strategic Management – An Integrated Approach*, New York: Houghton Mifflin Company.

Reynolds, J. (2002), *Practical Guide to CRM: Building More Profitable Customer Relationships*, New York: CMP Books.

CHAPTER 19

Clustering on the Island of Ireland

Paul McCormack
Environmental Technologies Cluster (ETC) and
New and Emerging Technologies Cluster (NETC)

Introduction

How can Irish industry be, and continue to remain, competitive in today's global marketplace? How can small and medium enterprises (SMEs) – typically time, skills, resources and finance bound – play the innovation game? How can Ireland rise to meet the challenges of rapidly changing market forces?

Companies are at the frontier of new market-driven global demands and internationalisation challenges that can only be met by ensuring they rise to the innovation and creativity challenge and thus achieve continued economic prosperity. In the rapidly evolving and increasingly uncertain international business environment, the need for new, collaborative working models and practices is emerging as an important strategic necessity for EU firms struggling to cope with an ever-changing commercial landscape.

The core of this report is based on my experiences as manager of the Border Vision Programme, working with the Cluster Facilitators Forum (CFF), and my knowledge gathered working in the field of business clusters and collaborative networking.

Networks and Clusters

The emergence of collaborative networks and clusters in Ireland is currently empowering firms and professionals to improve their flexibility, innovation capabilities and performances in the global market.

While networks typically provide a meeting point for businesses, clusters advance beyond these by identifying and focusing on commercial opportunities presented through company collaboration.

Clusters enable companies to re-design and to integrate business processes across enterprise boundaries, allowing them to cooperate closely among themselves and with professionals to achieve shared business objectives.

A cluster intrinsically links the natural alliances that previously existed between business members and importantly acts as the 'prime network' for each of the smaller, individual networks that inevitably emerge.

What Is Clustering?

Porter (1990) defines clusters as 'geographic concentrations of interconnected companies, specialised suppliers, service providers, firms in related industries and associated institutions ... in particular that compete but also cooperate.'

The Organisation for Economic Cooperation and Development's (OECD) definition of a cluster stresses the importance of value chain and creating added value: 'Networks of interdependent firms, knowledge producing institutions, bridging institutions and customers linked into a production chain which creates added value.'

The Governor's Guide in the USA includes a definition of clusters as 'geographically bound concentrations of similar, related or complementary businesses with active channels for business transactions, communications and dialogue that share specialised infrastructure, labour markets and services that are faced with common opportunities and threats.'

Cluster Success

Clustering has delivered many successes internationally and, importantly, in Ireland.

Visionary companies that actively participate in clusters inevitably reap the benefits of economies of scale, strength in numbers, credibility through membership, knowledge transfer, collaborations and joint ventures.

The Border Vision Environmental Technology Cluster has achieved collaborative commercial successes in excess of £100K within eighteen months of formation. Other clusters, including the Company of Irish Bakers network, have realised sales increases of 20 per cent and developed five new product lines just after one year of collaboration.

Supply Network Shannon has helped members adapt to a major change in the sub-supply manufacturing sector. Some companies have transferred totally since 2001. Some companies have changed from being

100 per cent manufacturing to global supply chains. The Renewable Energy Skills network has assisted members to enter the renewables market and transformed some businesses where renewables now form the majority of their business. These and many other success stories throughout the island are testimony to the collective commercial potential that clustering helps companies achieve.

Sustainability

These successes are currently being realised by the participant companies; however, the real challenges lie in ensuring continued success, sustainability, growth, expansion and institutional acceptance.

Whilst 'traditional' aims and objectives are achievable through clustering and can be measured, it is believed that significant additional benefits to companies and regional economies will arise from the non-obvious, second-order effects of networking and clustering. These are realised through the improved inter-company communication and collaboration.

When the companies participating in networks build a secure base of mutual trust, this leads to open communication and interaction. This develops a culture allowing for new levels of interactivity, which will accelerate and improve participants' abilities to collectively innovate and work creatively.

Clusters have the ability to produce a qualitative shift in business achievement through interaction. The enhanced communication, idea sharing, innovation and continuing contact will act as a catalyst and accelerate traditional activities, including management processes, business strategy, production techniques and marketing.

Clusters and Creativity

Networks and clusters create mutually supportive groups with a diversity of perspectives and backgrounds that provide an atmosphere where 'collective creativity' is encouraged and developed.

This creativity allows companies to become more agile and to develop 'adaptive foresight' in order to position themselves to predict future opportunities by exploiting changes in the business environment and anticipating customer behaviour. The companies within the networks and clusters are unrestrained by the daily bonds that affect their own businesses and often develop parallel commercial opportunities. Through these alternative commercial routes they are able to develop their adaptive foresight skills and recognise other collective opportunities. This allows the cluster companies to anticipate changes, to prioritise forward-looking customer needs and develop a collective approach to significantly develop their customer base.

By participating in networks and clusters, companies are involved in a 'culture of creativity', which creates openness and a process whereby they can begin to think laterally. This culture of openness and collective brainstorming prepares the companies to recognise serendipitous opportunities and act accordingly. Operating within the confines of their own companies means that executives are restricted by the normal daily time and task restrictions and are limited to their workplace environment of expectations and intentions. Cluster participation allows the executives to step outside this environment into a collective creative culture where they can cultivate their abilities to think laterally and create what Louis Pasteur called the 'prepared mind'.

Asset Utilisation in Cluster Firms

In general business terms asset utilisation focuses on financial management and does not consider one of the strongest assets in any company, i.e. its people and their knowledge and expertise, and how these can be applied. The clustering attempts to maximise these personal skills for the collective benefit of all the cluster members. An example of this can be found in the Environmental Technologies Cluster, which successfully maximises and utilises members' skills, e.g. leadership, technical expertise, entrepreneurial spirit and in-depth market knowledge. These skills are often ignored under traditional process-driven initiatives.

Facilitation: The Key to Cluster Success!

Clusters also provide a gateway for entrepreneurial endeavour. They allow for ease of process engagement, less bureaucracy, and quick and simple access to up-to-date information when it is required. Good facilitation creates an ambiance where entrepreneurship is the norm and not the exception.

In recognising the many specific and inter-cluster benefits that standardised facilitation and training can help deliver, an organisation that is hoping to help achieve these goals has been formed. The CFF has been expanded from its Northern Ireland base to include the whole island and it continues to seek, establish and engineer creative, intelligent and proven sector-specific networking programmes that will develop and preserve intellectual capital while optimising commercial opportunity on the global stage and ensuring that there is a systematic process in place for information collection and dissemination. This step will be of immense benefit to facilitators and clusters alike in providing the vital links that are required for success, internationalisation and sustainability.

Facilitation is a key in the ultimate success of clusters. A facilitator holds a neutral position and ensures good communication (leading to increasing trust between members), helps develop cluster strategy and drives collaborative initiatives. Ifor Ffowcs-Williams states that the facilitator ideally 'acts as the lubricant rather than the engine'.

Networking the Networks

Sustained success for the companies involved in clusters depends on facilitation of networking with commercially advantageous networks on the island and internationally. This will provide the catalyst for primary and secondary network gains for the clusters whilst also giving individual network members the scope to expand their own businesses.

By working in partnership, clusters can achieve increased gain but there has to be a 'roadmap' identifying these partners and their potential. This networking will act as a multiplier and will provide the additional knowledge, strength, links and acumen necessary in reaching global markets.

Return on Investment

The successes of clusters are many and go beyond the immediately identifiable traditional numerical-based return on investment measurements. Time frames within clusters are based on long-term gains, there are few quick wins and, as such, measurement techniques need to reflect this and reflect the commercial realities of life.

There are many 'intangible' benefits achieved through clustering (such as knowledge transfer, increased creativity, commercial confidence, innovation awareness and entrepreneurial activity) that must be included as measurement indices. Methodologies, metrics and performance indicators for clusters can not only be based upon 'hard' measurable achievements but can be also expanded to measure impact as well as output.

Within the clusters I facilitate we have companies now embarking on collective research, companies with increased skills and management expertise. All are 'soft' gains, but they are of immense importance to the companies, their commercial growth and success, and the ultimate success of the island. These gains do not fit on today's measurement charts and are therefore not officially recognised. New measurement methods are being explored to fully catch the role and potential of networks and clusters and their regional embedded impact.

Government Challenges

Historically, the economic prosperity of the island of Ireland depended on (mass) manufacturing, inward investment, grant aid and cheap labour. As market forces of the world change rapidly, how do governments ensure economic prosperity and growth in an uncertain future? They must work in partnership with industry to ensure that Ireland is skilled and equipped to meet these global challenges. By placing business networks and clusters at the centre of economic development plans, government can future proof prosperity and success by allowing opportunity to develop though attracting, retaining and mobilising innovation from all sectors.

Government needs to facilitate and encourage cluster linkages and help build a commercial atmosphere where collaborative potential is recognised. They need to ensure that the primary assets of infrastructure, education, skills and a conducive regulatory environment are put in place to enhance the growth potential of companies and help them compete in the global marketplace.

The clustering approach will allow Ireland to become a society of mass innovation in all sectors and to be recognised as the leading collaborative centre with a collective ethos, excellent collaborators, adept problem solvers and an acknowledged reputation for openness, innovation and creativity.

As recognised in Michael Porter's 'Diamond of National Advantage' (Porter 1990), government policy has an important role to play in shaping national advantage. Through supporting clustering and collaborative networking, government can raise the odds of gaining competitive advantage, but, importantly, it is industry participation that has the power to create real competitive advantage.

Conclusion

The commercial arena is constantly changing; competition is no longer readily identifiable. To survive, companies must develop flexible strategies in order to remain competitive. Cluster engagement will provide participant companies with the necessary tools and access to the knowledge, skills, expertise and technologies to help achieve competitive success.

Clustering provides companies with the commonality, concentration and connectivity to ensure that they remain knowledge focused, innovative, entrepreneurial and ultimately competitively successful. Managers must be visionary and actively participate in clusters and networks; they must implement long-term strategies with global markets and innovative processes at the core.

References

Porter, Michael E. (1990), *The Competitive Advantage of Nations*, New York: Basic Books.

CHAPTER 20

Managing Complexity in Business Integration Projects

Pierre-Henri Baviera

PA Consulting Group

It is increasingly important to manage large, complex integration projects well. Projects play a major role in most firms – whether the firm is delivering a contract or developing new products. The stakes are high because business success depends on a few key projects. The performance relies on integration between the partners in an enterprise.

PA Consulting Group's research on more than 3,000 projects and its direct experience over 100 large, complex projects shows that only 10 per cent exceeded their targets and over 50 per cent failed to reach their targets. Even the *New York Times* (2002) is exasperated:

> Cost overruns (totalling hundreds of billions of dollars) for large public works projects have stayed largely constant for most of the last century ... No learning is taking place among the professionals doing these budgets.

These projects are so complex due to the number of interdependencies, the level of uncertainty, the capacity of the enterprise to manage risk and the high rate of change and disruption to business as usual.

How to Best Manage this Complexity?

It is not good enough to analyse and simplify complex challenges, as profound new solutions can emerge from complex and unstable situations. Complexity can be a source of radical performance and insight, provided that the particular aspects are handled in distinctly different ways.

PA Consulting Group's experience in delivering transformation projects across all sectors and industries enabled the creation of a point of view on how to make the best of complexity.

What is Complexity?

Murray Gell-Mann (1995), in *The Quark and the Jaguar*, defines complexity as follows: 'Complexity is how long a message needs to be to describe the structure and behaviour of something.' The more intricate the system, the longer the message. This intricacy can arise from the nature of its technical elements as well as its architecture. Business systems and projects consist of people as well as things, and their number and personalities and political interrelationships also add to the intricacy.

The length of the message increases with both the intricacy of a system and the uncertainty of its behaviour. The complexity of any undertaking can be mapped across a two dimensional space (see Figure 20.1). This space reconciles many different management theories and models (see Figure 20.2).

Most management techniques have been developed by engineers and accountants who tend to view the world as a perfect machine, governed by exact mathematical laws, following the great tradition established by Galileo, Descartes and Newton centuries ago. The usual approach is to simplify and structure every complex situation in order to 'stabilise' it. This thinking persists in the face of ample evidence of continual randomness and uncertainty in the real world.

Case Study
In 1998, a project was underway to merge the two major downtown branches of a retail business. The work had been carefully organised and was planned to be completed in six months. Then a terrorist bomb destroyed one of the branches and made the plan unstable in an instant. Planning that had been done to date became irrelevant in an 'edge to chaos' situation.

This management wisdom is efficient for getting 95 per cent of any activities to be done efficiently. However, the remaining 5 per cent linked to the 'edge of chaos' area is a fantastic source of creativity and radical change.

Case Study
Some projects are purposefully thrust in the 'edge of chaos' direction to achieve 'mould breaking' change. An example was the establishment of an Internet bank by a long established and traditional financial services company. A group of creative free thinkers were assigned the task of setting up the new business on an entirely new IT platform and with a completely different culture to the parent company. Just like many other dot-com initiatives, this project was very intricate with its multiple stakeholders and technical elements, and there was

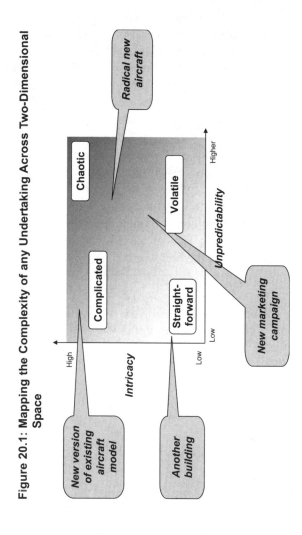

Figure 20.1: Mapping the Complexity of any Undertaking Across Two-Dimensional Space

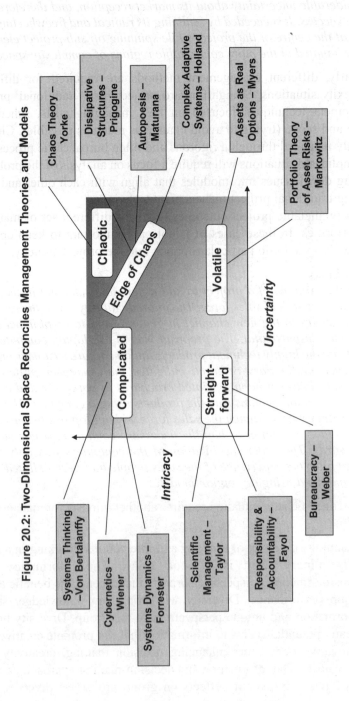

Figure 20.2: Two-Dimensional Space Reconciles Management Theories and Models

*considerable uncertainty about its market reception, and therefore ulti-
mate success. It succeeded by retaining its radical and freewheeling culture at the centre of the project while spinning off sub-project elements
to be handled in the more controllable regions of complexity space.*

Clearly, different management methods are required for different
complexity situations. Straightforward projects use 'traditional' project
management techniques focused on best managing costs, schedules,
quality and scope (trying to avoid change as much as possible). Change
is tightly managed through a rigorous and often bureaucratic process.

Complicated situations will require a focus on analysis of the problem,
breaking down issues into modules that align with each other and then
applying traditional project management techniques.

Less predictable project outcomes require a different set of management priorities. In these cases, it is not only important to keep options
open, but also to build particular options into the project strategy.

Case Study

*Take the example of a project to add a new sales channel in the form
of a dedicated field sales force. The unpredictability lay in the reaction
of customers to the new channel in general, and to its planned sales
approach in particular. The proposal was to use laptop computers to
illustrate the highly technical products and to capture customer orders.
However, preliminary research indicated that customer preferences
were split between having printed brochures to pore over and having
the sales person demonstrate the products using a computer. The project strategy was to launch the sales force without laptops to start with,
but to have an option to buy the necessary computers a few months
afterwards. The exact specification of the computers was only to be
settled after the experience of the sales people had been collated. This
was managed using an 'option model'.*

The 'edge of chaos' situation requires another mindset for managers so
that they:

- Encourage diversity of thinking and interactions. Working in a multidisciplinary team is a good thing. The information and
  decision-making perspective purports that diversity is beneficial for
  group performance. Diversity will bring new knowledge, skills,
  information and unique perspectives to the group. Diversity brings
  greater potential access to information that can promote creative and
  innovative behaviour, enhancing decision making, creativity and
  innovation. The information and decision-making approach predicts
  three positive diversity effects on group processes: diversity will

increase the cognitive processing demands of work groups; diversity will improve analysis in the group, leading to more careful analysis of issues; and diversity will lead to better use of information in the work group.

- Participate in and facilitate free-flowing conversations. Managers need to move from playing a god-like role above the process and descend into it with little more authority than anyone else.
- Allow emotion and anxiety. A high level of uncertainty and the incapacity to use traditional, rational management techniques as reference will create anxiety and emotions within the team. Traditional wisdom in the Western World generally associates emotions and anxiety with lack of control over events. This should not apply to 'edge of chaos' projects as greater innovation and trust in individuals' instincts will be required and should be encouraged.
- Tolerate mistakes. Many mistakes will be made on 'edge of chaos' projects, as no clear roadmap can be identified to the target. The path to success will be structured around mistakes and are corrective. In this context, fear of failure or fear of making mistakes cannot happen as they will restrain creative and innovative thinking. Mistakes must be tolerated.
- Constrain rather than control. Traditional and rational management methodologies are centred on control system based on the definition of monitoring factors or indicators. Controls are put in place if a monitoring factor is acting out of the norm. 'Edge of chaos' projects, with high levels of intricacy and uncertainty, make the identification and formulation of these indicators very difficult. Managerial focus should be on constraining group dynamics to keep the project's broad objectives in mind, rather than on controlling the work.
- Allow extinctions.

What is in it for Ireland?

Ireland has experienced unprecedented growth in its economy over the past ten years. This period has seen the rapid development and improvement of key industries (financial services, pharmaceuticals, biotechnologies) that are not limited to the construction sector. Ireland has (and continues to) built 'parity' with other key global economic players regarding key infrastructure services, for example, mobile telecommunication, national infrastructure (transport, health, etc.). In many respects, managers have been able to build on the lessons learned from other countries to reduce the level of risk and uncertainty linked to the development of these sectors. As a result, the traditional paradigm linked to project management activities has prevailed.

The development of new service-oriented or high-tech industries (e.g. biotechnology) through which Ireland competes in the global marketplace will impact the application of the traditional project management paradigm by Irish managers. The intensity of competition, the high number of market driving forces and the associated intricacies will create so many likely scenarios that it will be impossible for a normal human being to become master of all of them. It will leave Irish managers with no other option but to adapt a different management methodology that should accommodate high levels of uncertainty and intricacy. Learning from the 'edge of chaos' situation will be a 'must do' in the very close future – the time of the god-like manager is well and truly gone.

References

Gell-Mann, M. (1995), *The Quark and the Jaguar*, New York: W.H. Freeman.

New York Times (2002), 'International Survey on Major IT Projects', 11 July.

CHAPTER 21

Primary Health Care in Ireland: Change, Challenge, Opportunity

Mark Rowe[1]

Rowe-Creavin Medical Practice, Waterford City

Primary care needs to become the central focus of the health system. The development of a properly integrated primary care service can lead to better outcomes, better health status and better cost effectiveness. Primary care should therefore be readily available to all people regardless of who they are, where they live or what health and social problems they may have. Secondary care is then required for complex and special needs which cannot be met solely within primary care. (Department of Health and Children 2001)

In 2001, the Department of Health and Children issued the publication *Primary Care – A New Direction* as part of their health strategy. This aimed to bring primary care to the forefront over the next ten years, recognising the major beneficial impact that an effective and efficient primary care infrastructure, underpinned by well orchestrated, integrated teams of health professionals, would have on the health of the nation. In this context, notable changes, challenges and opportunities exist.

Need for Change and the Development of Primary Care Teams

It is said that the only constant in life is change. This is very true in the rapidly changing landscape of Irish health care delivery where the following issues are of particular relevance to primary care.

Development of Primary Care Teams

The European Working Group on Quality in Family Practice has identified team building as one of the major targets for development in primary

[1] The author gratefully acknowledges comments from Chris O'Riordan, Waterford Institute of Technology, on a previous version of this reflection.

care. In Ireland, the development of community-based teams in primary care is now the official health policy. This means the provision of additional professional services, such as physiotherapy, speech and language therapy, dietetics and counselling others in the general practice setting. Research has shown that team working provides a more responsive service to patients who benefit more when health care professionals work together. Patterson *et al.* (2000) note that being a team player is an important competency for a general practitioner.

The development and management of enhanced teams in primary care have significant human resource management implications. For these teams to be effective, there must be clearly defined team roles with emphasis on clinical governance and accountability.

Role of Group Practice

General practitioners (GPs) are community generalists with a focus on individuals. They specialise in people and provide people-centred cradle-to-grave care in communities.

Good primary health care ensures that services are coordinated and integrated across the boundaries of health and personal social care to the benefit of the patient (i.e. the consumer) in terms of better quality, better outcomes, better cost-effectiveness and better health status.

There is a growing tendency towards group practice where natural synergies and economies of scale kick in. Greater scope exists for sub-specialisation, which in turn allows for a greater range of services to be provided while at the same time giving greater patient choice.

Patients as Consumers of Health Care Services

This is a sea change in terms of the culture of health care delivery. Traditionally, an imbalanced relationship existed between the doctor and patient, which favoured the professional who literally held all the aces in terms of knowledge, diagnosis, treatment, etc. Now we are in the information age with an explosion of health information (however biased that may be) readily available. As a result, peoples' expectations from health care have risen commensurately.

This concept of patient as 'consumer' not only pertains to providing patient-friendly, evidence-based information and timely use of investigations and appropriate treatments. It includes the principle of treating the patient as an equal partner in the health care experience. To me, this is a core value in the delivery of primary health care. This means that waiting times do matter and that the patient's experience of the health care journey matters. Feedback on service provision is not only valued, but is also an essential element to allow for continuous improvements in service delivery.

Information and Communication Technology (ICT)

The enhanced role of ICT in the delivery of primary health care is multifaceted, from computerised records to more user-friendly websites making health care more accessible. This advent of the paperless practice, with electronic links to secondary care for real-time test results, is a potential quantum leap towards patient care. This facilitates clinical audit and quality assurance initiatives.

Wellness vs. Illness

In the past, patients only accessed health care either when they were ill or thought they were ill. But, in recent times, there has been a cultural shift in medicine towards health promotion and disease prevention. This paradigm shift has been matched by increasing demand from the public for wellness services. This has led to an explosion of health care activity related to screening and health promotion.

Feminisation of General Practice

Recent figures suggest that about 75 per cent of entrants to medical school and between 70 and 90 per cent of GP trainees are female. Female graduates value flexible working hours, good conditions, good colleagues and job satisfaction. They may well be less interested in the management side of health care. However, incorporating flexible working rosters, part-time practice and adjusting these to cater for the business needs of the practice is a fine balance, and it requires increasing management skills.

Chronic Disease Management

The huge increase in numbers of people with chronic illness such as diabetes and heart disease has massive resource implications for primary care. Many of these people can have most of their conditions managed in primary care, using dedicated practice nurses who follow clinical protocols based on the best international practice. This requires that appropriate infrastructure is provided in the primary care setting, which in turn requires investment, business planning and cost-benefit analysis.

Advocacy

The advocacy role of general practice is important, especially for patients with social or educational disadvantage. This helps to ensure the equity of access to health care services and to address the inverse care law which states that those in most need of health care are least likely to access it due to a variety of factors, including poverty and disadvantage.

It is also important to campaign politically for targeted investment in primary care. Currently, it receives miniscule funding relative to hospital-based secondary care. Yet, research in the USA by Starfield has shown that every dollar invested in primary care can lead to savings of ten dollars in the overall health care system. A case, perhaps, of a stitch in time saving nine (or ten!) (see Example 20.1).

Example 20.1: Responding to Change – A Case Study of Innovation in the South-East

The Rowe-Creavin Practice was founded in 1999 in Waterford City with four staff. Currently it has eighteen staff, including doctors, nurses, a part-time phlebotomist, two job-sharing practice managers and support staff. We have allied professionals, including a counselling psychologist and a dietician working with us. In addition, we are fully computerised and have a teaching practice for both medical students and GP trainees.

However, due to lack of space, our future growth is capped at our current location. Therefore, a strategic decision was taken to develop a 'one-stop shop' of primary care services. An opportunity presented itself to purchase the Presentation Convent in Waterford City and to develop a signature building for primary care of about 30,000 square feet, encompassing general practice, nursing, optician services, a community pharmacy, dentistry, physiotherapy, speech and language therapy and occupational therapy, complementary health professionals and community-based specialists. There will be an onsite café and space for community groups to meet. In addition, there will be mini conference facilities for small groups and for health promotional talks. There is protected car parking for about eighty cars. This will be Ireland's first health park for primary care services and is a model for future primary care development. It will allow for considerable synergy by facilitating a greatly enhanced range of services, all under the one roof. The key location in the city allows it to be a 'walk-to' as well as a 'drive-to' location. Health is much more than the absence of disease. This signature building will create a 'feel good' factor for the community by uplifting the spirits. It will also be a healthy building from a green energy and sustainability point of view. It is to be hoped that a project of this magnitude, which has the potential to take considerable pressure from the hospital sector, will be able to attract some degree of capital support. However, there are no guarantees and the decision to proceed has been based on strategic growth principles, coupled with an innate pursuit of excellence in primary health care delivery.

The Challenge: Moving Forward

They say that quality is the intelligent application of effort. The sea change that is occurring in the health care sector provides many challenges for primary care. Given its increasing complexity, primary care must be treated as a business, whereby management principles are married to the best medical practice. This should incorporate the following business management concepts:

- Financial management: a sensible approach to understanding the financial basis to health care.
- Strategic growth and management.
- Developing and providing value-added services.
- Human resource management.
- Developing and delivering team-based care with clear lines of responsibility and accountability.
- Change management.
- Innovation: 'innovate or stagnate'.
- Standardising quality assured administrative processes: 'Do it right, first time, every time.'
- Valuing feedback, especially negative feedback. All observations are useful and give an opportunity to strengthen your service.
- Striving for continuous improvement with measurable outcomes.
- Education, training and research as integral components of health care activity.
- Building a reputation for excellence.
- Reputation management.
- Total quality management.

The challenge here is to ensure that those involved in the delivery of primary care services recognise that they may be, first and foremost, clinicians, but that they also need to implement business practices that enhance their efficiency and their ability to provide a top-class service. As the demands increase on primary care providers, as the health strategy effectively intends, it will be a case of not necessarily working harder but of 'working smarter'. Thus, the principles that surround the functions of human resources, finance, marketing and information technology, amongst others, have a home in the surgery or clinic as much as they do in any other small and medium enterprise. In addition, providers will need to think strategically, looking at the direction their businesses are taking and will take in the future. If the world is changing, but we are not, we have missed out on the opportunity that such a challenge presents us with.

References

Department of Health and Children (2001), 'Primary Care: A New Direction', *Department of Health and Children*, 7.

Patterson, F. and Ferguson, E. *et al.* (2000), 'A Competency Model for General Practice: Implications for Selection, Training, and Development', *British Journal of General Practice*, 50, 188–93.

Index